Ver

An Integrated Defence

Verdun:
An Integrated Defence

An Outline of the French
Fortifications of the Great War
based on a Detailed Review
of the Defences of Verdun

Neil J. Wells

The Naval & Military Press Ltd

Published by
The Naval & Military Press Ltd
Unit 10 Ridgewood Industrial Park,
Uckfield, East Sussex,
TN22 5QE England
Tel: +44 (0) 1825 749494
Fax: +44 (0) 1825 765701

www.naval-military-press.com
www.military-genealogy.com
www.militarymaproom.com

Contents

Photographs

(All photographs are from the author's collection unless otherwise noted)
in between 106 & 107

1. The *redoute de Regret* (*Le camp retranché de Verdun*) looking south obliquely, taken from an USA Air force Reconnaissance Aircraft, summer 1918

2. The *fort de Douaumont* (*Le camp retranché de Verdun*) looking east obliquely. No date, but probably taken pre war. (No copyright)

3. The *fort de bois borrus* taken on 14 May 1916. (Bibliotheque Municipale de Verdun MS819-39)

4. The *fort de Marre* taken on 9 April 1916. (Bibliotheque Municipale de Verdun MS819-40)

5. The *Entrée* to the *batterie des Ayville*. No date, circa 1914. (Bayerisches Hauptstaatsarchiv - Abt. IV Kriegsarchiv BS-IIf59)

6. The *caserne* and *cour* to the *fort des Ayville*. No date, circa 1914. (Bayerisches Hauptstaatsarchiv - Abt. IV Kriegsarchiv BS-II1f60)

7. Photograph taken within a *fossé*, (fort unknown - *Le camp retranché de Verdun*) showing the *escarpe* on the left, the *contrescarpe* on the right and a *caponnières* built onto the corner of the *escarpe* – pre-war / no date

8. View of the *fossé* of the *fort de Bondues* (*Le camp retranché de Lille*) showing the *escarpe* on the left, the *contrescarpe* on the right and a *coffres simple* located at the corner in the *contrescarpe* – No date (IWM Q37114)

9. A *canon de 'Lahitolle' 95 mm modèle 1888*) shown in position upon an unknown fort's *baquette d'artillerie*, also showing some details of the *caserne* (*Le camp retranché de Verdun*) – pre-war / no date

10. A *canon de 'De Bange' 120mm longue modèle 1878*) shown in position upon an unknown fort's *baquette d'artillerie*), pre-war photograph – pre-war / no date

11. A *batteries* (gun emplacement) believed to have been Toul Hill. – Post-war / no date (American Official Photograph via IWM Am O 23355)

12. The *Réduit central – la Citadelle* (*Le camp retranché de Verdun*), looking north taken with the city of Verdun in the background. Photograph taken from an USA Air force Reconnaissance Aircraft, summer 1918

13. The *Réduit central – la Citadelle* (*Le camp retranché de Verdun*) photograph taken on the eastern wall from street level with *Bâtiments extérieur* in the foreground, pre-war photograph – pre-war / no date

14. The *entrée* to *Ecoute N° 1* of the *Réduit central – la Citadelle*, (*Le camp retranché de Verdun*) wartime photograph – c1916

15. The *fort de Moulainville* (bottom centre) and the *ouvrage d'Eix* (top left) on 9 April 1916. The batterie 1.2 can be seen (centre left) and the *abri de combat* LLM2 (centre) (Bibliotheque Municipale de Verdun MS812-180)

16. The *fort de Michel* taken on 30 March 1916 with the *Batterie 7.9* (top right) and the *Batterie 7.7* (bottom left). (Bibliotheque Municipale de Verdun MS812-222)

17. The *fort de Tavannes* (top left) the *abri du Projecteur* (centre right) and the *Batterie 6.8 - Batterie du Mardi-Gras* (bottom right) on 28 April 1916. (Bibliotheque Municipale de Verdun MS812-191)

18. The *fort de Douaumont* taken before the Battle of Verdun. No date c1915 (Bayerisches Hauptstaatsarchiv - Abt. IV Kriegsarchiv BS-II1g644)

19. The *fort de Douaumont* taken on 7 May 1916. Most of the shell damage seen here was inflicted by French artillery after the Germans captured the fort. (Bibliotheque Municipale de Verdun MS812-116)

20. Later photograph of the *fort de Douaumont* taken during the Battle of Verdun, 1 October 1916. (Bibliotheque Municipale de Verdun MS812-149)

21. Oblique photograph of the *fort de Douaumont* taken during the Battle of Verdun. 10 October 1916. (Bibliotheque Municipale de Verdun MS812-118)

22. The *redoute de Souville* (with the *redoute de Saint-Michel* in the middle-ground and the city of Verdun in the background), looking west taken from a German Air Force Reconnaissance Aircraft, (*Le camp retranché de Verdun*) summer 1915

23. The *fort de Vaux* (*Le camp retranché de Verdun*) looking northeast, taken after the battle and showing damage from shellfire, from an USA Air Force Reconnaissance Aircraft, summer 1918.

24. The *fort de Vaux* taken during the Battle of Verdun. No date, c.1916 (Bayerisches Hauptstaatsarchiv - Abt. IV Kriegsarchiv BS-II1g648)

25. The *fort de Vaux* (lower left) and the *fort de Tavannes* (upper left) taken during the Battle of Verdun. 5 August 1916 (Bayerisches Hauptstaatsarchiv - Abt. IV Kriegsarchiv BS-II1g643)

26. The *caserne* (barracks) of the *fort de Vaux* (*Le camp retranché de Verdun*) taken after the battle probably in the winter of 1917 and showing damage from shellfire (IWM Q81472)

27. The *fort de Souville.* No date, circa mid 1916 (Bayerisches Hauptstaatsarchiv - Abt. IV Kriegsarchiv BS-II1g647)

28. The *fort de Manonviller* taken during the Battle of Lorraine. Most of the shell damage seen here was inflicted by German artillery. No date, c.1914 (Bayerisches Hauptstaatsarchiv - Abt. IV Kriegsarchiv BS-II1g249)

29. The *fort de Manonviller* after its capture by the Germans. This view was taken from the *fossé* showing the *entrée*, the *pont* and the *pont mobile*. No date, c.1914 (Bayerisches Hauptstaatsarchiv - Abt. IV Kriegsarchiv BS-II1g250)

30. The *fort de Manonviller* after its capture on 27 August 1914 by the Germans. This view shows a *Tourelle de mitrailleuses (GF4)* in its firing position. No date, c.1914 (Bayerisches Hauptstaatsarchiv - Abt. IV Kriegsarchiv BS-II1g255)

31. The *fort de Manonviller* after its capture by the Germans. This view shows a *Tourelle de 75mm (T75) Galopin* in its raised firing position and shows damage to the *avant-cuirasse* caused by German shelling. August/September 1914. (Bayerisches Hauptstaatsarchiv - Abt. IV Kriegsarchiv BS-II1g260)

32. The *fort de Manonviller* (*Forts d'arrêt - en avant de Toul*) showing the bombardment damage to the fort. No date, circa September 1914

33. The *fossé* of the *fort de Manonviller* (*Forts d'arrêt - en avant de Toul*) showing the bombardment severe damage to the *Bétonné spécial* of this reinforced structure. 28 August 1914.

34. The *fort de Manonviller* (*Forts d'arrêt - en avant de Toul*) taken by the German Air Service, and also showing the clear outline of the fort a long with bombardment damage to the outer surface. No date, possibly early war.

35. View of the *fossé* of the *fort de Boussios* (*Le camp retranché de Maubeuge*) showing the *escarpe* on the left with the *pont* leading into the *entrée* and the *contrescarpe* on the right. c.1914. (IWM Q57542)

36. Damage by shellfire to the *fort de Malmaison* (*Frontière du nord - le groupe Nord/ Deuxième ligne /Forts d'arrêt – Soissons*). No date, post-war. (IWM Q44751)

37. The *fort de Vacherauville*, 4 June 1916 (Bibliotheque Municipale de Verdun MS812-47)

38. A *Locomotive Péchot-Bourdon modèle 1888* of the military *Voie ferré de 0.6m* (600mm military railway) – Pre-war / no date

39. Three quarter front view of a *Locomotive Péchot-Bourdon modèle 1888* with artillery officers and men including the locomotive crew – Pre-war / no date

40. A *Plate-Forme du Tablier de Truck modèle 1883* mounting a *canon de 'De Bange' 155mm longue S.P. modèle 1888* – pre-war / no date

41. Two *Affûts Trucks du général Peigne* mounting *Canon de 'De Bange' 120 mm court modèle 1878* and a *Plate-Forme du Tablier de Truck modèle 1883* loaded with shells being hauled by a *Locomotive Péchot-Bourdon modèle 1888* – Pre-war / no date

42. Three *Affûts Trucks du général Peigne* mounting *canon de 'De Bange' 120 mm court modèle 1878* during peacetime manoeuvres – pre-war / no date

43. An *Affûts Trucks du général Peigne* mounting a *canons de 155mm Court modèle 1912* - wartime/no date (French Official Photograph via IWM FO W674)

44. Locally recruited infantry (regiment unknown, but possibly from the *164e, 165e* or *166e régiments d'infanterie*) marching through a village in the Verdun area (*Le camp retranché de Verdun*) – pre-war / no date

45. Locally recruited cavalry (regiment unknown, but possibly from the *2e, 4e* or *5e divisions de cavalerie*) riding through a village in the Verdun area (*Le camp retranché de Verdun*) – pre-war / no date

Maps
in between 106 & 107

xiii

Roof and Floor Plans

in between 106 & 107

1.   The *Fort de Vaux* as built in 1884,
     (Based upon German Intelligence Report)

2.   The *Fort de Vaux* after modification in 1906,
     (Based upon French Army Engineers Drawings)

3.   The *Fort de Vacherauville* as built in 1910,
     (Based upon French Army Engineers' Drawings)

Sections

1.   Cross-Section of The *Fort de Vaux* as built in 1884,
     (Based upon German Intelligence Report)

2.   Cross-Section of a *'tourelle de 75mm (T75)'*,
     (Based upon German Intelligence Report)

3.   Cross-Section of an *'Observatoire Cuirasse Fixe'*,
     (Based upon German Intelligence Report)

4.   Cross-Section of a *'Tourelle de Mitrailleuses (GF4)'*,
     (Based upon German Intelligence Report)

5.   Plan and Section of a *'Casemate Bourges'*.
     (Based upon French Army Engineers' Drawings.)

6.   Section through a *'Casemate Pamards'*,
     (After M. & J. Barro's sketch Copyright ©1995)

7.   Side Elevation of the *Locomotive Péchot-Bourdon modèle 1888*,
     (After Christian Cénac Copyright ©1991)

Sketches

1.   Artist's impression of the *Fort de Vaux* as built in 1884

2.   Artist's impression of the *Fort de Vaux* after modification in 1906

3.   Artist's impression of the *Fort de Vacherauville* as built in 1910

Introduction

Early in 2001, I took a small private party of Americans around the fortifications of Verdun, and for a period after I was engaged in answering a number of questions relating to them. I gave a brief history of the fortifications to one of the party members and it became apparent that there is an interest in them, especially after the recent publication of books on the Battle of Verdun.[1]

The purpose of this study is to give a history of the permanent French fortifications of the Great War. These fortifications were designed and constructed over the years 1874-1914. I have used the defences around the town of Verdun in the French northeastern region of Lorraine as the basis for this study, since it was one of the most modern of the French defensive establishments in 1914. Verdun was also of course at the centre of one of the longest and bloodiest battles of the Great War, in which the fortifications played a significance role.

It should be noted that French fortifications consisted of a whole range of structures that formed a complex system - not just forts on their own, but of blockhouses, gun emplacements, infantry positions, depots, etc. - all forming an interlocking defence. It is for those reasons that I have named this book 'Verdun: An Integrated Defence.'

Since the fortifications were all pre-war designed and constructed, I have not only given detailed descriptions of them but also the background history to them. This history includes the leading characters, the politics, the policies and the strategies of the French, both civilian and military, whilst the fortifications were being built.

It is not the purpose of this study to give an in-depth analysis of the Battle of Verdun, nor any other battle that included one or more of the French Forts during the Great War[2] (in the same way that a study on types

---

[1] Recently published books are as follows:

Verdun 1916, by Malcolm Brown, published by Tempus Publishing Ltd, 1999

Verdun, by David Mason, published by The Windrush Press, 2000

The Road to Verdun, by Ian Ousby, published by Jonathan Cape, 2002

German Strategy and the Path to Verdun, by Robert T. Foley, published by Cambridge University Press, 2005

The Price of Glory, by Alistair Horne, published by Macmillan and Company Ltd., 1962, (following multiple reprints it is now available in Penguin paperback.)

[2] A number of the forts not including those of Verdun that saw action during the Great War, including the following: the *fort de Boussois* and *de Cerfontaine* (of *Le camp retranché de Maubeuge*), the *forts de la Malmaison* and *de Condé-sur-Aisne* (both of the *Frontière du nord - Groupe nord*; *deuxième ligne*), the *forts de Brimont* and *de la Pompelle* (*Frontière du nord-est – groupe Meuse*; *deuxième ligne*), the *forts de Troyon, des Paroches, du Camps des Romains,* and *de Liouville* (*Frontière*

of artillery would not attempt to cover every battle in which those artillery pieces were used.) However in the conclusion I have noted how the fortifications stood up to the aggressive actions of the warring armies at the time of the battle, and what remains are left to be seen.

There were 526 forts and other major fortifications[3] along the French frontiers and around major French cities immediately before the Great War. By 1914, Verdun was the most heavily fortified city in France, with thirty major fortifications in its defences. Twenty-two of Verdun's major fortifications had been built late or modified later on in the fortification program, incorporated some of the most modern designs concepts. This left eight of the fortifications in an unmodified state, giving a clear picture of original design concepts. Therefore, I have used the defences of Verdun as typical of all the defensive structures along the French frontier.

Although Verdun included an almost full range of defence structures, unfortunately there were a small number of defensive design features that were not used there. Where examples of a type of defensive feature are not to be found at Verdun, I have used examples from outside the Verdun defences. Generally all the forts and major fortifications were individually designed, especially in the mountainous regions of eastern France, but they still followed the same general pattern. The secondary fortifications and ancillary buildings were generally built to standard designs, although there were variations to be found (For example the small intermediate depots were design as single room masonry constructed buildings with an earthen covering, but there were a number that were built into the ground either into an embankment or built underground with a ramp descending down to the doorway).

The building program lasted 40 years from 1874 through to 1914, with modifications starting from 1885 continuing into the war years and beyond into the period between the world wars. With so much building work undertaken over such a long period, ideas in design threw up a lot of variations in details (For example the French designers developed five completely different types of drawbridges that were used within the fortification program). In consequence I have tried to describe all the variations of details, giving examples in each case.

Unfortunately, the local authorities at Verdun have started to seal off some of the fortifications, with the result that at the time of writing some of

---

du nord-est – groupe Meuse; forts rideau) and the Fort de Manonviller (Frontière du nord-est – groupe Meuse; fort d'arrêt).

[3] This total includes 118 earlier forts and fortifications (pre 1870) that were included in the new defences, but excludes the numerous battery positions, which were built during this period and that form an integral part of the defences. See appendix 2 for the fortifications as originally planned by général Séré de Rivières.

these details cannot be seen anymore. However, the details were standard and can be found in other fortifications though not necessarily within the fortifications located around Verdun.

The French Technical descriptions, place names and titles (ranks) are used throughout this publication, which are all shown in *italics*. The English translations are given within the text after the first use and can also be found listed within the Glossary. Some of the fortifications' type descriptions changed over the course of time and in such cases I have used the original fortification name within the text throughout, for example the *poste des Sartelles* became the *fort des Sartelles* – I have used the original title *poste des Sartelles*.

I have used footnotes to expand upon details in the text or to give reference that would be out of place within the text. Similarly I have used a large number of appendices to give listings and details that again would be out of place within the main text such as the brief description of French military railways during the fortification period – a subject that deserves a book in its own right and since they were an integral part of the fortification system requires more than just a passing comment within this study.

Acknowledgements

I would like to thank a number of people: Firstly, my American friend, Paul (Pete) Guthrie for his interest, which prompted the idea to write this book.

Tom Bull, a dear and close friend, who has accompanied me on numerous private visits to the Western Front and especially to the battlefield of Verdun to investigate the forts and fortifications of *général* Séré de Rivières. On one such visit he volunteered to help me in my researches in the French Archives and reproduced a number of the photographs used in this book.

My gratitude goes to the following: Claire Ben Lakhdar-Kreuwen, Directrice of the Bibliotheque Municipale de Verdun and her staff; Isabelle Remy Documentaliste of the Mémorial de Verdun: Dr. Achim Fuchs and his staff at the Bayerisches Hauptstaatsarchiv - Abt. IV Kriegsarchiv, München; and to The Keeper and his staff of the Photograph Archive, Imperial War Museum, London, for photographs.

Another good friend Ingrid Ferrand in her role as Verdun battlefield guide has not only shown me the forts of Verdun, but also given me a lot of useful information concerning their operation along with small details relating to the forts.

For the researches that have helped in the writing of this study I am indebted to Mark Conrad, Martin Egger, Florian Garnier, Alain Lecomte, Guy Le Hallé, J. Harlepin, Marcus Massing, Guy Pedroncini and Roland Scheller for their articles and publications M. & J. Barro for their illustration of the '*Casemate Pamards*' published in Guy Pedroncini's 'De L'Oppidum a L'Enfouissement - L'Art de la Fortification a Verdun et sur les marches de l'Est', which is the basis of a similar sketch included within. Christian Cénac published in 'La Voie de 60 sur less Fronts Français de la Guerre de 14-18' for his side elevation of the '*Locomotive Péchot-Bourdon*', which is the basis of my illustration also included within.

Finally my appreciation must go to Glyn Gibson and Raymond Lundquist for their help with the initial proofreading and a very special thank you to DEW for his multiple proofreading of the finished manuscript.

Any mistakes that might appear within the book are of course mine and mine alone.

The last thank you must go to my wife Barbara who not only had to put up with my obsession for the past four years whilst engaged in this project, but also did the final proofreading.

Background – French Fortifications up to 1873

After their defeat by the Germans in 1871 at the conclusion of the Franco-Prussian War, the French High Command developed a series of contingency war plans known sequentially as *Plan Nr. I* through to *Plan Nr. XVII*.

The final plan, *général* Joseph Joffre's *Plan Nr. XVII* became active in 1913. The *Plan Nr. XVII* was a mobilisation and deployment plan that was based on a huge, aggressive, offensive strike against the assumed enemy, the Germans. This materialised when war came in the summer of 1914. However the earlier plans up to the *Plan Nr. XV* were mainly defensive plans based around *centres de résistance* (centres of resistance) and *lignes de défense* (defensive lines), mostly based upon the then modern 'state-of-the-art' *forts* (forts) and their associated defences. The *Plan Nr. XIV* of 1898 was designed as a defensive plan however allowed for limited offensive operations in front of the defensive curtains to support their fortified positions. *General* Brugère's *Plan Nr. XV* was the first of the series of plans to move away from the previous defensive plans, it being an aggressive offensive plan. It was to be developed into the *Plan Nr. XVII* by *général* Joffre.

As already mentioned above there were a small number of slightly older forts that pre-dated this new planning from 1871, but due to their location, were also incorporated into the overall scheme. These were known as *vieux forts* (old forts). However the majority of the forts required for this new scheme were additional forts being built during the following forty years, most of them in the first ten years, including all of the forts centred around Verdun. An example of an old fort is the *fort des Justices,* which was part of *Le camp retranché de Besançon*. It should be noted that many of these old forts and indeed a number of the new forts that were added later were modified during this period to keep them up-to-date with advancing technology.

The man originally responsible for these 1871 fortifications was the serving '*directeur du Service du Génie au ministère de la Guerre*' (The Ministry of War's Service Director of Engineers), *général* Raymond Adolphe Séré de Rivières (1815-1895). Séré de Rivières' ideas were a direct development of the ideas established by his predecessors.

The first of the modern fortress designers in France was *Maréchal* Sébastien Le Prestre de Vauban (1633-1707) who in the seventeenth century fortified a large number of towns on the northern borders of France for King Louis XIV. His designs went away from the medieval castle concept with single high walls. He developed through various schemes culminating in the system that consisted of gunnery bastions giving the defenders the use of modern cannons. These gunnery bastions were essentially wide platforms that were arranged in such a way that the defenders not only had fire power directly against any besiegers or frontal attackers, but also crossfire across the face or front of the defences, against any attackers engaged in close up assault – making sure that there were no blind spots for the attackers to hide from the defending artillery or small arms fire. In effect Vauban replaced the tall thin walled medieval castles complete with high towers with modern forts that had low broad walls and squat bastions.

Vauban's successors continued to develop his ideas based upon this, his 'third system'. The most important of these developments were by the military engineers Montalembert and Haxo.

The *Marquis* Marc-René de Montalembert (1714-1800) developed the idea, which he formulated in his '*La Fortification perpendiculaire*' (1776-1786) of his small '*polygonal*' forts – polygonal in plan with smaller bastions and surrounded by a defensive ditch. This was a major development away from the fortified towns that Vauban had developed.

The *général* François-Nicolas Benoit *Baron* Haxo (1774-1838) developed his own ideas relating to the placement of the artillery within casemates, which became known as '*casemates à canons*' (gun casemates). These casements gave the guns and their crews a much greater degree of protection from incoming enemy artillery fire.

Probably the two people who had the most important influence on Séré de Rivières were the strategists *général Baron* Joseph Rogniat (1767-1840) and *général* Casimir-Charles de Poitevin *Baron* de Maureillan (1772-1829) who developed the idea of distance defence. Their concept was based on the principle that the best way to protect a city from enemy artillery was to prevent the said artillery from being placed within range. This was done by building a number of outer defences at the same distance as that of the range of the enemy artillery. Consequentially it would be highly dangerous for the enemy to position his artillery in range of the city without coming under intense direct artillery fire from the outlaying defences. In effect, deterring the enemy from doing so.

After completing his army officer training, Raymond Adolphe Séré de Rivières saw active service from 1840 to 1859 in Algeria and Italy. In 1862 he was posted to Nice where he reorganised the defences of that city. During the period 1864-70, he was posted to and planned the defences of Metz, which included the construction of four outlaying *forts* [4] creating a

---

[4]   There were eight forts originally planned although only four were completed before the outbreak of the Franco-Prussian War. Under the terms of the Treaty of Frankfurt at the conclusion of the Franco-Prussian War, France ceded Metz to the Germans. The four French forts were handed over and incorporated into the new

camp retranché (entrenched camp - fortified town). Promoted to *Colonel* in 1871, he was given the responsibility for the engineering aspects of the defence of Lyon during the Franco-Prussian War of 1870-71.

Following Séré de Rivières promotion to *Général de Brigade* in early 1872, Séré de Rivières was given a command in the Bourbon Army. He was made responsible for reinforcing the defences of Besançon and the Pontarlir-Joux region. However he was forced, due to set backs, to make his escape to, and was subsequently interned in Switzerland. His interment, however, was short and on returning to France later that same year, saw action involving the recapturing of the *forts d'Issy*, *de Vanvres* and *de Montrouges* all being part of the Parisian defences then under siege - thus giving him first hand experience of attacking forts.

With the Franco-Prussian war now over, Séré de Rivières became the secretary of Adolphe Thiers' *Comité de Défense* (Defence Committee), taking up his post on 30 June 1872. The chairman of the Committee was the *Maréchal* de MacMahon. This Committee reviewed the surrender of Metz and then went on to review all the Defence Procedures with regard to the defence of France, especially its eastern borders during the Franco-Prussian war. Based on the review work undertaken by the committee, Séré de Rivières produced a number of studies that formed the basis for the future defence of France and the construction program for fortifying the French borders. In 1873 *Maréchal* Canrobert replaced *Maréchal* de MacMahon as chairman of the *Comité de Défense*.

He wrote three studies between 1871 and 1873 with regard to the defence of the eastern Franco-German border, followed by a fourth more general study in 1874 covering the defence of the whole of France – namely all of the borders. Finally from 1876 to 1877, he wrote two more detailed studies concerning the defence of the northern border facing Belgian and the mountainous eastern borders (the Jura) bordering onto Switzerland and Italy.

The Germans kept a small army of occupation in France after the war until the French had paid the reparation demanded at the Treaty of Frankfurt as part of the peace agreement. The French paid the reparations in full by the late summer of 1873, and on 18 September 1873 the last of the Germans left France when they evacuated the city of Verdun.

German defences of the city. They were the *forts des Carrières, Diou, de Saint-Julien* and *de Queuleu*. The Germans renamed them *Feste Frederich Karl, Feste Alvenslebenn, Feste Manteuffeil* and *Feste Goeben* respectively. When they were returned to the French after the Great War they reverted to their original French names with the exception of the *fort des Carrières*, which was renamed the *fort de Plappeville*.

In February 1874, Séré de Rivières was appointed the '*directeur du Service du Génie au ministére de la Guerre*'. It was this appointment that empowered him to put his ideas into practice.

***

The Defence Committee set up a number of sub-committees and commissions to look at the various aspects of defences. The most important commission in relation to the fortification program was the *Commission des Cuirassements* (the Commission for Armouring). Created on 9 May 1874, it had as its first chairman *Général* Cadart. Over the years, a number of artillery and engineering specialists sat on the commission. This included a number of French Naval engineering officers who had had first hand experience of armouring as related to the new armoured warships[5]. Within a short time *Général* Cadart handed over the chairmanship of the Commission for Armouring to *Général* Secrétain.

However, the first officer to make a real impact on the committee was an army engineering officer, *Capitaine* (later to be promoted *commandant*) Henri Louis Philippe Mougin (1841-1916).

Mougin, a former aide-de-camp to Séré de Rivières, started to investigate the possibility of protecting the guns and the gun crews of the forts using various forms of armour constructed out of different materials that new technology was developing.

By 1876, Mougin had come up with a number of ideas and required experiments to take place in order to test and develop his ideas further. Of particular interest was the strength of armoured plates of different materials against shellfire. Therefore the commission decided to set up an experimental centre that became known as *the polygone d'essai de Gâvres* (The Gâvres' Testing ground) near to Lorient in Brittany. Consequently, the commissioners relocated to the testing ground to be near to the testing, with the result that the commission became commonly known as the *Commission de Gâvres* (Gâvres' Commission).

---

[5] The members of the *Commission des Cuirassements* that first sat on 9 May 1874 consisted of:

Général Cadart (committee chairman)
Capitaine du génie Mougin (army engineer captain and committee secretary)
Colonel d'artillerie Dards (army artillery colonel became chairman of the *Commission de Gâvres)*
Capitaine d'artillerie de Terre Guérin (army artillery captain)
Capitaine d'artillerie de Marine Bertin (naval artillery captain)
Capitaine d'artillerie de Terre Camps (army artillery captain)
Chef d'escadron d'artillerie de Terre Mugnier (army artillery major)
Monsieur F. Godron (civilian marine engineer)
Monsieur M. Bourdelles (civilian bridge and roadway engineer).

The Overall Plan for the Defence of France as Proposed by Séré de Rivières, 1872 - 1877

On 15 November 1873, Séré de Rivières published his third study for the defence of the eastern border in his memorandum *'Considérations sur la reconstitution de la frontière de l'Est'* (Considerations for the reconstitution of the Eastern Frontier).

The logic followed that with the defeat of the French army during the Franco-Prussian War of 1870-71 along with the internal fighting in the aftermath of that defeat, the French army was left shattered. The Treaty of Frankfurt relocated the eastern border between France and Germany across central Lorraine and the western boundary of Alsace. This new frontier, of approximately two hundred kilometres in length, consisted of two stretches of flat lands divided by a mountainous area. Both the German and the French armies regarded this mountainous area, known as the Vosges, as impregnable. Nevertheless, the flat lands either side of the Vosges would be extremely difficult for the French to defend, even with a well-equipped army with good morale. However these were luxuries the defeated French army at that time did not have - having neither the equipment nor the morale to defend it.

This new frontier ran through Central Lorraine, which consists of a flat plain known as the *plaine la Woëvre* ('The Woëvre Plain', which is commonly known as the Woëvre), which covers the area from the border with Belgium in the north to the boundary with the French region of Franche-Comte in the south. It then followed the eastern boundary of Franche-Comte (opposite to the western border of the southern part of the new German region of Alsace) down to the border with Switzerland. The northern section of the Franche-Comte frontier passed across the south western part of the Vosges mountain range before it dropped down onto a relative level area known as the *Trouée de Belfort* (the 'Belfort Gap') before climbing up again into the foothills of the Alpine mountains.

Initially after the Franco-Prussian War, the German chancellor Otto von Bismarck sought to isolated the French from other European powers by creating a series of international understandings and alliances, first with the Austrian-Hungarians and the Russians, and then later with the Italians. They were as follows:

The *Dreikaiserbund* of 1873 (the League of the Three Emperors) signed between Germany, Austro-Hungary and Russia, which was renewed in 1881,

The *Zweibund* (Dual Alliance) of 1879 between Germany & Austro-Hungary,

The *Dreibund* (Triple Alliance) of 1882 signed between Germany, Austro-Hungary and Italy

The *Rückrersicherungsrertrag* of 1887 (the Reinsurance Treaty) signed between Germany and Russia.

With the Belgians being neutral and the British being aloof from European politics, the Germans were successful in their endeavours until the Russians were forced out of this cordon of hostile neighbours in 1890 by the blundering diplomacy of the new Kaiser of Germany – Wilhelm II.

With the French isolated from other powers and with their Army decimated and therefore undermanned, the concept of offensive operations was not an option. A defensive plan had to be developed especially against the new German empire, the relations to whom were strained – there being a number of false diplomatic alarms during the period after the Franco-Prussian War. Therefore Séré de Rivières proposed a new system of defence consisting of lines of forts and fortified positions set back from the new eastern border along the nearest high ground. Working on the assumption that the Germans would be the aggressors launching a surprise attack with superior forces, he foresaw that the French army would have little time to mobilise, with the result that the Germans would gain a huge advantage over the French. One should bear in mind that the French mobilisation and deployment plans in the early 1870's would be dependent on the limited number of the then existing railway and road networks. This would be less of a problem for the Germans since they would be dictating the time and place of their offensive, and would have therefore already pre-planned their troop movements, unlike the French who would have to react to the situation that the Germans put them under.

The original strategy, behind the lines of fortifications was therefore threefold:

i   to prevent a surprise attack.
ii   to slow down and stop the German advance.
iii   to allow time for the French army to mobilise and to form up under the cover of the defensive line of fortifications.

It was assumed by Séré de Rivières that if the Germans launched an attack it would be around the Vosges Mountains from either end; in the north across central Lorraine into western Lorraine or through the *Trouée de Belfort* into Franche-Comte to the south. However he also assumed that the Germans could not or would not launch an attack directly over the Vosges Mountains - there being an inadequate road and railway system over the mountains at that time to support such an attack. Even to this day, communications across the Vosges is limited – there are no railway lines that run through the mountain range and the road system, although much improved by the construction of military roads during the Great War as well as the construction in the nineteen-eighties of a major road tunnel through the northern part of the mountains; the links are still sparse. He therefore felt that there was no need to defend the area in the shadow of the mountain range with fortifications. (See Map 1 for The First two Groups of Fortifications; *le groupe de la Meuse* and *le groupe Vosges*.)

Based on the proceeding logic, the eastern border was to be defended by two lines of forts, a northern and a southern section. The northern section, located between the cities of Verdun in the north and Toul in the south, forming the defensive line on the hills above the River Meuse to the west of the *plaine la Woëvre*. The southern section located between the cities of Épinal in the north and Belfort in the south, forming the defensive line on the hills above the River Moselle. The four above-mentioned cities were to become *camps retranché*. This would then leave an un-fortified gap of about ninety kilometres between Toul and Épinal, located behind the central part of the mountains. It was considered that this un-fortified area could be defended by the weak sections of the active French army stationed within the area during normal peacetime, who would use delaying tactics against any German forces that managed to find a passage across the mountains. Once the French army had been mobilised, any Germans that had found their way through this gap could then be dealt with.

This was the basis of the first contingency war plan, and was named the *Plan Nr. I*: it was published in 1880. It was a mobilisation plan based on a purely defensive strategy devised by Séré de Rivières, and it envisaged an armed concentration waiting behind the defensive curtains. The *Plan Nr. II* that followed shortly after in 1882 was a straight development of the *Plan Nr. I*; however, with Séré de Rivières removal from office, the strategies behind the later plans began to move away from those of Séré de Rivières.

The lines of fortifications that consisted mainly of forts between the *camps retranché* were to be located at strategic points guarding the main routes (major roads, railways, mountain passes, river crossings and tunnels) into France that the potential enemy presumed to be the Germans, but later the Italians as well, would take. A fine example of one of these strategic fortifications was the *fort de Manonviller*, which is located on a hill that overlooks the main Strasbourg-Nancy road just to the east of Lunéville. The site of the *fort de Manonviller* was at the time of its construction approximately ten kilometres from the then Franco-German border.

It was also hoped that the defensive lines of fortifications would have a deterrent effect on any would-be attacker, especially the Germans, but also included the Italians further to the south. It was indeed this deterrent effect that led to *Generalfeldmarschall* Alfred Graf von Schlieffen (1833-1913), the German Chief of Staff between 1891-1905 to develop his contingency war plans as based on his memorandums. The last of his memorandums of 1905 which was accepted by his successor, *Generalfeldmarschall* Helmuth von Moltke, the Younger, led to the German offensive against the French with a 'powerful right wing' through Belgium so as to outflank the French fortifications on the eastern border of France in August 1914.

The only flaw in Séré de Rivières' plan was that the city of Nancy, to the east of the Moselle and very close to the relocated Franco-German border, was to be left only semi-defended in front of the main line of defence, and although there were several plans (the *Plan Nr. VIII* of 1887 for instance) to somehow link the defence of Nancy into the overall defensive program, none of them ever materialised. According to a German intelligence map of Nancy dated 1873, the French were going to build a ring of twenty-three *forts* - five of which were to be very large ones. Of the twenty-three *forts* only one, the *fort de Frouard*, was actually constructed. However Nancy, being located on the attack route that the Germans would possibly take into France through the gap between Épinal and Toul, did have a number of fortifications built in its vicinity guarding the potential attack routes of the Germans. This cluster of five fortifications was known as the *Forts d'arrêt - en avant de Toul* (arresting forts in front of Toul). Two of the Nancy fortifications; the *fort de Frouard* to the north and the *fort de Pont-Saint-Vincent* to the south, caused the German military planners before the Great War a lot of concern regarding the feasibility of using this particular attack route in a future war. The two forts were located on the heights just above major crossing points on the river *Moselle*, the former to the north of Nancy and the latter to the south, thereby dominating the crossing points as well as the surrounding countryside. Von Schlieffen in 1894 suggested this attack route into France as one of two possible routes (the other being north of Verdun, which became the operational plan), but was criticised by *Generalfeldmarschall* Alfred *Graf von* Waldersee and *Generalmajor* Ernst Köpke, both senior members of his staff, on the basis that the *fort de Pont-Saint-Vincent* dominated the area and would be costly both in time and manpower to capture. Schlieffen held on to his idea until he dropped it at the turn of the twentieth century due to new factors. (This situation was reminiscent of what actually occurred during the battle for the monastery at Monte Casino in Italy during the Second World War. The Germans held the monastery up on the mountainside that dominated the valley below and the route towards Rome. This prevented the Allies' progress to Rome, until they had captured the monastery from the Germans, which they did at a very high cost in both time and manpower.)

The northern group of fortifications became known as *la frontière du nord-est* (*hauts de Meuse*) - *le groupe de la Meuse*. The southern group of fortifications became known as *la frontière de l'est* (*côte de Moselle*) - *le groupe Vosges*.

On 17 November 1874, *la Chambre des Députés* (the French Chamber of Deputies) passed a law to construct the defences based upon Séré de Rivières' memorandum, voting in the first instalment of 29 million *Francs d'Or* (Gold Francs), out of an estimated 88 million *Francs d'Or* for the realisation of this defence project.

At the beginning of 1875, Séré de Rivières suggested additional lines of fortifications. A new main line on the northern border (becoming known as *la frontière du nord - le groupe Nord*) in case the Germans used Belgium as their line of attack into France and thereby violating Belgian neutrality. He also suggested secondary lines (*Deuxième ligne* - the front lines becoming the *Première ligne*) to reinforce the lines on both the eastern and planned northern border.[6]

Existing fortified towns on the northern border (Dunkerque and Lille for example) were modernised and the overall plan was extended towards the south to cover the Alpine and Italian borders. The major cities of Paris and Lyon also had their existing fortifications updated.

It was hoped by the French politicians that the Belgians would remain neutral in any future Franco-German conflict and that the Germans would honour that neutrality, therefore the need to defend the northern border was questioned. Consequentially the northern border was not defended quite as forcefully as the revised defences on the eastern border, where the main threat was foreseen. The estimated cost rose to 400 *Franc d'Or*.

So, as can be seen, Séré de Rivières ideas were a straight development of the ideas as laid down by Maureillan and Rogniat, but on a much larger scale, using the fortified lines to protect the whole of France as opposed to just a town or city. Indeed the Germans at that time felt that Séré de Rivières had turned the whole of France into one giant *camps retranché*.

In the autumn of 1879, Séré de Rivières came under attack from the French Parliament, especially from the *Comte* de Roy for exceeding the original budget. *Général* Gresley, *la Ministre de Guerre* (the Minister of War), therefore came under pressure to reduce spending. With a change within the government and a new minister, *général* Farre, Séré de Rivières was removed from office in an attempt to reduce the expenditure. Séré de Rivières was retired and played no further part in the planning of the defence of France. He lived for another 15 years in quiet retirement in Paris, dying there on 16 February 1895.

To give an idea of the amount of over expenditure during this original planning and construction period, Verdun was to have six *redoutes*; this was increased to a total of sixteen *forts* and *redoutes*. A seventeenth one - the

---

[6] Indeed the French military command were very wary at this time of the Germans using Belgium as a possible attack route into France with the result that they developed two contingency plans to cover this possibility. The *Plan Nr. VI* of 1883 was an appendix to the *Plan Nr. III* and covered the possibility of Germany violating Belgium and the *Plan Nr. VII* also of 1883 was another appendix to *Plan Nr. III* covering the possibility of Germany forming an alliance with Belgium with a view to attack France.

fort de Vacherauville - was planned and built much later in 1912 but was not part of this original planning budget. Épinal likewise had eight planned, which was increased to seventeen. However there was a successful cost reduction at Reims where only seven out of the total of twelve originally planned were actually built.

Although Séré de Rivières was removed from office to reduce the spending on the defences, his successors continued along the same lines of defence development with an equally high rate of expenditure, consequently from 1875 to 1885 the cost of the defence of France had risen to a total of 564 million *Franc d'Or* for the permanent structures and another 229 million *Franc d'Or* for the required armaments.

By 1885 the borders of France were defended as follows:

The entire borders of France (including the updated old forts)
> 158 *forts*
> 40 *ouvrages*
> 254 *batteries*

The above totals included on the Northern and Eastern borders:
> 105 *forts*
> 25 *ouvrages*
> 162 *batteries*

As a postscript, there were two more major developments to the strategic plans for the defence of France, after Séré de Rivières had left office.

The first change to the strategy was the *Plan Nr. X* of 1889, which was the first of the plans to move away from a purely defensive scheme. It was still based on the defence using the fortified lines, but it would allow a limited offensive towards Metz and Strasbourg if the circumstances were favourable. The next two plans were straight developments of *Plan Nr. X.*

The second change occurred in 1896, the then *Commandement en Chef* (Commander in Chief)[7], *général* Miribel, produced his mobilisation and deployment *Plan Nr. XIII.*

The concept behind his plan was fourfold:

i   to prevent a surprise attack.
ii   to slow down and stop the German advance on the defensive line of fortifications.
iii to allow time for the French army to mobilise and to form up under the cover of the defensive line of fortifications.

---

[7] The *Commandement en Chef* was more formally known as the *chef d'état-major général de l'armée* (the Chief of the General Staff of the Army.)

iv   In addition to the earlier plans, to force the German advance to be funnelled through pre-determined gaps, within the fortified lines. The first gap was located between Verdun and the Belgian border, known as the *Trouée de Stenay* (The Stenay Gap) and the second gap between Épinal and Toul, known as the *Trouée de Charmes* (The Charmes Gap). Instead of using delaying tactics as previously planned, the weak sections of the French army would retreat slowly luring the German army forwards into a massive trap. Once the main part of the French army had mobilised and deployed behind the fortified lines, it could then enact a pincer counter attack either side of the German break through. The consideration being that once the Germans were stopped, a heavy defeat could then be inflicted upon them – the line of fortification would then become the springboard for an overall counter offensive which would lead to the conquest of the 'lost' regions of Alsace and Lorraine and perhaps even into the homeland of Germany.

This defensive-offensive doctrine behind *Plan Nr. XIII* remained active in the following French plans until 1911 when *général* Michel produced his purely defensive *Plan Nr. XVI Variant Nr. 1* (the first revision of *général* de Lacroix's defensive-offensive *Plan Nr. XVI* of 1909), which changed the concept by making use of reserve troops to cover the whole of the Northern border with Belgium. The defensive concept was dropped altogether when *général* Joffre in 1913 revised Michel's plan into the purely offensive *Plan Nr. XVI Variant Nr. 2*, which he then developed in 1914 into his totally new offensive plan, known as *Plan Nr. XVII*.

The General Development of the Defences 1874-1914

There were three distinct chronological stages in the development of the fortification program within the French defences between 1874 and 1914:

First period	1874-1884	Original Séré de Rivières planning using masonry construction coupled with the armoured designs of Mougin using iron and standard builder's concrete.
Second period	1885-1891	Reinforcing the original structures with special hard concrete.
Third period	1892-1914	Reinforcing and constructing with Ferro concrete and steel armour.

There was to a small degree a continuation of the first phase of development work well into the later two phases.

***

The first period 1874 to 1884 saw the construction of the fortifications based on the original design concept as lay down by Séré de Rivières.

As previously noted Séré de Rivières based the defences of France around *centres de résistance*, which were then linked together by *lignes de défense*. The *centres de résistance* consisted mainly of *camps retranché* using the concepts as laid down by Rogniat and de Maureillan for 'distance defence' and using de Montalembert type polygonal forts.

The *camps retranché* were laid out to withstand a siege and as such consisted of the following elements:

i   Permanent Fortifications of various types – forts, field works, artillery positions, command posts, etc.

ii   Independent Army Camps that included Barracks to house the required manpower, animals and equipment to man not only the permanent fortifications listed above but also the adhoc field fortifications that would also be required to fill the gaps between the above fortifications,

iii Artillery Parks including Arsenals for the storage and maintenance of the required artillery weapons,

iv   Ammunition and supply depots,

v   Warehouses especially for food stores – enough to last a siege for up to six months for military personnel, civilians and livestock,

vi   Exercise and Parade Grounds for training,

vii Communications – consisting of heliograph (visual signalling) and telegraph,

viii Permanent Roads and Railways networks,

ix Permanent Flying Grounds for Balloons.

Once aeroplanes had been developed in the early twentieth century flying grounds for them were added to the *camps retranché*, however during the original planning period only balloon flying was possible and hence only flying grounds for balloons were considered. As with the development of the aeroplane, the development of communication especially the telephone led to a telecommunication networks being installed at a later date.

The *lignes de défense* consisted of permanent fortifications mainly of forts linked together by a network of military permanent roads and communications.

The main structural material used in the construction of the first generation of fortifications was masonry, which at the time had sufficient strength to withstand bombardments by the then in-use black powdered propelled and black powdered filled iron projectiles. Brickwork was used where the strength to withstand a bombardment was not required, such as underground structures.

At the start of the fortification program Mougin of the *Commission des Cuirassements* seeing the danger to the guns and their crews in exposed positions began work on his Haxo style casemates, which he then developed into his armoured turrets. This work was limited to the materials available to him - namely standard builder's concrete of moderate strength and of iron, both cast and rolled. However at the time these materials were quite adequate to withstand the projectiles then in use.

***

By the mid eighteen-eighties, with the development of high explosive, which was invented by the French industrial chemist Eugene Turpin (1848-1927) especially those based on picric acid (known as *mélinite* in France and lyddite in Britain), it was quickly realised by the French that masonry and the standard builder's concrete were not strong enough to withstand the force imparted by such modern explosives. What made the situation worse was that with the new explosives came the development of a greater selection of heavy artillery firing more substantial steel shells at greater angles of trajectory – namely howitzers. This made the roofs of the building within the fortifications particularly vulnerable from plunging fire. In effect this made all of the French masonry fortifications obsolete overnight.

To confirm the truth of the situation, the French military authorities allowed the *Comité de Défense* to conduct a series of experiments on an existing 'modern' fort using the new explosive. The fort in question was the *fort de la Malmaison* of the *deuxième ligne* of *le groupe Nord* between La Fère and Soissons[8], which was, between 11 August and 25 October 1886, used in two experiments; the first to determine the effects of modern shellfire using modern artillery pieces on a masonry fort. The fort was bombarded by 120 millimetre and 155 millimetre cannons and then by 190 millimetre and 220 millimetre mortars. The second experiment was to determine the effect of modern high explosive on a masonry fort, with charges of up to 32 kilogrammes of *mélinite* being placed and then detonated within the fort. In both cases the effect of the explosions was devastating to the superstructures of the fort, prompting the conclusion that indeed the masonry fortifications were obsolete! It was noted that the shells penetrated as deep as six and a half metres and that in the case of the heaviest shells (of 220 millimetre calibre) the underground chambers with six metres of soil above proved to be insufficient to withstand the explosions.

With the majority of the defences of France completed, this proved to be a very serious disappointment to the French authorities. Having put so much effort and money into the construction program of the defences, a solution had to be found to counter the new high explosive shells – quickly and as cheaply as possible. To redesign and to rebuild all of the fortifications would be far too expensive and therefore out of the question, so it was obvious that the existing fortifications would have to be somehow upgraded and strengthened to withstand future bombardments. Any new fortifications would have to be similarly built to withstand the future bombardments by the harder hitting artillery.

Noting that the Belgium fortress designer *Lieutenant Général* Henri Alexis Brialmont (1821-1903) had in the eighteen-sixties used concrete as the main structural material in the construction of the forts around the city of Antwerp, the French turned their attention to this material as a solution to their problem. French industrial chemists developed an extra hard concrete known as *Bétonné spécial* (Special concrete), which was believed to be strong enough to protect against the new harder hitting shells. It was tested and indeed found to be secure against the new generation of shells. So the decision was taken to use the *Bétonné spécial* to reinforce the vital parts of the existing fortifications. The development and testing of the *Bétonné spécial* took the two years from 1885 to 1887.

---

[8] In 1912 the *fort de la Malmaison* was finally decommissioned and in 1914 was being demolished when the Great War broke out. Even in its semi-demolished state, it went on to play an important role during the Great War especially in the Nivelle's Spring Offensives – The Second Battle of the Aisne of April 1917 and Pétain's Limited Offensives – The Battle of La Malmaison of October and November 1917.

After the *fort de la Malmaison's* experiments; a follow up series of experiments were conducted at the *polygone de Bourges* (the Bourges Firing Ranges and Testing Ground) with various ideas for modern fortifications and structures being built out of *Bétonné spécial* and tested against modern heavy artillery and against *mélinite* charges. The experiments proved to be quite successful even though the tests were conducted before the *Bétonné spécial* was given enough time to fully set. Further experiments found that by combining the *Bétonné spécial* with a layer of sand below and a layer of soil above, a very strong and impenetrable surface was formed.

By the time that the problem with regard to the new high explosive had occurred Séré de Rivières had already been removed from office due to the earlier cost over-runs of the initial fortification programs. Therefore it was his successor who took the decision to reduce costs by strengthening only a selected number of the fortifications. It was the fortifications in the potential future war zones, namely *la frontière du nord-est* and *la frontière de l'est* (the border with Germany) and of those the ones mainly within the *camps retranché* that were chosen for modernising. Of the ones in the *camps retranché*, it was the fortifications that were located furthest from the towns and therefore nearest to the perceived attack that were chosen for updating. In another attempt to cut costs a large number of the other fortifications were downgraded, mainly the ones that were in secondary positions and those that were believed to be outside of the future war zone. A large number of the forts that were downgraded which had been originally believed to be outside of the future war zone actually ended up being within the future war zone. For example the forts of *Le camp retranché de Reims.*

Starting in 1887, the strengthening program consisted of the roofs of the main buildings within the interiors of the selected *forts* being reinforced with a thick layer of *Bétonné spécial* sandwiched between two layers of ballast to act as a cushion against in coming shells. In a small number of cases a layer of *Bétonné spécial* was also applied to exposed walls of these buildings so as to strengthen them. The main defensive bastions, which originally were positioned as part of the inner workings of the forts, were reconstructed so that they were positioned outside of the *forts* to lessen the likelihood of them being destroyed by shellfire.

As well as the forts, a number of the infantry field positions were selected to be upgraded by rebuilding them as defensive fortlets using *Bétonné special.*

This initial work of upgrading lasted from 1885 to 1891 and formed the second period of development.

***

However the next and final period of the fortification upgrading lasting from 1892 to the start of the Great War consisted of the introduction of armoured steel into the forts and fortlets.

This consisted of replacing the open and somewhat exposed gunnery positions upon the forts with armoured turrets for all-round fire and by the addition of Haxo style 'flanking casemates' using *Bétonné special* which from 1897 had reinforcing steel bars added for greater strength and protection. The 'flanking casemates' were to be used to cover the intervening ground between the fortifications and as such were positioned upon the sides of the fortification with restrictive fields of fire – that being sideways along the line from the fortification towards the next fortifications.

Also during this third period, large numbers of small infantry bunkers were built between the major fortifications - also constructed out of reinforced *Bétonné spécial* to give the covering infantry manning the interval areas between the major fortifications a degree of protection from the new artillery shells.

Finally, during later phase of this construction and modernisation period, the last group of fortifications were built, incorporating some if not all of the new design features and innovations mentioned above.

The Initial Planning and Construction of Verdun's Defences 1872-1884

As noted previously, in 1873 Séré de Rivières initially divided up that part of the frontier perceived to be the most threatened (the north eastern border with Germany) into two defensive regions. The northern border with Belgium was added in 1876 followed in 1877 by the eastern border with Switzerland and Italy. The remainder of the French borders followed, being completed by 1900. These regions were known as *groupes* (groups), each *groupe* consisted of a *première ligne* (first line) and the borders that were most threatened had a *deuxième ligne* (second line). (For the Regional Grouping of the Fortified Zones, see Appendix 1.) The fortified lines were made up of a combination of fortified towns; *camps retranché*, and *lignes de défense* consisting of; *forts de liaison* or *forts de rideau* (linking or curtain forts). Individual *forts* were added to the defensive system at key locations in front of these fortified lines and were known as *forts d'arrêt* (arresting or blocking forts) or *forts isolé* (isolated forts). Verdun was one of the towns selected to be fortified and thereby becoming a *camps retranché*. (See Map 2 for France's Frontier Defences Regions (Groups) as defined by *général* Séré de Rivières).

The town of Verdun was ideal for this purpose being sited on two natural defensive barriers – *La Meuse Fleuve* (the River Meuse) and the line of hills, known as the *Hauts de Meuse* (the Meuse Heights), which, from 1871 to 1919, were the nearest natural barriers to the Franco-German border within the region. Known as *Le camp retranché de Verdun*, it was also known as *La place fortifiée de Verdun*. However during the war the whole *zone de défense* (defensive zone) that consisted of all the defences within the area including the adhoc wartime defences outside of the original Séré de Rivières structures became designated as *La région fortifiée de Verdun (RFV)*.

Verdun also had an advantage in that it had an existing fortification – namely *la citadelle* (the citadel), which Vauban had designed with construction being completed in 1699. Verdun had been fortified from its earliest beginnings. Founded by the Romans as a border garrison town to the Roman Empire, it consisted of a Roman fort around which the town grew. It became a walled city during medieval times and the first construction work on its citadel pre-dates Vauban - work starting in the sixteenth century. The *Marechal* de Tavannes designed and started the work on this first citadel in 1567 with the completing it in 1591. However Vauban completely redesigned the citadel prompting the total reconstruction of it.

Le camps retranché de Verdun formed the northern end of *le groupe de la Meuse* with the next major town upstream from Verdun, sixty-seven kilometres to the south, *Toul* (also a *camp retranché*) forming the southern end of the *première ligne*. To complete *le groupe de la Meuse*, the *deuxième ligne* was formed by *Le camp retranché de Reims* one hundred kilometres to the west. The *deuxième lignes*, which although completed by the mid 1880's were downgraded in 1885, due to armament and explosive developments that made the *forts* out of date.

The military engineers in the areas that were to be fortified were asked to put forward schemes for fortifying their areas. In the case of Verdun, the *chef du Génie de Verdun* (Verdun's Chief of Engineers), Lieutenant Colonel Marchand, devised a plan in 1874 that consisted of five *forts* (forts), five *redoutes* (redoubts) and nine *batteries* (artillery positions or gunnery emplacements). They were to be position in a ring around Verdun. The forts were to have sixteen to twenty cannons each, the *redoutes* ten to twelve cannons, and the *batteries* from two to seven cannons. He estimated that his scheme would cost 18 million *Francs d'Or*.

Although Marchand's conception was generally accepted, modifications in the locations and types of fortifications were made. The number of forts and *redoutes* were reduced. There was to be a single ring of six *redoutes*, which were located from two and a half to six and a half kilometres from the centre of the city affording the city all round protection. Originally, each *redoutes* was to be spaced about five kilometres apart so that the then current heavy guns using black powder propellant would cover all of the intervening ground. All of the *redoutes* were built and later re-designated as *forts*.

By 1878, another four *forts* and *redoutes* had been added to the original six *redoutes*; however, the distance out from the centre of Verdun for these new fortifications was increased. This new line of fortifications, with the addition of other fortifications built between 1881 and 1887, was to become a second, outer ring. Once completed, this second ring consisted of ten *forts* and *redoutes*, five to eight kilometres from the centre, positioned so as to give each other, including those of the original ring of fortifications, covering or supporting fire. (For the organization of *Le camp retranché de Verdun*, see Appendix 3.) Thus the fortifications were spaced within the range of the guns, which were to be the intended main armament for the original forts. As a result, the *forts* were spaced about one and a half to two and a half kilometres apart, except for the three and a half kilometres gaps across the *Meuse*.

This created an integrated defence system, for example, the *redoute de Souville* was designed to be locked into the defence of its neighbouring *forts* and *redoutes* of *Saint Michel*, *Tavannes*, *Vaux* and *Douaumont*. The outer ring of *forts* was known as the *ligne principale de résistance* (main line of resistance), the inner ring as the *ligne de soutien* or *ligne intérieure* (support or inner line). For administration purposes the defences of Verdun were divided into a number of *secteurs* (sectors), by the start of the Great War there were three *secteurs*. (See Map 4 for The Main Fortifications of Verdun – *Le camp retranché de Verdun*.)

Redoutes and *Forts*[9]

Construction of the new *redoutes* started in 1874, with all the *redoutes* and *forts* being individually designed to suit the neighbouring surroundings. (For the Dates of Construction and Modifications of the Principal Fortifications of *Le camp retranché de Verdun*, see Appendix 5.) As noted above there were a number of old forts that were included into the new defensive system, and which were constructed well before this date. However there were no old forts utilised in *Le camp retranché de Verdun*. Strategically local high points were selected providing a commanding position with unobstructed views enabling direct fire of the surrounding countryside[10]. At the height of the fortifications' construction program, all available local labour was committed, and it was still found to be inadequate and so ex-patriot labour from Germany and Italy was used.

The size of the *forts* varied considerably; however, they did follow the same general pattern. To give a general idea to the size of the forts; the *fort de Vaux* (one of the smallest forts) covered an area of approximately 135 metres by 195 metres and had a planned garrison of 157 officers and men, compared with the *fort de Douaumont* (one of the largest forts) which had dimensions of approximately 280 metres by 380 metres with a garrison of 484 officers and men. In plan they were commonly based on either a four- or five-sided irregular shapes. Although irregular shapes were the norm for the plans of the forts there were a few forts that had perfectly regular shaped plans. There were no regular shaped forts located in *Le camp retranché de Verdun*, however the *fort de Lucey* of *Le camp retranché de Toul* and the *fort de Frouard* part of the *Forts d'arrêt - en avant de Toul* were both based

---

[9] As noted above these fortifications were originally called '*redoutes*' however these earlier, smaller forts were all re-designated as '*forts*'. Some of the '*postes*' were modified and also re-designated as *forts* however others were not (for example, after modifications the *poste des Sartelles* was re-designated as a *fort* but the un-modified *poste de la Belle-Épine* did not remain as a *poste*.)

[10] 'Direct fire' is where the artillery gunners can observe their targets directly, as opposed to 'indirect fire' were the gunners position their cannons where they cannot observe their targets (due to the range of the guns coupled with the lay of the land) and therefore rely on instructions from remote observers who would locate the targets and signal back details. With the advent of modern artillery using the modern high explosive propellants that allowed increased ranges, along with the development of telecommunications, the latter method became the norm during the Great War. However when the layout of the original defensive zones was being considered, a mere forty years before the war, the former method was the norm, hence the original spacing between the forts.

on perfect square shapes, whilst the *fort de Pagny-la-Blanche-Côtes* of the *Forts d'arrêt - entre Toul-Langres sur la Meuse* had a perfect lozenge shape.

At the core of the forts were a series of buildings mainly to house the fort's garrison and to store the required provisions and munitions. Around these central buildings was a wide outer wall for general protection against enemy shellfire. On top of but to the rear of these outer walls was a series of gunnery positions. Finally to prevent incursion by enemy infantry into the fort, there was a wide, deep ditch in front of the outer walls that surrounded the entire fort.

The *redoutes* and *forts* were built to face the expected direction of any attack (generally towards the frontiers or in the case of a *camp retranché*, outwards from the centre of the town), with the main armament on the front and sidewalls. This not only allowed the cannons to face the enemy in the front of the fortification but also to cover the ground that lay in-between the individual fortifications.

Each of the *redoutes* and *forts* were surrounded by a *fossé* (ditch) twelve metres wide and five to six metres deep, with masonry retaining walls that had a slight batter. The rear *fossé* was often split into two, directed slightly inwards from the corners towards the main gate at the midpoint.

Entry into the earlier *forts* was via a *pont* (bridge) over the *fossé*, the last part – immediately in front of the entrance - being a *pont mobile* (drawbridge) and then through the *entrée* (entrance) past the *corps de garde* (guardhouse) into a small *cour* (courtyard) in front of the *caserne* (barrack block). Both the fixed bridge and the drawbridge had hand railings, which in the case of the drawbridge, was hinged so that it did not interfere with closing the bridge.

Some of the earlier *redoutes* and *forts* had *postes de ravelin* (ravelin bastions) built to protect their entrances. The *postes de ravelin* were designed to cover the approach tracks as well as the entrance and the bridges. They came in different sizes, the larger ones being artillery casemates and were surrounded by a continuation of the *fossé* necessitating an outer bridge and drawbridge, thereby the entrance track passed into the *poste de ravelin* before passing on across an inner pair of bridges into the fort. A fine example can be seen at the *fort de Troyon* of the *Forts de Redeau – Ligne Verdun-Toul*. The smaller *postes de ravelin* tended to be casemates for riflemen located externally to the *fort* again covering the approach track; the entrance to it being located at the rear next to the bridge - the *Redoute de Belleville* has an example.

The *caserne* was normally on a single level (a ground floor), however some of the bigger forts had a second level (a basement or a first floor) and a very small number had a third level. The *fort d'Ecrouves* of *Le camp retranché de Toul* had three floors above ground level and a basement. It also had chambers located above the second floor just in front of the exit points onto the roof that in effect made a fifth level. However the *fort d'Ecrouves* was an exception. The *caserne,* as with all the other above ground buildings of the first generation of fortifications, were vaulted structures and constructed out of one metre thick masonry, covered with two to five metres of soil for added protection. The intermediate floor levels and the non-structural partition walls within the *caserne* were constructed out of normal brickwork. Normally the *caserne* consisted of officers' rooms and the men's dormitories, for the intended garrison of 150 to 750 officers and other ranks, based on the size of the fort, offices including the commanding officer's office, the communications room, the first aid post or hospital, the kitchen, the officers messes, the latrine or toilet block, the magazines and a number of water cisterns (for the French translations of the various rooms see the Glossary). The cisterns were normally located within the basement. (For a breakdown of the manpower requirements for the forts see Appendix 10.)

The frontage of the *casernes* at ground level consisted of large doorways between two large glazed windows or three large glazed windows for the floors above ground level. On the outside of the door and window frames were vertical slots set into the masonry; one on either side with the top part of the inner edge of the slot cut away. This allowed the defenders to slide into then drop steel slats into the slots, one on top of the other, up to the loading feeding point. Then all the slats were in place a solid armoured shutter was formed.

A typical dormitory would normally have ten double bunk beds sleeping four men each – two men to each level. There were four pairs of hooks mounted on the ends of the bunk beds for the storage of the men's rifles. Next to the beds mounted on the wall were shelves with hooks on for the storage of the men's equipment, and finally there were chests for their clothes and small stools for them to sit on.

The kitchens had large 'Aga' type cooking ovens/stoves built into an alcove and a walk in pantry adjacent.

The courtyard in front of the *caserne* was mainly used for organising and distributing incoming men and material, but in my opinion not for parading the men, generally being too small; parading was probably done externally of the fort.

Originally there were two lifting types of drawbridge, as well as a sliding type. The first of the lifting types was the *système Poncelet,* which consisted of a simple chain and gear operated drawbridge pivoted at the entrance opening. The second of the lifting type was the *système Tripier,* which did away with the chain and gear and relied on pivoted cantilevered counter weights. Again the *pont système Tripier* was pivoted at the entrance opening; however it had two weighted beams, one on either side of the entrance roadway that extended back into slots in the entrance floor that formed the cantilevered counterweights. The *pont système Tripier* was closed when the cantilevers were swung down into a lower chamber located immediately below the entrance. The sliding type, known as the *pont roulant* (roller bridge), lay on rollers and slid backwards into a cavity just below the floor or sideways into a slot set into the side wall to receive it. Like the *système Poncelet*, it was operated by a chain and gear system, from a chamber located next to, but below the entrance. The *système Tripier* and the *pont roulant* were used either on the *extérieur* (externally) over the *fossé* or *intérieur* (internally) within the entrance above a *haha* (ha-ha – a two metre deep, slab sided pit), whilst the *système Poncelet* was only used on the *extérieur*. All *pont mobile extérieur* were mounted in the *longitudinal* (longitudinally in line with the entrance), whilst all *pont mobile intérieur* were mounted in the *latéral* (laterally across the entrance). Example of the various types of *ponts mobile* used, are as follows: the *redoute de Saint Michel* had the *système Poncelet longitudinal extérieur*, the *redoute de Belrupt* had a *système Tripier longitudinal extérieur,* the *redoute de Belleville* had a *pont roulant longitudinal extérieur,* the *redoute de Regret* had a *système Tripier latéral intérieur*, and the *fort de Liouville* had a *pont roulant latéral intérieur*. There were no examples of the *pont roulant latéral intérieur* used independently in *le camp retranché de Verdun*, however the *fort de Liouville* as one of the *forts de rideau de la Meuse* – part of the *groupe de la Meuse* has one, so is presented here as an example.

The main defence of the *redoutes* and *forts* was based on the *fossé*, and the covering fire therein – leaving no blind spots were an enemy that found his way into the *fossé* could seek refuge. Using Haxo style covered casemates, these earlier forts had *caponnières* (caponiers or bastions) on the *escarpe* (inner *fossé* wall). They were usually located at the corners of the *fossé*. The *caponnières* were built with loopholes or embrasures in alignment to the line of the *fossé* that they were covering, and were often paired to cover two lines of the *fossé*. A vent hole was located above each loophole to allow the smoke from the black powder propellant (then in use) to escape from within the firing bays of the *caponnières*. There were also small gunnery embrasures with steel shutters, which allowed for the use of small-bore short-range cannons. The single ones were known as *caponnières simple* and the paired ones were known as *caponnières double*. As an alternative to the *postes de ravelin* there was a third type of *caponnières* known as the *caponnières de gorge* (the gorge's caponier - bastion covering the gorge or entrance), which was located on the *escarpe*, close by to the entrance. The *caponnières de gorge* covered the rear *fossé*, which in this case the *fossé* being of the straight or non-split type. Another alternative system for rear defence was a pair of *casemates de flanquement du fossé* (flanking casemates covering the *fossé*) covering a split rear *fossé*. These *casemates de flanquement du fossé* were located on the *escarpe*, built at an angle to and on either side of the entrance at the apex of the split rear *fossé* so that they faced square on to the line of the *fossés* that they were covering. All of these types of rear *fossé* defences were used throughout the fort building program.

The single storey *caponnières* had the firing bays located at the same level as the floor of the *fossé* and had a *fossé-diamant* (diamond ditch – a secondary ditch) to give added protection to the defenders – a secondary loophole was built at floor level angled down in alignment with the floor of the *fossé-diamant* to allow the defenders to cover this area. The earlier *caponnières* were built out of masonry and had a two and a half to five metre thick earthen covering.

Apart from the fire bays that covered the line of the *fossés* there was an elongated curved fire bay that faced outwards from the *fort* to cover the corner areas of the two *fossés* that were within the blind spot of the main fire bay of the *caponnière*. There were also secondary fire bays built into the *escarpe* adjacent to the main fire bays so that they were at right angles to the *fossés-diamant* and were intended to give extra cover to the front faces of the *caponnière.*

The *redoute de Belleville* gives a good example of the original *fort* defence systems, in that its five-sided *fossé* had five bastions, - a *caponnières double*; two *caponnières simple*, and two *casemates de flanquement* – one either side of the entrance. The *redoute de Belleville* was upgraded and renamed the *fort de Belleville.*

The *fossé-diamant* was a localised two metre deep, two metre wide *fossé* normally cut into the *fossé* floor local to either the *caponnières* or *entrées*. However there were a number of the earlier forts that had the *fossé-diamant* that covered the entire width of the *fossé*. An example of this can be found in the *fossé* of the *fort de Landrecourt.*

It was foreseen that the enemy infantry would attempt to enter the fort by two methods, either by entering the *fossé* or by bridging over the top of the *fossé*. Therefore apart from small arms, the following light artillery weapons were developed and were intended to be used for the main defence of the fort:

> i *Canon revolver de 40mm Hotchkiss modèle 1877* [11] (40 millimetre calibre revolver gun model 1877, manufactured by *Hotchkiss*).
> ii *Canon de 12-culasse modèle 1858 modifiée 1880* (gun firing shell with 12 'lugs' model 1858, modified 1880).

The first weapon, the *canon revolver Hotchkiss*, was based on the Gatling gun and had five barrels each of 40 millimetre calibre rotating

---

[11] The Hotchkiss et Cie., of Saint-Denis, Paris was a French engineering manufacturing Company that produced armaments along with other non military produces such as cars.

around a central shaft. Like the Gatling gun, it was operated by a hand crank next to the breech and was fed from a magazine located above the breech mechanism. It had a rate of fire of 50 rounds per minute. It was mounted on a special small wheeled fortress carriage, the *affût modèle 1882* (mounting model 1882) – a modified Reffye 70 millimetre gun carriage, which had a small armoured shield (the shield was for the protection of the gun crew and covered the area between the gun barrels and the gun embrasure in the wall of the *caponnières*). Its main employment was to cover the area inside of the *fossé*.

The second weapon, the *canon de 12-culasse*, was a breech-loading rifled cannon of 121 millimetre calibre. It was converted from the 125 millimetres calibre muzzle-loading 12 pounder bronze *canons 4 rayé de campagne modèle 1858*. It was set upon a new fortress carriage, which had a free elevation mounting allowing it to fire at quite a high angle upwards. The conversion from a muzzle-loader to a breach-loader was by the addition of a Lahitolle breach system. It fired a shell with twelve zinc lugs located around the base of the shell wall in two rows of six, which acted like early driving bands, engaging with the rifling of the barrel. This weapon could be manoeuvred out into the *fossé* when the fort was under direct infantry assault and used against the enemy whilst they were engaged climbing their scaling ladders and bridging equipment. It had a rate of fire of 2 to 3 rounds per minute.

The *fossés* were originally floodlit with oxyacetylene torches; however this was soon abandoned due to the danger of internal explosion from the oxyacetylene storage tanks, which were located inside the *caponnières*.

In a small number of cases, there was a two metre extension to the top of the *escarpe* wall. This extension, which had loopholes positioned at regular intervals formed a *parapet* (parapet) providing cover for defending infantrymen. This parapet being located above the level of the *fossé* level with the top of the *contrescarpe* (outer *fossé* wall) allowed the infantry defenders to bring extra firepower not only into the *fossé* but also on to the ground just in front of the fort. The addition of the parapet to the *escarpe* wall also made scaling the wall by enemy infantry more difficult. There was no example of this type of parapet at Verdun, but an example can be found on the *fort du Bois* of the *forts d'arrêt - Ligne Maubeuge-Longwy*. The *fort du Bois* was later renamed the *fort de Hirson*.

On top of the six metre high *contrescarpe* was a two metre high *glacis* (bank sloping downwards away from the *fort*), erected on top of which was a three metre high *grille* (iron-railing fence). At the top of the five metre high *escarpe* was a ten metre high embankment so designed to deflect in-coming projectiles, consisting of the *talus extérieur*, a gently sloping bank upwards at the same angle and in alignment with the *glacis*, that flattened out (to being almost flat) into the *plongée*, at the top of which was the main *parapet*. Behind the parapets were the *baquettes d'artillerie* (artillery ramparts). The total thickness of the walls between the *fossés* and the *parapets* ranged from 20 to 30 metres. At the time of the design and construction of the *forts* almost all artillery cannons were 'flat' trajectory field guns – high trajectory howitzers were only available in very limited numbers and of small calibres, hence the concept of the gently sloping embankment designed to deflect in-coming flat trajectory projectiles. However by the time of the Great War, the Germans had developed large calibre howitzers that could deliver high angle plunging shellfire, rendering the original defences outdated.

There were numerous *baquettes d'artillerie* – up to sixteen depending on the size of the fort – each one being a gunnery position for one or two modified field or heavy guns side by side. It was these cannons that made up the main "counter-offensive" armament of the forts, which in theory, would respond to any offensive action by an aggressor.

Located directly behind the *baquettes d'artillerie* was the *rue du rempart* (rampart's road), the main artery of the fort, which generally linked into each end of the courtyard in front of the *caserne,* forming a ring, thus allowing the movement of men and materials - the guns and munitions - around the fort. Since the *baquettes d'artillerie* were slightly elevated to the *rue du rempart* there were *rampes* (ramps – for gun access) linking them together, providing access for the guns.

The uncovered *baquettes d'artillerie* had a wood planking floor and either wooden or masonry retaining walls to the front and sides. There were railings at the rear to prevent the men from accidentally falling over the edge onto the *rue du rempart,* which was normally only about a meter below.

Between each pair of *baquettes d'artillerie,* but buried within the main walls with two and a half to five metres of soil on top, were the *casemate de tir direct* (primary magazine rooms) linked to the *canons* and the *rue du rempart* by a pair of corridors forming a 'T' shape in plan, with an entrance onto the *rue du rempart* and side entrances leading up to the *baquettes d'artillerie* via some steps. Located off the corridors were four rooms, two shell rooms either side of the entrance corridor and two powder or propellant rooms side by side located on the cross or exit corridor – the right hand pair of rooms (one powder and one shell room) of the *casemate de tir direct* serving the right hand *canon* and the left hand pair likewise serving the left hand *canon*. The concept was that the gun crew which consisted of the *chef de pièce* (gun commander – normally an N.C.O.), *tireur* (the layer), *chargeur* (the loader) and a number of *pourvoyeurs* (ammunition carriers), would have the ammunition carriers forming a line outside the entrance of the *casemate de tir direct* on the *rue du rempart*. They passed through it in turn, collecting a shell and a bag of propellant, then passing up onto the *baquette d'artillerie,* where the shell and propellant would be handed over to the loader, they would then pass down onto the *rue du rempart,* via the ramp to rejoin the back of the queue at the rear of the *casemate de tir direct,* ready to collect the next load, thereby following a 'one-way' system, making sure of a continuous supply of ammunition to the cannons.

A *casemate de tir direct* that served a single cannon had only two rooms off a 'L' shaped corridor again with one entrance on the *rue du rempart* and the other up on the *baquette d'artillerie.*

Where a *casemate de tir direct* served two *baquette d'artillerie* it formed a barrier between the two sets of cannons and thus formed in effect a blast wall against exploding shells, especially against the destructive effect of shrapnel balls[12]. The *casemate de tir direct* thereby prevented the effect of an explosion in one of the *baquette d'artillerie* from passing directly across into the next.

Located at regular intervals on the *caserne* side of the *rue du rempart* were a small number of *casemate de tir indirect* (secondary magazine rooms) where extra munitions were stored. On some of the larger forts there was even a second covered *rue du rempart,* running parallel to the uncovered one to allow the movement of men and material safely during hostile shelling.

Although there was a wide range of artillery weapons used in the *forts,* the following types of cannons were the most commonly used on the non-modernised *forts*:

    i   *Canon de 'Lahitolle' 95 mm modèle 1888* (95 millimetre calibre gun model 1888 invented by *Colonel* de Lahitolle).

    ii   *Canon de 'De Bange' 120 mm longue modèle 1878* (120 millimetres calibre long barrelled gun model 1878 invented by *Colonel De Bange).*

    iii *Canon de 'De Bange' 155 mm longue modèle 1877* (155 millimetres calibre long barrelled gun model 1877 invented by *Colonel* De Bange).

---

[12] The shrapnel shell was invented by a British army officer, General Henry Shrapnel (d. 1842), and consisted of a shell full of small spherical metal balls or bullets, along with two small charges of propellant – one behind the nose cap of the shell and therefore in front of the bullets. The other charge located behind the bullets with a metal divider plate in between. The fuse was set to ignite the first charge, which would blow off the nose cap of the shell just in front but above the target. A spark from the first detonation would pass along a central tube between the two charges and ignite the second charge. This would then propel the bullets out of the shell case onto the target, in effect like the spray of shotgun pellets. The bullets were about the size of a standard rifle bullet – about eight millimetres in diameter. There were also a smaller number of shrapnel shells that had larger bullets designed for use against cavalry horses. The shrapnel shell was cheap to fabricate and its main propose was as an anti-personnel weapon, although during the Great War it was used mainly for cutting barbed wire – however this employment of the shrapnel shell unfortunately proved to be very unsatisfactory.

Colonel Henri de Lahitolle and *Colonel* Charles de Bange were the designers of the cannons that bore their names. The basic difference between their designs was the breach block mechanisms. The *Canon de 'Lahitolle' 95 mm modèle 1888* quickly replaced the earlier *Canon de 'De Bange' 90 mm longue modèle 1877*. (For a complete list of armaments and a comparison of the main armament of the *forts* within *Le camp retranché de Verdun*, see Appendix 11.)

The *magasins à poudre* (powder magazines) were normally located within the centre of the forts. At the time of the construction of the forts, the use by the army of black powder explosive, which could become unstable over a comparably short time, potential internal magazine explosions were a considerable risk. To counter this problem, the *magasins à poudre* were buried extremely deep underground in an attempt to remove the risk of the black power becoming unstable, but in the advent that it did become unstable and explode, to limit the effects to the rest of the fort. By burying the *magasins à poudre* underground also gave them greater protection against hostile shelling. Alternatively, some forts had the *magasins à poudre* located externally to the fort, access being from an opening in the rear *contrescarpe*, close to the entrance, again so as to reduce the effects of an explosion to the fort. In a similar vane, within the *magasins à poudre* false wooden floors were mounted above the normal masonry floors, to minimise the risk of sparks from the soldier's boots. It was standard practice during this period that, as another safety measure, the soldiers employed within the *magasins à poudre* wore special boots made out of felt, to prevent any spark being produced from their standard army issue hobnail boots. The cavity below the wooden floors served to prevent ground moisture from seeping up and impairing the black powder. Finally, the *magasins à poudre* (as did a number of other underground rooms within the fortifications) had wall linings made up of tarpaper mounted on light wooden frames mounted onto the masonry walls and ceilings, so as to prevent water seepage into the rooms. Vents were provided high up on the end walls to keep the *magasins à poudre* and the black power stored within well ventilated, again to reduce the risk of an internal explosion. The *fort de Marre* had, when originally built, an external magazine, whilst the *fort de Vaux* had its magazine located underground, internally.

With the exception of the *fossé* floodlighting, the forts, and indeed all the fortifications at the time of construction, had no fixed internal lighting, there being no gas or electricity supply to the individual fortifications. Kerosene oil lanterns, even in the magasin à poudre, provided the lighting. To reduce the danger of a naked flame coming into contact to the black power explosive within the *magasin à poudre*, small lighting niches known as *chambres aux lampes* (lamp recesses) were set within the walls with permanent glass barriers between the lanterns and the *magasin*. Access to the lantern housings was from corridors that ran externally around the *magasin* (there being no access to the lanterns from inside the *magasin*).

The *Fort de Douaumont* and the *Fort de Vaux* had electrical lighting installed by the Germans only after they had been captured in 1916.

The *redoute de Belleville* and the *redoute de Belrupt* are examples of the early *forts* and *redoutes* that were not later rebuilt or modernized.

Bâtiments Extérieur

A number of the forts had *bâtiments extérieur* (external buildings). These ancillary buildings were built, set back at the rear and often next to the *route militaire* (military road - fort entrance track).

The common uses for these *bâtiments extérieur* were *logements d'officiers* (officers' quarters), *maison de pompe* (pump house for water supplies) and *magasin du génie* (Engineers storerooms).

These building were not intended to be defensible structures and, as such, were not built to withstand any form of battering. The *bâtiments extérieur* to the rear of the *fort de Douaumont* were quickly destroyed by the bombardments as can be seen from the aerial photographs taken before and after the bombardments. However there are some remains of a group of them that can be found to the rear of the *Ouvrage de Déramé* although they have deteriorated due to the weather, having been abandoned many years ago.

La Telegraphie Optique

Although Alexander Graham Bell invented the telephone in 1876 and the first telephones reached France in 1879, there was not a nationwide telephone network in France until 1889. This only occurred when the French Government passed a law nationalising all of the early telephone companies that had been created in the intervening ten years, thereby uniting all of the private networks.

During the initial fortification-building program of 1872-84, the telephone was too early in its development to be considered and therefore was not incorporated at this stage. Communication between the fortifications within the same locale was done visually during daylight hours by the use of the heliograph or by flags, and after nightfall by runners. However there was a problem in communications between the fortifications over longer distances where the heliograph proved to have insufficient range and the distances were too great for runners, therefore another solution had to be found.

The solution was to install powerful oxyacetylene lamps inside special *abris* (shelters) that had precisely aligned signalling ports. Known as *La*

Telegraphie Optique, the ports measured about 200 millimetres by 200 millimetres and pierced through the thick walls of the shelter forming a straight tube. These ports were in perfect alignment with the next telegraphic station that could be ten miles or more away. When in operation, messages could be sent using beams of light flashed across the intervening gaps. Not every fort was equipped with a *Telegraphie Optique,* for instance within *Le camp retranché de Verdun* the only examples built were in the *fort du Rozellier,* the *redoute de Souville,* the *redoute de Duguy* and the *redoute de La Chaume.*

The development of the telephone soon superseded *La Telegraphie Optique* and other uses were found for the chambers. A fine example can be found in the *fort du Camp-des-Romains* of the *Forts de Redeau – Ligne Verdun-Toul.* Unusually this one was built outside of the fort in front of the forward *fosse* probably due to the alignment of the signalling beams.

Batteries

During the planning stage of the fortified zone, it was realised that the firepower from the forts alone was insufficient and so to increase the firepower, *batteries* were built from 1881 onwards located between the *forts,* so as to cover the potential lines of approach of an attacking enemy.

Built to accommodate up to four heavy *canons* or up to six lighter *canons,* the *batteries* consisted of a low, but wide earthen *plongée* with a *baquette d'artillerie* cut into the rear edge. There was a *fossé* type ditch located in front of the *plongée.* The guns normally being paired, had masonry built *niches à munitions* (ammunition niches) positioned in the rear of the *parapet.* Behind the emplacements ran a track (similar to the *rue du rempart* of the *forts*) built to allow access for and to the cannons. The earthen *plongée* extended beyond the rear of the guns as far back as the track forming a blast wall giving lateral protection for the gun crews and like the forts especially against shrapnel shells.

The bigger *batteries* had masonry built *bâtiments* (buildings) set a short distance behind; I have not found the original purposes of these buildings, however I would suggest that the possible uses of the rooms within those buildings would have been used as a command post, a first aid post, a magazine or a combination of all. The *batterie de l'Hopital* located between the *fort de Souville* and the *fort de Tavannes* is an example of one of the larger *batteries* designed to accommodate four 155 millimetre guns. The building that was built behind the *batterie de l'Hôpital* is listed as a *poste de secours* (first aid post), which possibly gave rise to the name given to the *batterie.*

It was quite common for *batteries* to be built adjoining a *fort.* An example was the *fort de Vaux,* which had a *batterie* position built next to its western corner. However this particular *batterie* was demolished during one of the *fort de Vaux* modernisations.

Village fortifié

Not part of the *Le camp retranché de Verdun*, the *Village fortifié de Villey-le-Sec* part of the *Forts d'arrêt - en avant de Toul* was an example of a fort with two *batterie* positions. The *Village fortifié de Villey-le-Sec* consisted of the small fort - the *fort de Villey-le-Sec* which was positioned next to the village of *Villey-le-Sec* along with two *batterie* positions which in effect enclosed the entire village making what appeared in plan to be a very large fort.

Casernes

It was never intended to fully man or equip all of the fortifications during peacetime, but to man them only during times of emergencies and even then only those that were directly required. During the whole period of constructing the *zone fortifiée de Verdun* (Verdun's fortified zone), from 1874 to 1914, a number of army camps, also known as *casernes* were built, or were being built in the rear areas to house the 54,000 men that it was estimated would be needed to man the fortifications. With two left uncompleted in 1914, there was accommodation for only 36,000 men at the outbreak of war.

The *casernes* were built to a standard pattern. They consisted of a main gate with two *corps de garde* – one either side of the gateway that housed the guardrooms. This led onto a large square parade ground with three large multi-storeys barrack blocks that faced onto it. Each barrack block was normally three storeys high with a cellar and a dormitory in the roof. There were other ancillary building located behind this central group and a number of smaller storehouses and stables. With the artillery and cavalry there were a larger number of ancillary buildings– there being more horses and equipment to house. The *casernes* down in the town were surrounded by a high perimeter wall except at the front, where on either side of the main gateway, there was a railing fence giving a clear view of the parade from the street outside. The *casernes* outside of towns had an all-round high perimeter wall that had loopholes at regular intervals for all-round defence.

Magasins aux Vivres and Magasins à Fourrages

In addition to the storehouses in the *casernes* there were a number of *magasins* (warehouses), some predating the fortification program and some added during the fortification development period to house the provisions for the garrison and civil population in times of war. There were two types of warehouse: the *Magasins aux Vivres* (food warehouses) for human foodstuffs, and the *Magasins à Fourrages* (fodder warehouses) for the animals.

In Verdun these warehouses were mainly located in the area between the railway station and the river, presumably near to the points of shipment. Theoretically, as mention before, there were enough foodstuffs for a siege lasting up to six months for both the garrison and civilian population.

Parc d'Artillerie and Arsenal

The *Matériel* (materials – guns and munitions) that was required for the armaments for the fortifications were stored in the *parcs d'artillerie* (Artillery Park). They consisted of a number of single storey warehouses and included a railway network for ease of transporting the Materials.

In order to maintain and to repair the cannons, *arsenals* (arsenals) were built at the same time as and located within the perimeter of the *Parcs d'Artillerie.*

Each of the *camps retranché* had a *parc d'artillerie* and in the case of Verdun it was called the *Parc d'Artillerie de Jardin Fontaine*, which was built circa 1878. This had an arsenal, which led to the *Parc d'Artillerie* being commonly called the "*Arsenal*". The *parc d'Artillerie* and its arsenal were located near to the centre of Verdun, just to the north of Verdun railway station in the suburb of Jardin Fontaine, and it was demolished in the late nineteen-nineties. At the time of writing (2006) the perimeter wall still remained and the site has been redeveloped as warehouses with an associated lorry park.

Routes Militaire

All the fortifications and their ancillary buildings, within the *zone de défense*, were linked together by a network of *routes militaire* (military roads).

This military roads network consisted of metalled tracks that allow the quick movement of men and materials between the defensive positions and fortifications especially in times of emergencies, such as times of mobilisation for war or during wartime.

The road system was also utilised by the building contractors when they were constructing the fortifications, especially in the early days of the armouring program when large, heavy pre-fabricated armour components were transported up to the fortification sites, normally on trailers towed by road steam engines.

***

During this first period of construction there were a number of developments that although important in relation to the general progression of the design of the fortifications no examples were built at Verdun. I have therefore listed those early designs for the sake of completeness.

Caves à Canon

Due to an outbreak of political tension between France and Germany at the start of 1875, it was thought in France that war between the two countries was imminent. This possibility of war, caused an atmosphere of fear, and with the fortification program in its early stages, the French military authorities had to act. In the knowledge that they did not have enough time to construct full-sized forts, the authorities asked the *Commission des Cuirassements* to produce a small 'armoured' blockhouse, armed with a cannon that could be quickly erected as a temporary measure.

Mougin responded to the situation and quickly designed what was to become known as the *cave à canon* (cellar with a cannon), a small one-room artillery emplacement.

This Haxo style casemate was large enough to house a reasonably large artillery piece and was constructed out of the standard builder's concrete that was the only material available to him that would allow building quickly, combined with an iron front shield. This front shield had a small diameter *sabord* (gun port) positioned in the centre just large enough to allow the cannon to be fired through. The gun port had a secondary small iron disc shield that was pivoted just to one side of the main shield opening. By simply turning the disc a quarter of a turn the gun port could be opened thereby allowing the cannon to be fired and by turning it back again the gun port could be sealed.

The weapon chosen was the *Canon de 'Reffye' 138 mm court modèle 1816 modifiée 1874* (138 millimetres calibre short barrelled gun model 1816 modified by General Reffye in 1874) that was commonly known as the *138 de montagne* (the 138 mountain [gun]). Reffye had updated this old smooth bore, bronze, breech-loading *canon* by re-boring and rifling it. By adding a breach block of his design, it could fire a cast iron shell. It was mounted onto a new fortress mounting, which was again designed by Reffye.

In the course of the emergency there were only four *caves à canon* constructed. The four were positioned to cover the expected attack routes that the Germans would probably take, however none of which were built near to Verdun. An example was built in the *ouvrage de Château-Lambert* of the *forts de Redeau – Ligne Épinal-Belfort*.

Once the emergency was over, the inadequacy of the *cave à canon* was realised especially with regard to the aiming of the *canon*. The cannon, with its specially designed wheeled carriage, which had the wheels located at the centre of gravity of the barrel, caused great difficulties for the crew to manoeuvre it for aiming, whilst keeping the muzzle located in front of the gun port. Therefore the *caves à canon* was quickly decommissioned and in the case of the above example, the gun port was soon bricked up and sealed, the chamber then being reused as a storeroom.

Casemates de Mougin

With the threat of imminent war receding, Mougin returned to design work on his first major defensive undertaking, which had been interrupted by the need to design the *cave à canon*. With the design well advanced before it had been stopped, it only took a short period of time to complete. This was done by the end of 1874, the new structure being called the *casemates de Mougin, modèle 1876* (casemate model 1876 designed by commandant Mougin). However after review and testing, the French army did not accept the design until 1876. It was then a few years before it was incorporated within the fortification program, with construction of them starting in the early eighteen-eighties. It is believed that this delay in construction was due to funding problems, namely the available funds were being using on fort construction during this period. The surveying of the potential sites took from 1878 to 1880 and construction of the *casemates de Mougin* was between 1880 and 1884.

Like the *cave à canon*, it was a covered artillery position based on the Haxo concept consisting of a *chambre de tir* (firing chamber or gun room) and was related to the earlier casemate design. The single gun room had a very short front wall and a much longer back wall. The rear portions of the sidewalls were parallel, whilst the front portions tapered inwards towards the cannon muzzle and, in effect, combined with the front and rear walls, formed an irregular hexagon in plan, the front part of the gun room being trapezoidal and the rear being rectangular. The gun room had an overall length of seven and a half metres and a width of seven metres across the back wall. As with the earlier *cave à canon*, the walls and floors were constructed out of non-reinforced standard builders' concrete that lacked the strength of the later high-strength concretes. The three metre high ceiling consisted of a multi-layered roof of iron, concrete and soil. Starting with four rolled iron ceiling panels weighing 42 tons with the joints leaded for waterproofing, there was then a layer of non-reinforced concrete above, and finally an earthen layer on top of that. The combined rolled iron and the concrete giving great strength whilst the soil absorbed the impacts from enemy shells. The top layer of soil had a grass covering giving camouflage against enemy observers as well as preventing soil erosion. At the rear of the gun room there was a large chimney type vent to allow ventilation of gun smoke and fumes after the firing of the cannon.

The *avant-cuirasse* (front armour) of the *casemate Mougin* was located immediately in front of the cannon and set in the concrete of the front wall. The front armour had a small gun port and in front of that it had a thirty-five to forty centimetre thick cast iron *bouclier mobile* (movable shield) that slid vertically down into a slot when the cannon was to be fired and back up again when the cannon was not in action such as when it was being loaded or not in use, thereby giving the gun and its crew protection. The seven and a half tonne movable shield had counter balance weights and was raised and lowered by turning two hand wheels located in a pair of ante-chambers either side of and at the rear of the gun chamber. The hand wheels were connected to the movable shield via shafts and gears that ran through the one and a half metre high basement. It took only five seconds to raise or lower the movable shield. A simple electrical device prevented the cannon from being fired when movable shield was in the upper, closed position thereby preventing accidents after reloading.

Armed with a single *Canon de 'De Bange' 155mm longue modèle 1877*, (155 millimetre calibre long barrelled gun model 1877 invented by *Colonel* De Bange) mounted on an *affût pivotant modèle 1883* (pivot mounting model 1883). The total weight of the gun and mounting was 22.7 tons.

The design of the *affût pivotant* rectified the main problem of the *cave à canon* in that it kept the gun muzzle in the same position at all times no matter what angle of elevation or transverse, and thus allowing the gun port to still be kept as small as possible. This was done by having the cannon mounted upon a cradle with vertical slots – the barrel trunnions being positioned within the slots that allowed the breech of the cannon to be raised and lowered, allowing the cannon to be angled for elevation. The front of the barrel was connected to a pair of struts, which in turn was connected to the single hydraulic recuperator that was anchored to the cradle in effect formed a parallelogram. The cradle had wheels and sat on a pivoted platform. On firing the cannon, the hydraulic recuperator took up most of the force of the recoil, and by allowing the cradle to move back on its wheels, the remaining recoil force was dissipated. The pivot of the platform at the front, just below the cannon muzzle with a pair of wheels at the rear mounted at right angles to the pivot, ran on a curved rail– thus allowing the breech to be traversed through an angle of 30°. In effect the gun muzzle remained stationary whilst the breech was moved to aim the cannon.

Altogether, ten *casemates de Mougin* were constructed; although again there were no examples used in the Verdun defences, the *batterie de l'Éperon* of the *groupe de la Meuse* is a fine example. (For a list of the *Casemates de Mougin* and *Tourelles de Mougin* see appendix 18.)

Cave à Mortier or *Casemate à tir indirect*

The main artillery weapon in the first generation of forts during the period of 1870-90 was the cannon. The mortar had gone out of military fashion and was not in common usage with most armies at that time, including the French army. Because of their flat trajectory, the cannons had to be placed high upon the fortifications and were thus exposed to enemy fire. This was a major problem that the fortress' designers sought an answer to, hence the *casemates de Mougin*.

However the French fortress' designers, during this early period of development, realised that the mortar with its high trajectory of fire could be of use in the defence of forts. Mortars, it was foreseen, could give great account in the fort's protection, especially against attackers who at short range were taking advantage of blind spots due to the lie of the land.

In earlier days when mortars were used out in the open field, they were commonly placed into specially dug pits. A straight development of these ad hoc pits was to add a roof for protection, against both enemy counter fire and the elements. This concept was developed into the fortification design simply by placing the mortar in a chamber below ground level within the fort, and a shaft added angled up at 45° directed towards the danger area. The size of the chamber varied based on the size of the mortar it was to house, and entry into the chamber was via an underground passage. Sighting the weapon was done by the indirect method using the observation of a remote spotter. These mortar chambers were known as *Cave à Mortier* or *Casemate à tir indirect*.

Tourelles fixes de Mougin

Although the *casemates de Mougin* provided cover and protection to the cannon and its crew, there was one disadvantage to it. This was the limited field of fire due to the small amount of transverse that the cannon could travel through within the confines of the shelter. In the years 1874 to 1875, in response to this problem Mougin worked on a new concept – a gun turret.

Accepted by the French army ten years later in 1885 (probably for the same financial reasons as the *casemates de Mougin*), the *tourelle de 155mm Mougin, modèle 1885* (155 millimetre gun turret model 1885 designed by commandant *Mougin*) was a *tourelle fixes* (fixed or non-retractable turret). Like the *casemates de Mougin*, the *tourelle fixes de Mougin* was not used in any of the Verdun fortifications.

The *tourelle fixes de Mougin* like all other turrets could be rotated horizontally through a full 360° to give an all-round field of fire. The cannons could be reloaded whilst the turret was being rotated, thereby saving time. The turret was aligned onto its targets by a method of placing a reference pin in line with the target onto an aiming disc located below the turret. The turret was then rotated around until a second contact pin mounted on the turret touched the reference pin, creating an electrical circuit that stopped the turret from rotating and then automatically fired the cannons. It had a six-metre diameter *chambre de tir* that consisted of a vertical cast iron frame supporting a curved iron plate wall. This frame and wall formed the lower part of the turret, which was located below the roof level of the standard concrete structure in which the turret sat. The frame also supported the curved armoured dome that projected one and a half metres above the structure's roof level. Originally designed to use cast iron for the construction of the dome, the design was modified replacing the cast iron with rolled iron. There were six rolled iron plates that made up the dome. Five curved pieces around the edges, with the sixth being the central capping plate – all the plates having a maximum thickness of 500 millimetres. The total weight of the *tourelle fixes de Mougin* was 166 tonnes, with the plate armour of the dome and sidewalls weighing 133 tonnes.

Placed on a central pivot mounted in a cup set in the concrete floor, the main weight of the *tourelle* was taken on a wheel race – there were sixteen wheels running on a circular rail track. A small hand hydraulic pump was used to pressurise (using a glycol - water mix) the space between the mounting cup and pivot lifted up the whole turret, thereby taking the weight off the wheel race. With the main weight (about 90% of the total) lifted from the wheel race, the *tourelle fixes de Mougin* was rotated by a simple hand wheel, which operated gear and chain located below the turret. The hand wheel required four to six men to operate it and so in a few cases a steam engine was used to save manpower.

The opening of the concrete structure that the turret sat in was reinforced with a cast iron *avant-cuirasse* (which in this case consisted of an armoured ring made up of four quadrants weighting 84 tonnes). Entry into the turret structure was through a pair of sliding doors located in the lower wall of the gun room and was reached via a small circumferential chamber around the outside of the turret base.

Armed with two *Canon de 'De Bange' 155mm longue modèle 1877*, they were mounted on a similar wheeled cradle with recoil system of the parallelogram of struts and hydraulic recuperators as that of the *casemates de Mougin*. This again kept the cannon's muzzles in the same position at all times allowing the gun ports to be kept as small as possible. The gun ports were cut into the dome roof of the turret.

The *tourelles fixes de Mougin* were the forerunners of the later *tourelles à eclipse*. There were twenty-five examples of the *tourelle fixes de Mougin* constructed, one can be found in the *fort de Barbonnet* of *la frontière italienne – deuxième ensemble*.

With the opening in the armour being limited to the gun ports the *tourelle fixes de Mougin* was without any observation ports and the gunners fired the cannons blind. Therefore they used the indirect method of ranging using observers in remote *postes d'observation* (observation posts).

Postes d'Observation - Cloche Digoin (Observatoires Cuirassé Fixe)

Since all casemates and turret – including the ones developed later - used indirect fire control, they were coupled to at least one remote *postes d'observation*. The observers who were required to spot for the cannons were in just as much danger from enemy shelling as the cannons and crews they were supporting. Therefore the *observatoires cuirassé fixe* (fixed armoured observation posts) were developed for the protection of the observers. (For drawings of an *observatoire cuirassé fixe* see section 4.)

Known as the *cloche Digoin* (Digoin's bell) they came in two types, the first type were the ones incorporated into the forts. However it was realised that they could be used externally from the forts. These independent *cloche Digoin* were given the name *petites cloches Digoin* (Digoin's small bell) and were used first in the *batteries* and later in the future infantry positions (see below).

The *cloche Digoin* consisted of a small room about fifty-five centimetres in diameter (just wide enough to accommodate the observer), which was normally reached from a corridor below via a ladder. The observer stood on a wooden platform with a trap door in its centre through which he had entered. Cast in early concrete (the later ones in *Bétonné spécial*) the *observatoires cuirassé fixe* had an armoured dome twenty-four centimetres thick – the earlier ones cast out of iron and the later ones cast out of steel. The dome had three observation slits about 300 millimetres wide by fifty millimetres high set at 80° apart giving a field of vision of 120°. Communication between the observer in the *observatoire* and the casemate or *tourelle's* gun crews, for fire control, was by speaking tube, later upgraded to telephone. There was also a wooden fold down seat mounted on the wall of the *cloches Digoin* on the opposite side to the central observation slit. The *cloches Digoin* was set down into the upper surface of the fortified structure so that the observation slits were just above the surface level. Examples can be found on the *fort de Vaux*.

The *petites cloches Digoin* consisted of the same cast armoured dome set into a small one-man *abri* (shelter) - entrance into it was through a doorway located in the rear wall of the *abri*, which had a steel plate door. The *petites cloches Digoin* were normally set into the parapet wall with the doorway opening out into gunnery or the infantry positions, and again with the observation slits located just above the surface level in front of the position. An example of a *petites cloche Digoin* can be found in the *Batterie du Mardi-Gras* (*Batterie 6.8*).

The Modernisation and Development of Verdun's Defences, 1885-1892

Although this second phase of development was spurred on by the development of high explosive, the work that had started during the first phase of construction continued with a number of additions to the defences.

Ouvrages Intermediare d'Infanterie and *Postes*

It was realized that there were blind spots and gaps in the lines of forts and *batteries* often due to the lie of the land, and so from 1887 it was decided to cover these blind spots with *ouvrages intermediare d'infanterie* (intermediate infantry field works[13] – they were commonly abbreviated as *ouvrages infanterie*) and *postes* (posts – fortified artillery positions.) For an example, the *ouvrage d'Hardaumont* is located about one and a half kilometres in front of the *redoute de Souville* and about half way between the *fort de Douaumont* and the *fort de Vaux* overlooking the dead ground in the *Ravin des Fontaines* between the three *forts*.

The early *ouvrages* were small fortifications or fortlets consisting of an all-round, low earthen bulwark with a shallow *fossé*, surrounding one or two small masonry constructed, earths covered building(s) of one to three rooms, and as their name suggests, were built for the sole use of the infantry. The building(s) faced away from the assumed position of the would-be enemy and the entrance gap in the bulwark was located in front of the buildings. The *Ouvrages de infanterie* had barred gates at their entrances.

The *postes* were similar to the *batteries*, but incorporated *ouvrages infanterie* type buildings. They were much larger than the *ouvrages infanterie* and included *remparts* (gun ramparts), with a *fossé* in front as fitting their intended use for artillery; however they did not have all-round defence so were not regarded as forts. Some of the *postes* were later rebuilt as forts, for example the *poste des Sartelles*.

Réduit Central

In the same year as the building work on the *ouvrages infanterie* started (1887), work started on adding to *la citadelle*.

---

[13] The term *ouvrages* was also applied to ad hoc defensive positions built throughout the war i.e. trenches, dug-outs, etc. – however, to differentiate between the earlier pre-war built *ouvrages infanterie* and the later wartime built ones, I believe a better description is a 'pre-war built defensive position in the field for the infantry'.

This upgrading consisted of an underground complex with a number of *galeries souterraines* (underground galleries or tunnels) totalling four kilometres in length. It was designed to house 71,000 men as well as the entire civilian population of Verdun, and was known as the *réduit central* (Central storage 'structure' or shelter). When completed, it had four main *ecoutes* (corridors) leading in from the entrances linking up the four main cross *galerie* (galleries or tunnels). Those were partitioned into rooms that included the commander's office, officers rooms, recreation room, lecture hall, chapel, hospital, sleeping rooms, a butchery, a telephone exchange, repair shops, an electrical power station along with powder and munitions' magazines.

Abris Cavernes

From 1889, a small number of *abris sous roc* or *abris cavernes* (Shelters within the Rocks or shelters caves/cellars - underground shelters) were built, which were to be used as *postes de commandement* (command posts).

These consisted of a long brick-built, single underground room three and a half metres wide, with an arched ceiling. They were tunnelled out of the ground and were of varying length - the larger ones being approximately seventy metres in length. They had two to four 'bomb proof' large diameter vent shafts, depending on the size of the underground room with steel caps as protection against the weather. The room had two brick built skins; an outer and an inner skin with gullies at the base of the wall cavities (between the outer and the inner skin) located below the floor level. Vent holes were set high in the inner skin, but out of alignment with the vent shafts, so as to prevent grenades from being dropped straight down the vent shafts into the room, instead they would be deflected by the inner skin and would roll down into the side gully where they would detonated harmlessly below the floor level. The double skin walls were also designed to prevent dampness seeping through from the surrounding ground causing humidity within the room.

Typically *abris cavernes* were positioned next to a hillside with the main room parallel to a slope, which allowed two entrances. The two *couloir d'entrée* (entrance corridors) normally had stairways leading down from the entrances into the underground chamber and were set apart at each end of the main chamber. Each entrance corridor had a grade room built outside next to the doorway.

There were three built in the defences of Verdun, an example being the *abri-cavrne de Froideterre* (commonly known to the French army at the time as the *abri-cavrne de Quatre cheminées* - the 'Four Chimneys' underground shelter, the name deriding from the four chimney-like vents).

Voie Ferré (Railways) and *Tunnel Fortifié*

Under French law in the last quarter of the nineteenth century, all railway construction required both civil and military authority approval. The military authorities often required changes in the routing of the civilian lines, as well as in detail design of railway structures, mainly for mobilization or for rearguard reasons. In some cases, where there were no plans for a civilian railway to be built but there was a military need, the military authorities had strategic railways built solely for the use of the military.

The railway line from Châlons-sur-Marne[14] to Verdun was routed to pass near the Military camp of Suippes and had incorporated upon its length a number of sidings for military use only. There were also extra long platforms designed for army mobilization – there were two platforms next to the camp, a third about half way between the camp and Verdun, and finally a fourth near Verdun station next to the Arsenal.

The section of line between the junction with the main line at Châlons-sur-Marne and Verdun (i.e. the section that was intended to be used for the provisioning of *le camp retranché de Verdun*) was constructed as a double track line thereby maximising supply to the town. However the following section along from Verdun that crossed the then Franco-German border to the town of Metz was constructed as a single-track line, so as to deny the German army any similar advantage in terms of victualling in the event of a German attack.

Natural obstacles that necessitated the construction of long railway tunnels or bridges, especially those that crossed wide fast flowing rivers, were designed to be defended. In the advent that they ever came under direct assault from an enemy and could not be defended, a system for quick destruction was incorporated.

When the Verdun to Metz railway line was built, the French railway engineers had to drive a one and a half kilometre tunnel under the *Hauts de Meuse*. Named the *tunnel de Tavannes*, it was built as a *tunnel fortifié* (fortified tunnel), and had grade rooms incorporated at its eastern portal (the tunnel mouth furthest from Verdun and therefore nearest to the expected direction of a possible attack), along with an iron grill gate.

The single railway track tunnel had four demolition chambers built into one of its sidewalls. These low ceiling chambers were positioned a short distance apart in the centre of the tunnel and were entered by short

---

[14] The town of Châlons-sur-Marne has recently been renamed and is now called Châlons-en-Champagne.

corridors. They were designed to hold a number of kegs of black powder explosive. [15]

Similarly the railway bridge that crossed over the River Meuse near to the centre of Verdun had demolition chambers built into its piers, entry being via vertical shafts located next to the track bed.

Magasin à Poudre de Secteur

The defensive structures - *forts, ouvrages infanterie* and *batteries* - had ancillary structures supporting them; the most important of which was the *magasin à poudre de secteur* (sector power magazine). The construction of the *magasin à poudre* started in 1889. (For names and designation of the *magasins à poudre de secteur* of *le camp retranché de Verdun*, see Appendix 7.)

The defences were grouped into *secteurs* and each *secteur* had at least one *magasin à poudre de secteur*, each of which were located behind the lines of forts, normally positioned next to one of the *routes militaire* that ran up to the fortified zone.

The *magasin à poudre de secteur* consisted of an underground, masonry-built complex centred on a main corridor with a number of rooms adjoined to it, each room being a *magasin à poudre* like the ones found within the forts, with wooden floors and oil paper linings. The lighting was again similar to the *magasins* found in the forts and was provided by oil lanterns. The lighting for the *magasins à poudre* were set in lantern niches with a glass shield set within the walls; access to the lanterns this time was from the main corridor; the lantern niches were located in the main corridor next to the doorways into each room.

Like the *abris cavernes*, the *magasin à poudre de secteur* were built into the slope of embankments with the main corridor parallel to the track allowing two entrances. Entry into the *magasin à poudre de secteur* was via the entrance corridors located at each end of the main corridor, with each having a guardroom covering the entrance. The entrance corridors were at right angles to both the main corridor and normally the track outside. It is believed that there would have been a 'one–way' system in place with the men using one entrance as the entry and the other as the exit.

By 1914 the use of black powder had fallen out of use by the French army; however the *magasins à poudre* were still in use for the storage of munitions.

---

[15] Of note, in August 1914, during the Battle of the Frontiers, the German Fifth Army had major transportation problems due to the demolition by the French Army of a number of essential railway tunnels in the Montmédy area that were required for the quick movement of German troops and supplies.

With the main fighting during the battle occurring in the *1er secteur* and to the north of the *3e secteur*, the *Magasin à Poudre de Secteur de Fleury*, commonly known as '*la Poudrière*', located in the *1er secteur* was used as a defensive position by the French and was actually besieged by the Germans for a couple of days at the height of the battle. The French defenders held out until the Germans were ordered to retire. This was the high point of the German attack. '*La Poudrière*' has survived quite well even with the scars of war and is a fine example of a *Magasin à Poudre*. (For the breakdown of the *secteurs* see Appendix 3 Organisation of *le camp retranché de Verdun* Map 4 for The Main Fortification of Verdun - – *Le camp retranché de Verdun* and Map 5 for The Fortification within the 1st sector.)

Dépôt Intermédiaire

After the main *Magasin à Poudre* there was still a need for a number of local stores. These small, masonry-built, arched, one room buildings were intended to supplement the Magasin à Poudre de Secteur, and to store not only ammunition, but equipment as well. They were known as *dépôt intermédiaire* (intermediate depot).

The *dépôts intermédiaire* were located at ground level near to the *batteries* positions, and close to the *routes militaire*. These *dépôts intermédiaire* were built from 1891, with an earth covering to give them added protection. However, some were built into natural embankments if the location allowed or in one case, at least buried underground with a sloping ramp cut into the ground down to the entrance. An example is the *dépôt intermédiaire "d"* which can be found next to the track leading up to the *ouvrages de Froideterre*.

Voie Ferré de 0.6m

Whilst there was a network of *routes militaire* connecting all of the defensive positions and depots where heavy equipment such as artillery had to be moved, (the forts, larger *ouvrages*, larger *batteries, magasins* and *dépôts*) a military light railway was added from 1887. Developed by *Capitaine* Prosper Péchot in 1887 as a temporary system for use in the field of battle, it was used on a permanent basis within the *camps retranché*. It was known as the *voie ferré de 0.6m* (600 millimetre narrow gauge railway) – the name deriving from the gauge of the track.

At Verdun, like the other *Places fortes de l'Est* (fortified places of the East), the *voie ferré de 0.6m - la système Péchot* (the Péchot system) – the network was quite extensive. *Le camp retranché de Verdun* had about twenty-eight kilometres of permanent way, 15 steam locomotives, and 252 bogie wagons. These bogie wagons could be used on their own; however by combining them with special chassis, various special purpose trucks could be created, for example two bogie wagons were combined to make up an *affûts truck* (rail mounted artillery wagon) which could mount either the *Canon de 'De Bange' 120 mm court modèle 1878* (155 millimetre calibre short barrelled cannons model 1878 invented by Colonel De Bange) or after 1912 the *Canon 155mm court modèle 1881 modifiée 1912* (155 millimetre calibre short barrelled cannon model 1881 modified 1912). By 1914, Verdun had 12 *affûts trucks* mounting the *Canons 155C modèle 1912*.

The *voie ferré de 0.6m* network at Verdun was routed into the *forts* and even underground into the *magasins à poudre*. They were also routed into the *parc d'artillerie* and *réduit central;* the latter had four kilometres of 0.6m tracks, laid inside the *galeries souterraines*. It was planned that in the event of a war, additional tunnels measuring 330 metre in length were to be driven toward the main railway line as well as the *parc d'artillerie* to the west of *la citadelle* in which another three kilometres of track was to be laid, making a total of seven kilometres; however this was not realised once the war actually began.

For a general overview of the French military railway system before the Great War, as well as a more in-depth view of the system at Verdun, see appendix 16: The *système Péchot* - French Military Railways.

Parc à Dirigeables

To keep up with the advancing technology of aviation in the last decade of the nineteenth century, an airfield was constructed for airships – known as the *parc à dirigeables* (dirigible balloon enclosure). It was located just behind the *redoute de Belleville* and was established circa 1890.

It consisted of a flat take off and landing field and it is thought that there were probably a number of permanent and temporary buildings located within the boundaries to give shelter against the elements to the balloons (wooden balloon sheds) and to the manpower required to operate them (wooden huts).

***

Even before this initial work had been finished in 1885, the French military engineers started to modify and update their *zone de défense*, mainly the forts in the *ligne principale de résistance*. This modification program continued up to the start of the Great War, albeit in two stages. Indeed the *fort de Bois-Bourrus* and the *ouvrage de La Laufée* were having modification work carried out in 1914, the work only being completed in the summer of 1914 just as war broke out.

Based upon the realisation that modern artillery using *mélinite* type high explosive, and especially using modern heavy howitzers, had made the structures of the original forts too weak to withstand the punishment that a potential future bombardment would subject them to; the structures had to be reinforced. The outer forts had their protection reinforced by having their earthen covers replaced by ballast; then with a minimum of two and a half metre thick layer of *bétonné spécial* and finally a second one metre thick ballast covering on top. Again the roof was overlaid with grass turf to prevent soil erosion and to act as camouflage. In some cases, where it was felt necessary, a covering of *bétonné spécial* was applied to the wall facings of exposed buildings. *Bétonné spécial* was extra hard concrete developed especially for the reinforcing of the forts and other fortifications and in later years was strengthened with steel bars for even greater tensile strength. During this period of modification of the fortifications, the *voie ferré de 0.6m* was utilised by the contractors for the transportation of their heavier equipment and of the materials required in the modification work. The contractors laid temporary sidings and branches were required for the work. The *système Péchot* was found to be particularly useful in the transportation of the huge armoured plates required for the construction of the *tourelles*. The *fort de Douaumont*, the *fort de Vaux* and the *fort de Moulainville* are all fine examples of this modification program. For drawings of the *fort de Vaux* after the modification of 1906, see plans 2 and sketches 2.

Coffres

As originally designed, the *caponnières* were set down low within the *fossé* below the normal ground level and were seen to be protected from the low trajectory artillery fire of the period. However with the development of heavier artillery, especially of the howitzer type using modern explosives that produced "plunging fire", the *caponnières* built on the corners of the *escarpe* became dangerously exposed. This can be seen very clearly at the *Redoute de Souville* where all of the *caponnières* were destroyed by artillery fire during the war with nothing left remaining of them.

To resolve this problem, a new type of casemate was designed. Known as *coffres* (coffers or casemates) they replaced the exposed *caponnières*. This was a Haxo style covered casemates built into the *contrescarpe* using *bétonné special* that had at least five metres of soil above. Being located in the *contrescarpe* of the *fossé*, the idea was that the incoming projectiles would pass above the *coffres* and not into them, which was the case with the *caponnières*.

As the *coffres* were located on the outside of the main fortified area of the *fort*, the defenders reached the *coffres* via *passages sous le fossé* (passageways or tunnels under the *fossé*), which gave them protection against enemy fire. Like the *caponnières*, they were located at the corners of the *fossé* and were built with loopholes in alignment to the *fossé* lines. Again they were often paired to cover two lines of the *fossé*. The single ones were known as *coffres simple* and the paired ones were known as *coffres double*.

Finally, as with the *caponnières*, the *coffres* were single storey and had all the firing bays located at the same level as the floor of the *fossé*. They had a *fossé-diamant* in front with floor level loopholes angled downward in alignment with the floor of the *fossé-diamant*. They often had a steel doored sally port complete with drawbridge set to one side of the loopholes.

The *fort de Vaux* gives a good example of fort defence systems, in that its four sided *fossé* originally had three bastions, one of each type - a *caponnières simple* (covering the *fossé* on the south-east side), a *caponnières double* (covering the northern two *fossés*) and a *caponnières de gorge* (covering the rear, south-western *fossé*). However these were replaced during the first modification with a *coffre simple*, a *coffre double* and a *coffre simple* respectively. For drawings of the *fort de Vaux* as originally built, see plans 1, section 1 and sketches 1.

Entrée de Guerre

Another addition to some of the forts, but not all, at this time was the construction of a secondary, more concealed entrance for use during wartime only. These entrances became known as the *entrée de guerre* (war entrance) and the original entrances were renamed *entrée de temps de paix* (peacetime entrance).

These later fort entrances (*entrées de guerre*) were developed in such a way that they were at the same level as the *fossé*, removing the need for the bridge, but still keeping the drawbridge over a localised *fossé-diamant* or haha. For example the *fort du Rozellier* was modified to have two entrances; the original *entrée de temps de paix* had a *système Poncelet longitudinal extérieur* and the later *entrée de guerre* had a *pont roulant latéral intérieur*.

The Modification of the *Redoute de Souville*

Like most of the forts, the *Redoute de Souville* was designed in such a way that it prevented any major internal building work to be considered. Although it had a *caserne* for 312 men, it was decided in 1888 to add another *caserne* for 300 men. It was built underground in *galleries souterraines*, externally to the fort, but linked into it by two corridors, both running parallel under the *fossé*. This new *caserne* had three entrances – a single external entrance connected to the two corridors - leading out onto the *route militaire* that became the *entrée de guerre* (with the result that the fort's existing entrance became the *entrée de Temps de Paix*.) The other two entrances were both located within the fort. The western corridor linked into the existing *magasin à poudre*, the magazine being converted into a barrack room, with the original magazine's entrance becoming the second entrance. Finally, the eastern corridor led directly up onto the *rue du rempart*, becoming the third entrance to this new underground complex.

The corridor were linked together by two large rooms, each room extended beyond the corridor, thus forming six barrack rooms for 50 men each and, similar to the *magasins à poudre*, they had wooden floors and tar-papered partitions lining the walls to reduce the dampness. There was a guardroom and a toilet block located either side of the *entrée de guerre*.

With the function of the existing *magasin à poudre* changed, a new *magasin à poudre* was added externally to the fort located underground, just to the north of the *entrée de Temps de Paix*, with the entrance sited in the *contrescarpe*.

***

In the mid 1880's, the *commission des cuirassements* asked the three main armour manufacturers in France - *Schneider et Compagnie* of *Le Creusot, Compagnie des Forges et Aciéries de Marine et d'Homécourt* of *Saint Chamond*, and *Compagnie des Forges de Châtillon, Commentry et Neuves-Maisons* of *Montluçon* – to develop an armoured turret each.

The commission reviewed each of the three turret designs, and then set up a series of tests that started on 8 October 1887. The turret's designs were pre-constructed within the manufacturer's factories, transported as components to, and then erected at the *camp de Châlons* (the artillery ranges in the Châlons Artillery Camp) where the tests were conducted. The main purpose of the tests was to determine the value of the different types of armour against modern artillery and, as such, was a straightforward test comparison of the three different designs.

When the testing was completed, the three turrets were repaired and then dismantled. Each turret was then reinstalled in different forts.

Tourelle de Bussière (T155L)

At the same time as the new *caserne* work was being undertaken on the *redoute de Souville,* the first of the three newly tested turrets, the *tourelle de 155mm (T155L) Bussière modèle 1888* (155 millimetre gun turret type T155L model 1888 designed by *colonel* Bussière) was re-erected in a location externally to the rear of the fort.

The five and a half metre diameter *tourelle T155L* was a *tourelle à éclipse* ('disappearing' or retractable turret) equipped with a pair of *canon de 'De Bange' 155mm longue S.P. modèle 1888* (155 millimetre calibre long barrelled gun model 1888 invented by *Colonel* De Bange). The gun ports of this turret were relocated in to its sidewall instead of the dome as with the *tourelle fixes de Mougin*. The advantage was that the dome became

68

uncorrupted - without any holes punctured in it and therefore kept intact its integral strength. As with the *tourelle fixes de Mougin*, it could be rotated horizontally through 360° to give all round fire and, in the case of a *tourelle à eclipse*, it could also be raised above roof level for firing and then lowered back down into the roof void leaving only the *tourelle's* dished armour iron plate roof flush with the upper surface of the fortification. In its raised firing position only 1.2 metres stood proud of the ground level and that being the upper half of the gun room enough to clear the gun ports off the ground. The *tourelle T155L* sat in a circular pit in the roof of its own *abri* and had a hydro-pneumatic system that operated a large piston device for lifting and lowering it.

The 4.1 metre long guns were housed completely within the gun room, hence the large diameter of the turret. Like the earlier turret, the gun mountings were designed to keep the cannon muzzles located in one position so as to keep the *sabords* as small as possible.

Immediately below the gun room but still part of the turret was the *chambre fonctionnante* (working chamber) where the shells and propellant cases were prepared before being passed up via a shell hoist to the cannons above. The concrete *abri* that the turret sat in also housed a steam powered hydraulic piston operating system along with the counter weights needed for lifting the 184 tonne *tourelle* (armour plate, cannons, gun room, working chamber, men and ammunitions). Like all turrets, the opening in the *abri* had an *avant-cuirasse* – a deep armoured iron ring around the edge of the opening in which the turrets sat to give protection to the chamber below.

After the testing at the *camp de Châlons* the *tourelle de 155mm (T155L) Bussière*, was dismantled and reconstructed in *Le camp retranché de Verdun*. It had a few modifications including the tightening up of the hydro-pneumatic system before it was reinstalled.

The *tourelle de 155mm (T155L) Bussière* was located next to the existing *batterie*, close to the original entrance track. Because it was located outside the fort, it was considered to be an independent *batterie* and as such was given its own designation number (*Batterie 8.2*). This was the only example of the *tourelle de 155mm (T155L) Bussière* to be built.

***

The other two turrets that the *commission des cuirassements* reviewed at the *camp de Châlons* were the *coupole de Saint Chamond* and the *coupole de Montlucon*. Unlike the *tourelle de 155mm (T155L) Bussière*, which was a *tourelle à éclipse*, both the other two turrets were *tourelles fixes*. They were not reinstalled in *Le camp retranché de Verdun*, but were instead reconstructed in two of the fortifications within *Le camp retranché de Toul*.

Detailed information in the French archives on these turrets has been lost. However the German intelligence report on Toul[16] has scaled drawings showing these turrets. The factories of *Saint Chamond* and *Chatillon-Commentry* supplied the Belgian military with turrets for their fortification program. The Belgians used the term '*coupoles*' instead of the French term of '*tourelles*'. It appears that since the two factories were familiar with using the Belgian terminology, they continued to use the term when asked to supply the French military with these turrets. From the German intelligence reports of both the French and the Belgian turrets[17], the drawings give the impression that the designs of the French turrets were very much related to their Belgian counterparts, although not copies.

Coupole de Saint Chamond

The *coupole de 155mm de Saint Chamond, modèle 1888* (155 millimetre cannon cupola design and built by the Saint Chamond factory, model 1888) was an improved *tourelles fixes de Mougin*; designed and constructed by the *Compagnie des Forges et Aciéties de Marine et d'Homécourt,*[18] armaments factory. It was presented to the French military on 17 March 1886.

The *coupole* was armed with two *Canon de 'De Bange' 155mm longue modèle 1877* that were mounted in cradles with curved slots for the gun trunnions. The breaches were lowered to the gun's maximum elevation for loading. This required a tall gun chamber – it being 4.3 metres high. Even though the turret had a six metre diameter, the muzzles of the long guns protruded out of the turret's domed roof. The cradles were built into an overall rolled iron chassis that supported the two curved rolled iron roof plates that were dove-tailed together along with three rolled iron wall plates mounted onto a cast iron frame. Below the wall frame was a roller race with twelve rollers. The chassis was mounted on a large central pivot, which sat

---

[16] The German intelligence report that covers these two French turrets has the title '*Großer Generalstab. IV Abtheilung. Denkschriften Toul*' and is dated 1911. The drawings within the report were tracings of the original French architectural and mechanical drawings.

[17] The German intelligence report that covers the Belgian *coupoles* has the title '*Großer Generalstab. 4 Abteilung. Die belgischen und holländischen Befestigungen und die Grundsätze ihrer Verteidigung*' and is dated 1908. This was the report that was commissioned by *Generalfeldmarschall* Helmuth von Moltke, the Younger and his chief of intelligence *Oberst* (later *Generalmajor*) Erich Ludendorff that led to the modification of the "Schlieffen Plan" with the abandonment of using Holland as a route into the France.

[18] The *Compagnie des Forges et Aciéties de Marine et d'Homécourt* was located in the town of *Saint Chamond* and was commonly known as such.

in a mounting sleeve – the sleeve being cast into the gun chamber's concrete floor. The lower part of the pivot projected through the floor and was attached to a counterweight located in the chamber below. It appears from the drawing that to rotate the turret, it was first lifted by use of the counter weight and then, with the majority of the turret's weight off the rollers, simply rotated using a capstan type device coupled to a gear on an azimuth at the level of the roller race. On each cannon there were two hydraulic brakes to absorb the forty-five centimetre recoil of the cannon when it was fired. A third smaller hydraulic brake acting in the opposite direction brought the cannon back into its firing position.

There were four cast iron parts that made up the *avant-cuirasse* that were then encased in the concrete roof of the *abri*.

The *coupole de 155mm de Saint Chamond* was reinstalled in the *fort de Saint Michel* part of *Le camp retranché de Toul*.

Coupole de Montluçon

The *coupole de 155mm Châtillon-Commentry, modèle 1888* (Châtillon-Commentry's 155 millimetre cannon cupola, model 1888), was also known as the *"coupole invisible de Montluçon"* (Montluçon's invisible cupola). It was designed and constructed by the *Compagnie des Forges de Châtillon-Commentry et Neuves-Maisons* armaments factory, which was located in the town of Montluçon, hence the names. It was presented to the French military on 18 June 1886.

This turret unlike all the other French turrets but similar to some of the Belgian *coupoles*, was armed with twin *Canon de 'De Bange' 155mm court modèle 1881*. The use of these short ranged howitzers instead of the longer ranged cannons of the other turrets had a number of impacts on the design.

Firstly, the use of the short-barrelled howitzers meant that the size of the turret could be reduced considerably, it having a diameter of only 2.8 metres and headroom within the gun chamber of only 2.4 metres.

Secondly, the shorter barrels could be accommodated entirely within the gun chamber even though the chamber was so small.

Thirdly, with the range being only 6,300 metres, this turret was left exposed to longer range hostile guns, but since these howitzers could only shoot with plunging fire, and with the firing elevational angle being in the range of +5° to +40°, this was used in the defence of this turret.

Being armed with howitzers, the *coupole de 155mm Châtillon-Commentry* was positioned upon the highest point of the fortification to give it the maximum possible range. Therefore by locating it within a small sunken hollow formed by an encompassing bulwark, the turret was given a degree of protection against the flat trajectory of the enemy's longer ranged field artillery. The inside of the bulwark, facing the *tourelle*, was sloped at the same angle as that of the guns' lowest elevation, 5°, so as to allow the howitzers to fire unhindered. The bulwark had a secondary function being that it completely hid the turret from outside horizontal view, as there was at that time no aircraft and hence no close range aerial observation, making ranging upon it by enemy ground artillery observers much more difficult.

The drawing of this turret in the German intelligence report is missing a lot of details, however what details are shown make it appear to be very similar to its Belgian counterpart. The Belgian turret sat on a roller race, with rotation being actioned by turning a hand wheel located in the gun chamber and was coupled to a gear meshing with an azimuth located at the same level of the roller race. There appears to have been no lifting device to take the weight off of the rollers, however there was a ventilation system operated by a hand pump located in the basement chamber. The Belgian turret had a rolled iron-plated roof and similar cradles with curved slots to carry the guns.

The *coupole de 155mm Châtillon-Commentry* was reinstalled on the *fort de Lucey*, of *Le camp retranché de Toul*.

The Final Modernisation and Later Construction of Verdun's Defences 1893-1914

As with the second phase of development, this third stage was also spurred on by the development of high explosive, and again like the previous stage, the work that had been started during the first two phases of construction continued with a number of additions to the defences.

From 1893 the *bétonné spécial* was made even stronger by the addition of reinforcing steel rods introduced into the concrete. From this date onwards all new above ground structures within the perceived battle zone were constructed using this new reinforced *bétonné spécial*.

Abris du Projecteur

With most of the defences built on high ground, it was felt by the military command that there was a problem with the low ground. In the deep ravines, especially after nightfall, the enemy could use the darkness of night or even the twilight of morning or evening to penetrate into the defensive systems. This was considered to be particularly dangerous to the defence. Even though the ravines were now covered by the *ouvrages infanterie*, it was judged that the most dangerous of the ravines needed to be illuminated.

To resolve this problem, the ravines considered to be most exposed were given permanent lighting using electric searchlights; temporary lighting was made available to others not so exposed. There were three ravines considered most at risk at Verdun and were covered by this permanent lighting system. Each of the permanent lighting stations comprised of an electric searchlight, along with an electric generator protected by small shelters known as *poste Photo-Électrique* or *abris du projecteur* (electric searchlight post or projector shelters). All three *abris du projecteur* were built in 1899 and each consisted of a small, reinforced *bétonné special* hut with a large doorway in the rear wall.

The first *abri du projecteur* can be found quite close to the *batterie du Mardi-Gras* and was used to cover the *ravin de Tavannes*[19]. The second was built to cover the *ravin de Eix* and is located close to the *ouvrage de Eix*.

---

[19] The *ravin de Tavannes* is not named on the modern French *Institut Géographique Nationales* (*IGN*) maps, but is the ravine located between the *Ouvrage de La Laufée* and the *batterie du Mardi-Gras*. The *ravin de Tavannes* has also been called the *ravin du chemin de fer de Metz* (since the railway line to Metz runs through it.)

The third was located to cover the *ravin de Fontaines* in the *Bois Fumin* and is located close behind the *Abris de combat 'DV3'*.

For the ravines that were not permanently covered there were five railway mounted – railway trucks designed for the *voie ferré de 0.6m* - and eleven lorry mounted searchlights that could be transported about the defence zone and manoeuvred into position quickly.

Casemate bétonnée pour Projecteur Électrique de 90cm

A development of the *abris du projecteur* was the *Casemate bétonnée pour Projecteur Électrique de 90cm,* an example being constructed on the *fort de Frouard - Forts d'arrêt - en avant de Toul.*

It consisted of three rooms – the operating chamber, the storage room set behind and to one side and, connecting them, a transit room. Due to its weight the *Projecteur Électrique de 90cm* (90-centremetre diameter searchlight) was mounted on a small railway trolley and was when not in use normally kept in the storage room. The 600-millimetre tramway ran from the storage room and then into the operating chamber via a wagon turntable located at the junction of the two sets of tracks in the transit room.

The semi circular front wall of the casemate had a large opening that spanned the entire front wall into the operating chamber. The front was protected from direct assault by a *fossé-diamant* and the opening had an armoured steel shutter, which was pulled across to seal the room against small arms and shell shards. The shutter was constructed out of hinged steel plates mounted on a pair of rails (top and bottom) and was pulled back when the *Projecteur Électrique* was in use. There was also a pair of steel doors between the operating chamber and the transit room.

Entry into the *Casemate bétonnée pour Projecteur Électrique de 90cm* was from a corridor located at the rear of the transit room opposite the storage room. There was a passageway directly from the storage room into the operating chamber for ease of manhandling the *Projecteur Électrique*, which also had a steel door.

***

Ouvrages Modernisée

It was decided to upgrade the *ouvrages infanterie* and *postes*, because of the development of the new high explosive projectiles, but only about a third of them were upgraded because of financial restrictions.

Of the twenty-five *ouvrages infanterie* and the four *postes* originally built around Verdun, six and three respectively were rebuilt as *ouvrages modernisée* ('modernized' *ouvrages*) and were converted into fort like structures, although generally smaller, they also had a modified *fossé*.[20] The *fossés* consisted of the normal fort type *contrescarpe* along with the *glacis* located in front, and the *grille* on top. However the *escarpe* was not included - the floor of the *fossé* running straight into the *plongée*, so designed to deflect incoming projectiles to a better degree than that of a slab sided *escarpe*. Since there was no *escarpe* creating a blind spot for the defenders, there were no *coffres* built into the *contrescarpe* - it being assumed that the enemy within the *fossé* would be neutralised by the *ouvrages's* defensive guns.

The *ouvrages modernisée* consisted of a combined *caserne - abri* built out of reinforced *bétonné special*. On some of the larger *ouvrages modernisée* a number of independent *abris* were constructed, also constructed out of reinforced *bétonné special*.

The requirement for the courtyard as included in the earlier fortifications was no longer deemed to be necessary (the uses of the courtyard being undertaken within the *fossé* or outside of the fort's perimeter on a specially prepared ground just beyond the *fossé*). Therefore on the later fortifications or on the rebuilds, the courtyard was not incorporated; the front face of the *caserne* formed a rear *escarpe*.

Entrances to the outside normally had an armoured steel door. However where doorways were to be used in peacetime only, a secondary removable door block 150 millimetres wide was positioned in front of the steel door. It consisted of vertical concrete slots on either side of the corridor – the inner runners of the slots finishing about 300 millimetres from the top of the doorframe. This allowed the defenders to drop 150 millimetres wide by 250 millimetres high slats into the slots, one on top of the other, up to the top of the inner runners, creating a solid block. There was a 300 millimetres gap left at the top, which could be used for observation.

As previously mentioned, some of the gunnery positions that were located in particularly exposed positions were later modified to give the gun crews improved protection. The *batterie de Damloup* (*batterie 6.1*) located on the edge of a steep ravine, which was considered to be extremely dangerous, had consequentially a couple of *abris bétonne* (concrete shelter) added for the protection of the gun crews.

Also mentioned above the *batterie du Mardi-Gras* (*batteries 6.7*) had a *petites cloche Digoin* added for the protection of the gunnery observer.

***

Abris de Combat

---

[20] It should be noted that the *Ouvrage de La Falouse* was a totally new *ouvrage* and was constructed in 1906. It was known as an *ouvrage moderne*. See below for a detailed description.

In the late 1890's a further review of the fortified lines took place about the same time as the upgrading of the *ouvrages infanterie* into the *ouvrages modernisée*. This review showed that there were still a number of gaps, or that some of the gaps which had been found earlier in 1887, were still thought to be a problem. This was due to the inadequate size of the *ouvrages infanterie* to provide sufficient cover.

The solution to these problems was to build *abris d'intervalle* or *abris de combat* (interval or combat shelters) to supplement the rebuilding and enlargement of the *ouvrages*. The new constructions covered the dead ground that provoked the concerns. They were to be used by the infantry in the field as *Centres de résistance*.

The *abris de combat* were therefore multi-room infantry shelters, built out of reinforced *bétonné spécial* with soil covering the roof. The reinforced *bétonné spécial* extended down the front and sidewalls. They came in two sizes, small for a half infantry company and large for a whole infantry company. A French infantry company in 1914 consisted of three officers and one hundred and ninety-seven other ranks – totalling two hundred all ranks. However this complement of officers and men had been introduced just before the outbreak of war, so that at the time that the *abris de combat* were being designed and built from 1898, the complement of an infantry company was about one half of the later wartime number (one hundred all ranks). The shelters were originally sized for one or two companies respectively.

The smaller *abris de combat* consisted of one large room for the half company and one small room for the use of the officers – probably as a sleeping chamber and command room. The larger versions had two large rooms to accommodate an entire company, and again they had an officers' room at one end. Each room had fold down wooden benches. The entire *abris de combat* had a water cistern located within the basement located under the main room(s). A latrine was located externally on the rear wall at one end of the covered entrance corridor furthest from the officers' room and a kitchen niche on the other side next to the officers' room.

Entry into each chamber was from the outside – there being a single entrance covered by a blast wall in front of it, the blast walls forming the outer supports for a shellproof canopy - an extention of the roof slab. The original design of the *abris de combat* had masonry supports for the concrete canopy, however this was changed quite quickly to concrete supports giving added strength to the canopy support and greater protection to the entrances. Each doorway had a steel grill door and faced away from the expected enemy position – i.e. towards the back. These blast walls in effect formed a corridor with entrances at each end as well as entrances backwards out of alignment with the doorways into the chambers. The *abris de combat* were purely infantry shelters and not fortlets like the "pillboxes" of the war period. They did not have any loopholes, firing slits or artillery gunnery slits. An opening within the centre wall linked the two main rooms in the larger abris de combat.

There was thirty-four *abris de combat* built around Verdun with four located in a line between the *fort de Douaumont* and the *fort de Vaux* to supplement the *ouvrage d'Hardaumont*.

In 1913 the design was changed again. The basic room layout was the same; however the outer corridor had the ends blocked in, in effect making it another room. The number of entrances was now reduced to two, being through the back wall at each end of the corridor. The entrances were given steel grill doors in addition to the ones at the entrances to each of the internal rooms. A small guard shelter similar to a *Caponnière de gorge* or a *postes de ravelin* constructed out of reinforced concrete was added. The shelter had two gun ports, one on either side in line with the back wall and gave cover to both the entrances and the approaches.

Retranchements d'Infanterie

At the same time as the construction of the *abris de combat*, there were a number of *retranchements d'infanterie* or *retranchements de campagne* built (infantry or field trenches and like the *ouvrages*, I would suggest that a better description would be a 'pre-war built trench') often in association with the *abris de combat*.

The *retranchements* were basically a shallow *tranchées bétonné* (concrete lined trench) supplemented by a number of small *abris* (shelters), built into the forward trench wall. These *abris* were mainly used for ammunition storage. Located on top of the front parapet of the trench were fold-down armoured steel shields with *echappatoires* (loopholes) cut into them to accommodate a rifle similar to the type of portable armoured shield used by the German army in 1914. These trenches were of varying length but on average were about 100 metres long and about 1.2 metres deep. They had a pair of short communication trenches, one at each end, leading back to the rear. There were sets of steps located at the end of the communication trenches for the ease of the men descending into them.

Another addition to the Verdun defences was an eighth *Magasin à Poudre de Secteur* to supplement the seven already built. The *Magasin à Poudre de Secteur de Fleury* (commonly known as '*la Poudrière*') was added in 1910.

Ouvrages en Terre de Infanterie

Just before the war in 1914, a number of infantry redoubts were built, which became known as *ouvrages en terre de infanterie* (infantry earth works.) The *ouvrages en terre de infanterie* basically consisted of a number of *retranchements d'infanterie* inter-connected to form an enclosed defensive position. These *retranchements d'infanterie* and *ouvrages en terre de infanterie* were intended to provided cover for the infantry, the location of which were chosen to give support to nearby fortifications – the *ouvrages infanterie,* the *abris de combat,* the *batteries* and the *forts.*

There were three *retranchements d'infanterie* built to cover the *fort de Vaux,* and three *ouvrages en terre de infanterie* built to cover the *ouvrage d'Hardaumont* – they were the *ouvrage de Lorient,* the *ouvrage de Josémont* and the *ouvrage du Muguet.* Unfortunately due to the heavy fighting in these areas, not much if any of them survived the battles and there are little of them to be seen today. However, a fine example that has survived intact is the *retranchements d'infanterie* located a short distance from the northern end of the *batterie du Mardi-Gras* (*batteries 6.7* and *6.8.*) They were probably the most economic of all the defence structures built, being quick and cheap to construct.

Terrain d'Aviation

The first decade of the twentieth century saw the rapid development of the aeroplane and, as such, the final defensive development to *le camp retranché de Verdun.* This was a second airfield, but instead of balloons this airfield was for aircraft.

It was known as a *terrain d'aviation* (aviation ground or airfield), which was located just behind the *redoute de Belrupt.* It was probably built just before 1908 – the date that the airfield first appeared on a map of the area. Like the *parc à dirigeables,* it consisted of a flat field for taking off and landing and had some building to protect the aircraft and men from the elements.

I assumed that from about 1910 there were a couple of aircraft hangers probably of the *hangars Bessonneau* (*Bessonneau* hangers) type to house the aeroplanes, and possibly a wooden hut or two for the officers and men of the fledgling French air service. The *hangar Bessonneau* had a wooden frame covered by linen fabric and was designed by the rope manufacturer Julien Bessonneau to meet the need of the budding civilian sport of aviation in 1910.

The Military Aviation Law of the March 1912 decreed that French Military Aviation had to increase in size to 334 aircraft. It also stated that some of the new aircraft would be assigned to the eastern fortresses.

Therefore the *terrain d'aviation* was probably developed later in the same year as the law or possibly during the following year.

The French Air Service was the world leader in military flying just before the start of the Great War. Although the French Air Service did not achieve the increase required by the 1912 Law, it still had 252 aircraft as compared to 232 in the German armed services (both naval and military) and the 113 in the British armed services (both naval and military) at the start of the Great War.

***

From the early nineteen hundreds, both of the *fossé* defence weapons, the *canon revolver Hotchkiss* and the *canon de 12-culasse* were replaced by the *mitrailleuse de 8mm Hotchkiss modèle 1899* (8 millimetre calibre *Hotchkiss* machine gun model 1899). This new machine gun was lighter, more movable and had a higher rate of fire than the older weapons which made them obsolete.

***

Further modifications, starting in 1902, to upgrade the counter-offensive armaments of the forts consisted of a new type of casemate, known as the *casemates de Bourges* and a number of more modern designed *tourelles à eclipse*, both of which were added to the fortifications in reasonably large numbers.

Casemates de Bourges

Reverting back to the Haxo style casemate, the *casemate de Bourges* was a type of *casemate de flanquement* (flanking casemate). The idea dated back to the early 1890's when the concept was first mentioned. The concept was that casemates, with their limited field of fire, could be used to guard the flanks of the fortifications and would be more economical since they were much cheaper to construct than the turrets. Following a long debate within the *commission des cuirassements* concerning the relative merits of the *casemate de flanquement* against turrets, the design for this type of casemate finally materialised in 1899. For drawings of *casemates de Bourges* see plan 5.

Commandant Laurent, who was a member of the commission des cuirassements, designed the *casemate de Bourges*. Since it was designed to cover the area between the fortifications, it was normally positioned on the side of the fortifications above the *fossé* with a limited field of fire sideways. The *casemate de Bourges* was named after the *polygone de Bourges* firing ranges where it was originally tested and not after its designer *commandant* Laurent as was the case with other casemates and the turrets.

The *casemates de Bourges* was a two-storey complex with its exterior walls and roof constructed out of one and three quarter metre thick steel reinforced *Bétonné spécial*. It had two gun chambers located side by side as well as an *observatoire* (observation room) on the ground floor. A magazine and a working chamber were located within its basement. The gun chambers were connected to the magazine and working room by shafts with hand operated shell hoists within. There was a staircase at the back of the casemate, which connected the two levels together, and a rear entrance to the outside with an armoured steel door. There was often an underground passageway that led back into the main part of the fortification.

Originally armed with a pair of *Canon de 'Lahitolle' 95 mm modèle 1888,* it was considered that the rate of fire of six rounds per minute of this type of *canon* to be too slow. Therefore by 1902 the design was modified so that the later *casemates de Bourges* housed two standard *canon de 75mm TR modèle 1897* (75 millimetre calibre quick firing gun, model 1897 – the standard French Army field gun of the period known as '*les soixante-dix cinq*' or 'the Seventy-Five'), mounted on an *affût à pivot modèle 1900* (pivot mounting, model 1900), firing over a limited field of fire. The *fort d'Haudainville* was the first fort to have incorporated a *casemates de Bourges* which was armed with the earlier *canons de Lahitolle 95 mm.*

The *casemates de Bourges* had a crew of one junior officer and sixteen men consisting a *chef de pièce*, a *tireur*, a *chargeur* and three *pourvoyeurs* for each gun and two *pourvoyeurs* under a sergeant operating in the magazine and working chamber below.

A fine example can be seen in the *ouvrage de Froideterre*.

Tourelle de Mitrailleuses (GF3)

The new *tourelles à éclipse* came in a range of sizes and types. The smallest of the new turrets was the *tourelle de mitrailleuses* (machine gun turret.)

The armaments factory Ateliers de Puteaux designed the first of the tourelles de mitrailleuses, which was for close range, anti-infantry work. The biggest problem with a lot of the French design work on the turrets during this period was the limitation of the available weapons. The problem in this case was the availability of a modern automatic machine gun. Consequently when work on the turret started in 1893, it was designed around the only reliable machine gun available at that time, the seven barrel Gatlin Gun.

The *tourelle de mitrailleuses (GF3) modèle 1895* (machine gun turret type GF3 model 1895) was a small turret that had 15 millimetre front and side plates and 120 millimetre thick plate on the roof of rolled iron.

(Presumably GF was an abbreviation of *Gatlin Fusil* (Gatlin rifle) and although in the later turret the type and manufacturer of the machine gun was changed, the initials for the turret remained.) The concept was that the turret would always be in the retracted position when there was a bombardment and therefore only the roof needed to be thick enough to withstand direct hits by incoming shells – the assumption was that the turret would only be in the raised position when it was engaging the enemy infantry and that the enemy artillery would not be shelling its own infantry. Based on that assumption the thin front and side armour was only required to protect the machine gunner against the enemy infantry's small arms. Due to the size of the Gatlin Gun relative to the size of the turret, it had a mechanism whereby the Gatlin Gun was retracted into the turret when it was being lowered, and then projected out again when the turret was raised. The turret had three balanced counterweights for elevating and lowering. The prototype was the only one built and this example was mounted onto the *fort de Manonviller* - a *fort isolé* of the *groupe de la Meuse* – not being part of the Verdun fortifications.

Tourelle de Mitrailleuses (GF4)

In 1899 the *Société Anonyme des Anciens Établissements Hotchkiss et Compagnie* produced their *8mm mitrailleuses Hotchkiss modèle 1899* (8 millimetre machine gun designed by Hotchkiss model 1899), which resolved the earlier problem of a suitable machine gun. The *tourelle de mitrailleuses (GF3)* was then modified to accommodate the new weapon.

The *tourelle de mitrailleuses (GF4) modèle 1900* (machine gun turret type GF4 model 1900), had a diameter of 1.3 metres and was armed with a pair of *8mm mitrailleuses Hotchkiss*, the right hand gun being mounted slightly above the other to allow access for the 26 round strip-fed ammunition to the upper gun (the strips being fed into the left-hand side of the gun.) A *mitrailleur* (machine gunner) operated it single-handedly and therefore only one gun could be fired at any given time. The second gun was kept ready in case of emergency such as a jam in the first gun. It was designed for close range defence against attacking infantry, it had a fast acting mechanism for quick operation – the *mitrailleur* used straps attached to his hips so that he could easily and rapidly rotate the turret on the target. There were also handgrips located on the inside as an alternative to the hip straps. The *mitrailleur* was supported by a *pourvoyeur* who stood below and handed up the ammunition strips when they were required. For drawings of the *tourelle de mitrailleuses* see plan 4.

Again it was assumed that the enemy artillery would not be active whilst his, the enemy's, infantry was in the vicinity of the turret and although the armour of the GF4 was thicker than that of the GF3, the armour was still relatively thin – having only twenty millimetre side panels, a 125 millimetre front plate and 320 millimetres on the roof. Like the Bussière's *tourelle (T155L)* before it and indeed the later turrets, this turret was moved up and down by the use of a counterweight that kept the turret in equilibrium, again making for ease of operation. Because of the lightness of this turret, it was not necessary to provide a steam engine to produce the power unlike the earlier Bussière *tourelle (T155L)*.

Projecteur à Éclipse

As a development of the earlier *abris du projecteur*, the *projecteur à éclipse* (retractable projector) was a special turret designed to illuminate areas close by the fortifications where it was installed.

The *projecteur à éclipse* was similar to the *tourelle de mitrailleuses (GF4)* except it was equipped with a search light with a ninety-centimetre lens. Designed in 1903, it was not accepted until 1908, the *projecteur à éclipse* was based on the design of the armoured retractable searchlights of the Belgian forts. It was about the same size as the *tourelle GF4* in terms of both armour thickness and overall size. The *projecteur à éclipse* was guided up and down between two rails and the mechanism made use of balanced counterweights. There was a working chamber below for its crew to operate.

There were only five constructed before the outbreak of war in 1914, an example of the *projecteur à éclipse* can be found on the *fort d'Arches* which was part of the *forts de Redeau – Ligne Épinal-Belfort*.

Leading on from the earlier *tourelles* a number of new design concepts for better turret defence mechanisms were put forward.

After his retirement from the French army, Mougin was employed by the *Compagnie des Forges et Aciéries de Marine et d'Homécourt (Saint Chamond)* working alongside M. Darnancier, the company's chief engineer. Between them, they developed an automatic system for the cannons' gun ports. They rejected the *tourelles à éclipse* concept; instead reverting back to the *tourelle fixes* using automatic movable armoured shields over the gun ports. The shields worked by being lowered as the cannons were just about to be fired and re-elevated after being fired, which was carried out automatically.

Another idea of the period originated from the work being carried out at the *Saint Chamond* factory, whilst engaged upon work for the Belgian and Romanians governments, was that of an oscillating turret. These ideas were put forward to the *commission des cuirassements*.

There were also other designs by *colonel* Bussière who was now working for the *Schneider et Compagnie (Creusot)* and *colonel* Souriau of the *Compagnie des Fives-Lille pour Construction Mécaniques et*

Entreprises (Lille). Both of them were working on *tourelles à éclipse* designs, which they submitted to the *commission des cuirassements*.

However all their ideas and designs were rejected by the *commission des cuirassements*. The commission's *commandant* Galopin, who had now taken on the role of lead engineering commissioner, had just developed his own system of '*éclipsage*' and therefore disregarded the competitors to his own design. Galopin felt that Mougin's *tourelle fixes* was out of date, as with Bussière's improved turret. Galopin regarded Souriau's design and that of the oscillating system as being not robust enough to take an enemy bombardment and disregarded them. Although Galopin had found technical problems with the *Saint Chamond's*, *Creusot's* and *Fives-Lille's* designs, he concluded that his own design appeared to be the better design overall. There still may have been a more personal reason for keeping his own design! Galopin submitted a comparison report to the *ministère de la Guerre* (The Ministry of War) on 19 April 1892 concluding with a recommendation for his own design.

Although Mougin's later designs were to be found in the Belgian and Romanian fortifications none of his later work was to be utilised in any French fortification after this date.

There were periodic experiments that were conducted over the years taking place at *Saint Cyr* (1890), the *fort de Pagny-la-Blanche-Cote* (1901) and the *fort de Pont-Saint-Vincent* (1910) to test various aspects of the armour systems, which included the use of electric lighting and ventilation systems.

Tourelles de Galopin (T57CF) (T75) and *(T155R)*

The development of *commandant* Galopin's turrets followed a quite logical path.

The larger calibre artillery was required for long-range, long-distance defence, whilst the smaller calibre artillery and machine guns with the shorter ranges were used for close range defence. The *commission des cuirassements* had come to the conclusion that for the longer ranges, the best form of protection for the larger cannons and their crews was to place them inside turrets. On the other hand, the best protection for the defenders for very close range defence was the casemates, namely the *coffres* that covered the *fossés*.

However there was still some debate within the *commission des cuirassements* concerning the best way to protect the cannons of medium calibres and their crews with regard to the intermediate ranges. *Commandant* Laurent was advocating the use of casemates for intermediate defence whilst Galopin favoured the turrets.

Laurent's argument stated that the casemate could house larger medium calibre weapons, for a much smaller cost. Galopin's counter argument was that their somewhat restricted field of fire limited the use of the casemates. To cover all the ground meant that more casemates had to be built with an increase in cost and greater possibility of them being damaged by enemy fire. The debate was finally resolved by the *commission des cuirassements* with the concept that the cheaper casemates with their limited fields of fire were ideal for sideward defence, hence the development of the *casemate de Bourges*. The turrets were better for intermediate distance frontal defence. The problem that faced Galopin was the weapon to use within the turret for the intermediate ranges (similar to the problem with regard to the machine gun).

About 1890 Galopin put forwards his ideas relating to the turrets and from those ideas he developed the design for his turret. The *tourelle de Galopin* was certainly an improvement on the earlier turret, but the biggest problem with his design was the large overall size of the cannons in respect to the small size of his turret – he wanted to keep the turrets as small as possible so as to reduce the target presented to the enemy artillery.

The solution to his problem initially was to use small artillery pieces, namely the *canons de Nordenfelt 57mm CF modèle 1889* (57 millimetre calibre gun type CF manufactured by Maxim-Nordenfelt, model 1889). Using two of the *canons de Nordenfelt 57mm CF mounted* side by side he produced the design for the *tourelle de 57mm (T57CF) modèle 1889*. The biggest disadvantage for this turret was the calibre size of the cannons; they were just too small, when compared with the first of the *casemate de Bourges* which mounted two *canons de Lahitolle 95 mm*. There were four turrets constructed during 1895, but none of them were positioned in any of the Verdun fortifications. Two examples were installed on the *fort de Manonviller* - a *fort isolé* of the *groupe de la Meuse*.

The small calibre size of the cannons was soon rectified with the development of the *canon de 75mm raccourci modèle 75-02* (75 millimetre calibre, shortened gun, model 75-02). This shortened version of the famous '75' (the *canon de 75mm TR modèle 1897*) was introduced in 1902 and had an overall size of the earlier *canons de Nordenfelt 57mm*. This allowed for the *canons de Nordenfelt 57mm* to be substituted for the later and more powerful *canon de 75mm raccourci*, thus creating the *tourelle de 75mm (T75) Galopin modèle 1902* (75 millimetre gun turret type T75 designed by Galopin model 1902). It had a diameter of 2.7 metres and apart from the change in the type of cannons; the working chamber was redesigned to eliminate problems that had been found in the earlier *tourelle de 57mm (T57CF)*. For drawings of the *tourelle de 75mm* see plan 2.

Since his design was seen to be superior to the earlier turrets, it seemed obvious to produce a version of the *tourelle de 75mm (T75)* with larger calibre cannons. During this period a lot of work was conducted to produce cannons with shorter barrels especially for turrets. Work was being done on shortening the *canon de 'De Bange' 120 mm longue modèle 1878* and so Galopin started his own work on a slightly larger version of the *tourelle de 75mm (T75)* to house the new projected cannons.

However before Galopin's work on the new turret could really begin, a new larger weapon became available. This was the *canon de 'De Bange' 155mm raccourci modèle 1902* (155 millimetre calibre shortened gun, model 1902), a shortened version of the *canon de 'De Bange' 155 mm longue modèle 1877*. The *canon de 'De Bange' 155 mm longue* had already been modified to have a short barrel in the shape of the *canon de 'De Bange' 155mm court modèle 1881* which was a short ranged high angle howitzer, but it was of no use for the intended purpose of a long range defence turret cannon. What the turret designers required was cannon that had the same range as the original version, but with the barrel shortened. So the barrel of the *canon de 'De Bange' 155 mm longue* was redesigned with the shorter barrel length but with its performance maintained.

Galopin therefore modified his proposed new turret design for the *canon de 'De Bange' 120 mm* to accommodate the new larger but shorter *canons de 'De Bange' 155mm raccourci*.

All of his turret designs up to this date housed twin cannons and the new turret was no exception. It became known as the *tourelle de 155mm (T155R) Galopin modèle 1903* (155 millimetre gun turret type T155R designed by Galopin, model 1903). A small number of the new turrets were manufactured and commissioned. None of the *tourelle de 155mm (T155R) Galopin modèle 1903* were used in the fortifications of Verdun, however they were used elsewhere, for example the *batterie de l'Eperon* of the *groupe de la Meuse*.

A debate soon developed with regard to the number of *canons* that were to be housed in this new larger turret. The case was put forward that if the twin gun turret was put out of action by a direct hit, and then both guns would be made inoperable. However if the guns were to be split and mounted into two separate single gun turrets, then it would be less likely that both the turrets would be hit at the same time with the result that at least one gun would always be in action. The counter argument was that by reducing the number of guns within a turret, the firepower would be severely reduced by half. The cost factor of the two types of turret probably decided the argument in favour of the single gun version – the cost of the single gun version being about two thirds of that of the two gun version.

Galopin again modified his design to create a single gun version, which became known as the *tourelle de 155mm (T155R) Galopin modèle 1907* (155 millimetre gun turret type T155 R designed by Galopin model 1907).

The 4.1 metre diameter *tourelle de 155mm (T155R) Galopin modèle 1907* was in effect a larger version of the *tourelle de 75mm (T75)* but was considerably smaller then Bussière's *tourelle de 155mm (T155L)* with its 5.5 metre diameter dimensions.

All of Galopin's *tourelles à éclipse* consisted of a circular gun chamber with armoured steel roofs and walls, along with the cannons mounted internally. Below the gun chamber and connected to it was a weighted cantilever (two cantilevers in the case of the *tourelle de 155mm* due to the extra weight) allowing the *tourelle à éclipse* to be elevated clear of the roof for firing and retract back into the roof slab for protection when the turret was subjected to an enemy bombardment. Again there was an *avant-cuirasse* ring located in the concrete of the roof opening for extra protection of the internals. The *tourelle à éclipse* was elevated by changing the balance of the cantilevers using two hand-operated cranks and once elevated the *tourelle à eclipse* could be locked in position. There was also a spring mechanism that was activated in the event of the *tourelle à eclipse* receiving a direct hit. The *tourelle à eclipse* would drop into its shaft thereby dissipate some of the force from the exploding shell and then bounce back up again into its firing position. It was said that a turret could be lifted up into position in about one minute.

Part of the turret immediately under the working chamber, within the fort's roof slab, was a working chamber for the preparation of the shells and propellants – the shells being lifted into the gun chamber again by a hand operated winch.

The weighted cantilever was located below the working chamber. The whole of the gun chamber was mounted on an azimuth or turret ring – a horizontal ring with gear teeth cut into the upper surface – forming the base of the lifting turret, and connected directly to the cantilever below. The gun chamber part of the turret had mating bevel gears that meshed into the azimuth. The mechanism operated via a transmission box by a hand-wheel located within the working chamber, allowing 360° rotation of the turret for all-round fire. The gun mountings on the cannons had a rack and pinion device for elevating the guns, which were hand operated by a simple crank handle located within the gun chamber. There was a ventilation system to clear the propellant smoke and gases from within the gun chamber using a hand pump, which was used after the firing of the guns.

The *tourelle de 75mm (T75)* had armour thicknesses of 350 millimetres for the domed roof, 250 millimetres for the sidewalls and 350 millimetres for the front plate. The *tourelle de 155mm (T155R)* had armour thicknesses of 450 millimetres, 400 millimetres and 450 millimetres respectively.

The first group of *ouvrages modernisée* and *forts* were modernised by adding either a *tourelles à éclipse* or a *casemates de Bourges* or sometimes a combination of both. The later built fortifications had this type of armament incorporated into their designs. A fine example of this reconstruction was the *ouvrage de Froideterre*, which was one of the larger *ouvrages modernisée* bigger than quite a number of the forts. It was armed with a combination of both *tourelles à éclipse* and *casemates de Bourges.*

All the equipment within the turret and the *casemate de Bourges*, with the exception of the *tourelle de 155mm (T155L) Bussière*, in the Verdun fortifications were manually operated. The weight of the lifting part of a *tourelle de 155mm (T155R) Galopin* was 70 tonne, which had to be moved by nothing more than the muscle power of the men below, coupled with gears and levers. The *fort de Douaumont* has examples of most of the preceding modifications.

The turrets were constructed from a variety of components, different components being fabricated by the four main constructers – *Châtillon-Commentry*, *Fives-Lille*, *Saint Chamond* and *Schneider* of Creusot, the last named taking on the bulk of the work.

The constructers utilised the *voie ferré de 0.6m - la système Péchot* for the transportation of these later turret components, especially the larger armour plates.

Once barbed wire had become commonplace at the turn of the twentieth century, the fortifications, especially those that were designed to be used as defensive positions, had a wide barbed wire field added to form an obstacle for all round protection to the defenders.

***

Ouvrages Moderne

In 1906 the last of the *ouvrages* was built. Named the *ouvrage de La Falouse*, it was built as an *ouvrages moderne* on *cote* 237 and was designed to cover the gap across the River Meuse to the south of Verdun between the *fort de Haudainville* and the *Redoute de Duguy*. Although the site chosen was originally the site of a proposed *ouvrage* and was quite close to the *ouvrage de Bois-Rogé*, which was then abandoned in 1910, the site had not been used by the military for any fortifications before, making the *ouvrage de La Falouse* a completely new development.

The design of it incorporated most of the then modern concepts so that it appeared to be similar to the *ouvrages modernisée* or a small modern fort. As such it was the ultimate *ouvrage* to be built.

The *ouvrage de La Falouse* was armed with a *tourelle de 75mm (T75R) Galopin* and a *tourelle de mitrailleuses (GF4)*. It did not have any *casemates de Bourges*, since it was assumed that the two turrets were adequate to cover the river as well as the ground on the non-riverside of the *ouvrage* thereby removing the need for a *casemate de Bourges*. Positioned on the left (west) bank in a bend in the river, it was built on a north-south axis facing south. The main armament, the *tourelle de 75mm (T75R)*, was located on the south east corner (closest to the river) so that it would cover both the front and the east (the river) side and by doing so covering across a long length of the curving river. The smaller *tourelle de mitrailleuses (GF4)* was located on the south west corner and was designed to cover the dead ground behind the *Redoute de Duguy* and also to prevent enemy infantry from infiltrating around on the west side of the *ouvrage*.

The *ouvrage de La Falouse* had a *caserne* built out of *bétonné spécial* in the centre in front of a small courtyard. It was surrounded by a wide sloping *plongée* that dropped down into the *fossé* with a standard *contrescarpe* on the outer side. In plan it was an irregular hexagon. There was a barbed wire field within the *fossé*, which extended up the *plongée* to just below the original ground level, namely just below the top of the *contrescarpe* elevation and in theory within a blind spot to the enemy artillery.

For observation the *ouvrage* had four *Observatoires* – two being located behind each of the two turrets and the other two located on the two rear corners. A single covered corridor connected the caserne, with all the turrets and observatories.

Fort Moderne

The last *fort* to be built, in *le camp retranché de Verdun*, was a *fort moderne* (modern fort). It was named the *fort de Vacherauville*, and was completed in 1910. Built on the site of the *batterie de Charny* (which was demolished in 1908 to make way for it), it was the ultimate fort.

The plan of this fort clearly shows the later fort designers' logic, especially in the way that its armament was laid out.

From the experience gained from designing and upgrading the *ouvrages modernisée,* and later designing and building the *ouvrage moderne* (the *ouvrage de La Falouse*), the designers decided that the main armament for this fort would be located in turrets. As such the *fort de Vacherauville* did not require *baquettes d'artillerie* for the older type of artillery nor a *rue du rempart* to provide access.

Due to its location to the north of Verdun on the left bank (west) that overlooked the river valley, the *batterie de Charny* had to cover both the ground in front of it and to its side across the valley. Although the *ouvrage de Charny* was located down in the valley, it was felt by the military authorities that this gap was still exposed to possible enemy infiltrations due to the insufficient firepower of the *batterie*. They therefore decided to replace the *batterie* with a fort. The fort was built on an almost north-south alignment.

The *fort de Vacherauville* had an armament of two *tourelles de 155mm (T155R) Galopin*, a *tourelle de 75mm (T75R) Galopin* and a *tourelle de mitrailleuses (GF4)*. The first *tourelle T155R* was mounted on the front (north) part of the fort in the centre and was intended to cover the ground in the immediate front of the fort to the north. The second *tourelle T155R* was mounted east of the first (northeast corner) and was to cover the area across the valley to the east of the fort. The third smaller *tourelle T75R* was mounted to the west (northwest corner) covering the ground between the fort and the next fortification to the west the *poste de la Belle-Épine*. Finally the *tourelle GF4* was located to the rear of the fort in the southwest corner and was to cover the ground on top of the fort and the ground behind the fort in case of enemy infantry incursions. The use of *tourelles* instead of *casemates de Bourges* upon the flanks of the fort allowed all the available firepower to bear in any direction.

A four-side *fossé* was used to form the main defence of the fort. Based on the concept that the enemy artillery would be located to the north of the fort – namely in front – then the fort would only be subjected to shellfire from that direction. Therefore the *caserne* was located at the rear of the *fort* adjacent to the *fossé*, the rear wall of the *caserne* being the *escarpe*.

The *fossé* was protected by a *coffre double*, a *coffre simple* and a *caponnière de gorge*. This arrangement was for the maximum protection against enemy shelling. The *coffres* were located to the front of the fort and covered the front and the sides; the *caponnière* was located to the rear. As with the *fosse* defence, the location of the *caserne* at the rear was again for maximum protection against enemy shelling. All of the buildings within the fort were constructed using one and a half metre thick re-enforced *bétonné spécial* walls and roofs

With the three turrets at the front taking up greater space than the *caserne* at the rear, the front face of the *fort de Vacherauville* was longer than that of the rear, so that the plan of the fort was an irregular rhombus.

For maximum effect, the *coffres* had to be square onto the *fossés* that they covered. To this end, the front (north) *fossé* was set at 90° to the west *fossé*. This arrangement allowed for the *coffre double* to be set into the north-west corner of the two *fossé* giving maximum coverage along the lines of the two *fossés*. However the east *fossé* was in plan angled back from the front *fossé* to the shorter rear *fossé*. In doing so, although the east *fossé* was longer than its western counterpart, it provided less of a target for enemy artillery by reducing their angle of sight when operating on the right (east) bank of the river. Nevertheless this did cause the designers two problems. The first problem was that the *coffre simple* had to be angled so that it was squared on and in line with the angled east *fossé*. To do this, the *coffre simple* was not flush with the front *contrescarpe* but angled into it. It was set back into the front *contrescarpe* so that it was out of alignment of the firing line of the guns in the west *coffre double*. The other problem also concerned the machinegun fire from the west *coffre double*. With the east *contrescarpe* being set at an acute angle to the front northern *fossé* there was the possibility that bullets fired from the western *coffre double* could ricochet off into the *coffre simple*. To prevent this from happening, the part of the east *contrescarpe* adjacent to the *coffre simple* was squared off to the *coffre* creating an obtuse angle and thereby reducing the possibility of any bullets from ricocheting into the *coffre*. Both the *coffres* had a standard *fossés-diamant* in front of them.

All the normal array of rooms was to be found in the *caserne* such as the commander's office, dormitories for both officers and men, a kitchen and a toilet block. The rear wall being part of the rear *fossé's escarpe* had loopholes with armoured plate steel shutters to allow individual riflemen to cover the area within the rear *fossé*. The rear *escarpe* had a *fossés-diamant* in front of the *caserne* for added protection. However the main rear defence was provided by the *caponnières de gorge* offset to the west end. A drawbridge over the *fossés-diamant* allowed access through the entrance into the *caserne* and the rest of the fort. The main entrance was located in the middle of the *caserne* and lead onto the main covered corridor, which linked up all the major parts of the fort (the *caserne*, the turrets, the *coffres* etc.) in effect becoming the replacement for the *rue du rempart* of the older forts. At the end of this corridor a short covered cross-corridor was located that connected all the turrets and their observatories as well as two covered secondary corridors leading to the *coffres*. There were also several stairs located off the side of these corridors, leading up onto the roof. All entry points including the main entrance had heavy armour plate steel doors.

For drawings of the *fort de Vacherauville* see plan 3 and sketch 3.

***

Great effort was put into making the entire pre-war fortifications blend into their surroundings, in the days when camouflage uniforms for the French Army was viewed with disdain. Forts, especially, being located on the high points, had their silhouettes designed to blend into the contours of the hilltops. As mentioned previously, the earlier masonry fortifications had earth covering for added protection and grass laid upon them. Even the later concrete fortifications had a layer of soil and grass added. Existing woods close by however were cut down and cleared to provide clear fields of fire. Wooden palings were also placed in front of the railing fence for added concealment.

***

The actual cost of fortifying Verdun (with approximately 230 structures), excluding the wartime modifications, has been given as 55 million *Francs d'Or* for the buildings, plus 15 million *Francs d'Or* for the engineering services, and another 8 million *Francs d'Or* for the cannons and ammunition that where incorporated within the forts.

Modifying *la citadelle* cost another 1.9 million *Francs d'Or* and if the cost of the field guns and ammunitions of 49 million *Francs d'Or* are included, a total of about 130 million *Francs d'Or* is reached. Finally, it has been stated that by 1914, 660 million *Francs d'Or* had been spent to complete all the defences on all the eastern border of France.[21]

For the total cost of the principal fortifications of *le camp retranché de Verdun* see Appendix 9.

---

[21] Quoted in Hew Strachan's essay "From Cabinet War to Total War" - one of the essays in Roger Chickering and Stig Förster's "Great War, Total War" Cambridge University Press, 2000. It is stated that this figure of 660 million was for "166 forts, 43 secondary works, and 250 batteries in a defensive scheme for the eastern frontier" which I assume relates to the fortifications of the *Frontière de l'est (côte de Moselle)* - *le groupe Vosges* and the *Frontière du nord-est (hauts de Meuse)* - *le groupe de la Meuse.*

Wartime Additions and Developments
1914 - 1918

From the earliest days of the Great War, modifications were carried out on the 'forts', initially corridor blockades, especially near to the exit points out into the open[22]. These ad hoc blocks varied considerably, and were made from rough masonry block-work, brickwork or reinforced concrete. Some had built-in loopholes. They ranged from full blocks closing off corridors completely to double blocks, one after the other but staggered to allow movement through, but also creating defensible positions in the event of an incursion by enemy troops. The *ouvrage de Déramé* has examples of full and double blocks. There were also semi-blocks namely simple barricades with a loophole that only partially blocked the corridors forming again a defensible position against incursion.

All defensive construction work and additions upon the fortifications were stopped, when on 9th August 1915 the *Grand Quartier Général* (General Headquarters – *G.Q.G.*) decided to decommission all the permanent defences. With this new doctrine of concentrating on field defences, work began on disarming and decommissioning of the fortifications. Engineers' drawings for the demolition of the forts were drawn up and work digging demolition chambers was begun in a number of the forts.

However, once the Battle of Verdun has started, the doctrine was reversed and the fortifications were rearmed.

Casemates Pamards

Once the Battle of Verdun started on 21 February 1916, it was found that there were still blind spots around the forts. These were thought originally to have been covered, but in the light of battle that ensued proved to be highly dangerous to the French defenders. These blind spots were

---

[22] I have not included within this study *Colonel* Emile Driant's *Poste de commandement* 'R2', since it lies well to the north of the original fortified zone area, and was not part of the original planning nor addition to the fortified zone.

Incidentally, Driant's bunker was probably not the small concrete building that is so marked today – if one compares the damage by shellfire to the ground surrounding the bunker and then review the lack of damage to the bunker itself, one quickly comes to the conclusion that this is not the original one. One just has to look at the destruction to the *abris de combat* close to the *Fort de Douaumont* to see what effect artillery fire could have on bunkers. Indeed the original one (as a command post) was a prime target for the German artillery and the location of which was well know to the German army as shown on their pre-battle military maps of the area.

covered, albeit from the end of the battle in late 1916 until the end of the war in 1918, with small armoured machine gun nests known as *casemates Pamards*.

The *casemates Pamards* was designed by *Capitaine* Léon Pamards in March 1916 and consisted of a small armoured steel dome set into a *bétonné spécial* base. Normally only the dome was above ground level. The cast steel dome had a thickness of fifteen centimetres on the roof and sides, increasing to eighteen centimetres at the front. It normally had a crew of three consisting of a *mitrailleur* (machine gunner) standing behind the gun, a *chargeur* (loader) sitting in front of the machine gunner, beneath the gun and an *observateur* (observer) standing at the rear. With one - *casemates Pamards simple* - or two machine gun ports - *casemates Pamards double* – they had fixed lines of fire. Each *casemate Pamards* (both *simple* and *double*) had a pair of *Mitrailleuse Modèle 1907 transformée* (converted machine guns model 1907 – abbreviated to *Mitrailleuse Modèle 07(T)* but commonly known as the *Mitrailleuse Saint Étienne* after the Saint Étienne works, and was a different gun to the type used in the *tourelle de mitrailleuses (GF4)*, which was the *8mm mitrailleuses Hotchkiss modèle1899*.) The guns were mounted on a horizontal, sliding spindle with one gun being mounted 180° out of alignment with the other (one above the other – the lower one being upside-down), so that only one of the guns, the upper and one in use, was in alignment with the port at any one time. In the case of a *casemates Pamards double*, the spindle was pivoted at the front end in between the two gun ports to allow the guns to be swung from one port to the other, thereby giving a wider field of fire. Entry to the *casemates Pamards*, like the *coffres*, was by a *passages sous le fosse* that led from the inside of the *fort* and then, like a *cloche Digoin* up a ladder up through a trap door in the wooden floor. There was no entrance from the outside into the *casemates Pamards*. For a drawing of a *casemate Pamards* see section 2.

The *Mitrailleuse Modèle 07(T)* was a 24 round strip-feed weapon firing at about 450 rounds per minute. Consequently it only took just over 3 seconds to expend all the rounds from the strip if fired in one burst! The gun was notorious for blockages, and I assume that *Capitaine Pamards* devised a system whereby if the gun in use jammed, the second gun could be swung up quickly to replace it, thereby allowing an almost uninterrupted fire whilst the blocked gun (now in the lower position) was freed from blockages by the loader. The mechanism to rotate the guns worked by the gunner unlocking the spindle pulled the gun assembly back along the spindle, so that the upper gun's muzzle was clear of the gun port and then rotated the whole assembly through 180°. This action brought the second unblocked gun in line with the gun port. The assembly was then pushed back into its original position and locked, with the result that the rate of fire could be kept up with very little interference due to blockages – that was the theory, anyway! There was a periscope mounted in the rear of the roof so that the observer could survey the effectiveness of the machine gunner. Being easy and cheap to build, the *casemates Pamards* were installed in numerous places. The *fort de Souville* for instance, had three added around it (one is in front by the road, the second is around the back by the *tourelle de 155mm (T155L) Bussière*, and the third is located in the woods between the first *casemate Pamards* and the *route militaire*, all providing fine examples.) One of the *casemates Pamards* located around the *fort de Tavannes* has an unusual variation – it has a rear compartment with a rearward-facing loophole (back towards the fort) to accommodate a grenadier armed with *Vivan-Bessières* rifle grenades.

Blockhaus Bétonné

A unique wartime structure was the *Blockhaus bétonné* (concrete blockhouse) located externally just to the rear of the *fort de Tavannes*. Constructed out of 1.5 metre thick reinforced *bétonné spécial*, in 1918, this large blockhouse (approximately ten metres in diameter by five metres high) is octagonal in plan and has loopholes for all-round fire – every second side has a machine gun port, the remaining sides have *Vivan-Bessières* rifle grenade loopholes. It does not have an earthen covering. Like the *casemates Pamards*, it was entered through a *galerie souterraines* leading from the inside of the *fort de Tavannes*, which it was built to protect.

The gun ports had steel inserts around the openings. The inserts were tapered inwards with the surface corrugated so as to deflect any inward coming bullets back outwards.

For major wartime additions to *le camp retranché de Verdun*, See Appendix 14.

***

Due to the high amount of shelling that the *forts de Douaumont* and *Vaux* received, quite extensive repair work was undertaken during and after the battle. The outer walls of the *caserne* that had been partially destroyed were rebuilt out of *bétonné spécial* with rifle slits added, with an ad hoc *caponnière de gorges* also added.

The forts were not the only structures to be modified during the 1916, Battle of Verdun; some of the *batterie* were modified to take different types of guns from the original design. Dating from about mid 1916, the *batterie 7.3* of the *3e secteur* (next to the *fort de Bois-Bourrus*, which overlooks the hill *La Mort Homme*) had two of its *baquette d'artillerie* modified so that each could accommodate a large platform mounted howitzer.

For the summary of defences of *Le camp retranché de Verdun* see Appendix 15.

***

In the aftermath of the battle, the French quickly learnt the lessons. The capture of the *fort de Vaux* by the Germans could have possibly been avoided. The Germans had captured the roof and surrounding area of the fort on June 3rd, thereby totally cutting off the fort's French garrison from the rest of the French army. However, it still took the Germans another four days of very hard and costly fighting before the fort actually fell on June 7th. The French therefore reasoned that if supplies and replacements could have been maintained to the fort, as well as the wounded and non-combatants evacuated, the fort could have held out against the German assault for a much longer period if not indefinitely. In conclusion it was decided to dig *sorties lointaine* (remote exits - commonly known in English as 'communication tunnels') to all the forts. Starting in late 1916 and continuing well into the post war years most forts had *sorties lointaine* dug. The *fort de Moulainville* has a fine example, which is one and a half kilometres long. Other *passages sous* (underground passageways or tunnels) were also dug within the *forts* linking areas together, allowing defenders to re-deploy quickly and safely in the case of an enemy break in.

A second problem relating to supplies was that in the *fort de Vaux* the water supply failed fairly early on when the cistern was found to be leaking. This problem was resolved by boring *puits d'eau* (water wells) making the forts self sufficient in water.

Finally, electrical generators were installed by the Germans to provide electrical lighting in the forts that they captured – the *fort de Douaumont* and the *fort de Vaux*.

Because of the damage to the superstructure of the *fort de Douaumont* during the course of the battle, most of the *observatoires cuirassé fixe* were rendered inoperable. Consequently after the French recaptured it, they were forced into building a small concrete lookout post on top to replace the original *observatoires*. The Germans quickly spotted the post and destroyed it with artillery fire. The French rebuilt it numerous times only for the Germans to destroy it on each occasion! The present one was the last to be built before the war ended.

Also referring to the *fort de Douaumont*, it was found that parts of the *passages sous le fossé* were damaged beyond repair and so new ones were dug to replace the older un-useable routes.

The *fort de Douaumont* was not the only fort that received damage to its *passages sous le fossé*. In the case of the *fort de Vaux*, the Germans fought their way into the fort via the *passages sous le fossé* using grenades and other explosive devices, in so doing, severely damaging the tunnel's original masonry walls and ceilings. This damage made the tunnels very unstable and therefore unsafe to use, so the Germans lined the walls and ceilings with concrete, thereby reinforcing them. This resulted in the considerable reduction of the width and height of the tunnels.

Towards the end of the Battle of Verdun, once the *fort de Douaumont* had been recaptured on October 24th, the communication to it was found to be subjected to heavy German shellfire. So in 1917 the French built a *boyau* (communication trench) out of pre-assembled concrete components. The trench was dug in the normal way, but pre-fabricated slotted concrete posts were then placed against the trench walls - the posts being dug in at their bases. Then concrete slats were slid down the slots in the posts to form a secure trench wall.

This trench was built to give protection to the troops moving to and from the fort, and was given the name the *'boyau de Londres'* (the London Trench.) I have not found the origins of this name, however all field defences built during the war were given names to aide navigation within the trench network where one trench or defensive position looked much the same as the next. They were named by the troops who constructed the defences and varied to the whims of the constructors. In this case the *'boyau de Londres'* may have been an "in joke" by the troops going up to the fort at night, which being under constant enemy artillery bombardment, was reminiscent to them of the bright lights of London.

After the war, due to expenditure cuts, there was little work done to the *forts* apart from the work mentioned above concerning *sortie lointaine, passages sous le fossés* and the *puits d'eau*.

Conclusion

Based upon the *Grand Quartier Général* pre-war *Plans Nr. XVI* and *Nr. XVII*, the French general staff had begun to regard the Séré de Rivières fortifications as obsolete. Although work on the fortifications continued up to the start of the war, they ceased to be included in the immediate pre-war planning.

On 15 August 1914 the Belgian *fort de Lonçin*, part of *Le camp retranché de Liège* was hit by a single 42cm shell, which triggered the main magazine to explode, which in turn forced the garrison's survivors to surrender. This had a knock on effect when it led to the surrender of the rest of the *forts* within the *camp retranché*. It should be noted that although the Belgian forts, which were designed by Brialmont in the 1860's and were modern forts constructed out of concrete with armoured turrets, thereby being much more advanced in their design then the French forts of the day - they were however constructed out of the types of material then available namely standard concrete and rolled or cast iron. The failure at the start of the war of the Belgium forts to withstand artillery bombardments, as well as some of their own older forts (for example, the *fort de Manonvillers* of the *Forts d'arrêt - en avant de Toul*), reinforced the *Grand Quartier Général's* view of their own fortifications in that they believed that the forts would no longer play any useful role in modern warfare. As such the fortifications were then declared to be unsafe, being seen as 'shell traps' for the defenders. The French troops were subsequently instructed to avoid sheltering inside the forts, The General Staff stated that it was safer for the troops to be out in the open rather than inside one of the forts, which would attract enemy shellfire.

However, the French fortifications that had been constructed or modernised after 1900 were constructed out of *bétonné spécial* (often reinforced with steel rods) and steel armour plate, making them far stronger than their Belgian counterparts. Even though a small number of their forts became the focus of operations (namely the battles for the *fort de Pompelle* part of *Le camp retranché de Reims* and the *fort de Condé-sur-Aisne* of the *Forts d'arrêt – Soissons* are both examples) in 1914-1915 provided a clear indication of their usefulness as *centres de résistance* as well as giving safe refuge to the local French troops. The *Grand Quartier Général* still refused to see the fortifications' usefulness and therefore they decreed on the 9 August 1915 that the forts were to be demobilised.

The shortage of heavy artillery within the French field army during the early part of the war gave rise to the redeployment of the cannons assigned to the fortifications. This led to the disarming of the forts and the emptying of the *camp retranché's parcs d'artilleries* of all artillery cannons to be used out in the fields of battle, mainly the *Canon de 'Lahitolle' 95 mm*, the

Canon de 'De Bange' 120 mm, the *Canons de 'De Bange' 155 mm* and the *Canons 75mm TR* that were installed in the *tourelles de 75mm (T75R) Galopin* and the *casemates de Bourges*, along with all the *8mm mitrailleuses Hotchkiss* from the *tourelles de mitrailleuses (GF4)*.

Once the main armament had been removed from the *fort de Vaux,* the French army engineers started to bore holes into its foundations to create detonation chambers for the demolition of the fort. Explosives where then brought up to the fort for the purpose of the demolition and were temporarily stored under the *tourelle de 75mm (T75)* working chamber until the chambers were ready. In the early autumn of 1915, a direct hit by a German heavy shell on the roof of the turret triggered the demolition explosives, with the result that the whole of the turret was destroyed, the roof of the turret being blown into the *fossé*.

As part of the general downgrading of the fortifications in November of that year, the General Staff reassigned the regular troops who were garrisoning the forts and replaced them with territorial troops.

It was not until the fighting in 1916 for the forts, during the Battle of Verdun, that the General Staff realised their mistake; their fortifications, especially those that had been modernised, still had a major role to play in modern warfare.

Although the exteriors received considerable damage, the interiors remained intact and provided protection to the defenders. The explosions and fires in the aftermath that caused so much loss of life inside the *fort de Douaumont* (on the 8 May 1916) and the *tunnel fortifié de Tavannes* (on the 4 September 1916) were both caused by accidents by the defenders and not by enemy action. In both cases, the damage to the structures was superficial. There was then a reversal of the previous doctrine by the *Grand Quartier Général* and the forts were quickly re-manned and, where possible, rearmed.

The modern and modernised fortifications with their *bétonné spécial* coverings withstood shelling very well indeed and were only seriously damaged by direct hits by the heaviest calibres of shells. Even so, there were a few examples of modern fortifications that were totally destroyed by direct hits by heavy shells; the *Ouvrage de Thiaumont* and the *abri de combat 'VLL1'* were two that were destroyed. The older and un-modernised masonry under shellfire tended to have their superstructures destroyed, but their underground interiors remained largely intact and fully operational.

The earlier *caponnières* being constructed out of masonry and located on the *escarpe* were prone to be hit and were generally destroyed. However the newer, more modern *coffres* being constructed out of *Bétonné spécial* and located on the *contrescarpe* - therefore under the cover of the fortification's *glacis* - tended not to be hit, with the result that they tended to survive.

Contrescarpes and *escarpes* being normally constructed out of masonry were likewise vulnerable to shellfire damage and in some cases were destroyed. The damage to the fortifications reflected the direction from which the shells were coming. Fortifications that were not captured by the Germans and therefore continually shelled by them from one side, caused the walls that faced in the direction of the shelling to be hit and damaged, whereas the walls facing away from the source of the shelling where the shells passed over the top of them, were frequently not damaged. A fine example of this is the *fort de Pompelle* of *Le camp retranché de Reims* which was built on the east side of Reims was orientated on an easterly axis. When the war stagnated, the two armies dug in, the front lines being just to the north of the fort (roughly were the modern duel carriageway road - the N.44 - is today). The result was that the northern facing walls of the fort – the *escarpe* on the north *fossé* and the *contrescarpe* on the southern *fossé* - were both totally destroyed by the German shelling. Whereas the south facing walls - the *contrescarpe* on the northern *fossé* and the *escarpe* on the southern *fossé* – were always in the shadow of the shelling and so not hit, and remained practically undamaged.

The fortifications within the fighting zone were captured often became subjected to shelling from both sides - German and French. As a result of the shelling coming in from both sides all of the *fossé* walls were destroyed. The shelling was normally from the direction of the side that were not in occupation of the fortification, so that first one set of walls were destroyed and then after the capture, the other set. However there were occasions when both sides shelled the same fortification at the same time. An example of where all the walls and caponnières were destroyed is the *fort de Souville*. At one point on 12 July 1916, the attacking Germans managed to force their way onto the top of the *fort*, but not inside it. It is said that the French artillery shelled their own fort even though it was known that there were Frenchmen still inside it to force the Germans off of the roof and at the same time the German artillery thinking that the mud covered men on the fort's roof were French troops mustering for a counterattack, also opened fire! The ten German soldiers who survived both the hostile and the friendly fire, surrendered to the French garrison who had survived quite safely within the interior of the fort.

The lightly constructed *Ouvrages infanterie*, the *Ouvrages en terre de infanterie* and the *Retranchements d'infanterie* in the fighting zone did not stand up to the artillery bombardment well and were quite often totally destroyed. However the *Abris caverns*, the *Abris de combat*, the *Dépôts intermédiaire* and the *Magasins de secteur* within the war zone tended to survive the attentions of the artillery. The *Batteries* being mainly earthen works but set back also tended to survive relatively well.

To sum up: the most modern and modernised *bétonné spécial* constructed fortifications generally withstood the actions of the German artillery extremely well and even the older un-modernised masonry fortifications gave refuge and safety to the soldiers who were under heavy shellfire. They provided *centres de résistance* in the overall defence of the areas being fought over. Although in a few cases men were killed within the fortifications when hit by the heaviest of shells, the fortifications saved a much greater number of the defenders' lives than they cost.

Finally it has been estimated that it cost the Germans 64 officers and 2,678 men to capture the *fort de Vaux* during the period of 3-7 June 1916 for a cost to the French of less than 100 casualties, of which about 20 defenders were killed. The lessons of Verdun were clear for all to see - that well constructed fortifications, defended by resolute defenders could and did stop a much greater number of attackers at minimum cost to themselves - but by the time those lessons were put into place, technology had made the lessons out of date[23].

With the political developments in Germany in late 1929, the decision was taken by *la Ministre de Guerre*, André Maginot (a veteran who had fought in the 1914 battles around Verdun[24]) to construct a new defensive line of fortifications along the frontier. This new defensive line was approved in early 1930 and it was then named after him, '*la Ligne Maginot*' (the Maginot line.) All the lessons from the Séré de Rivières' fortifications were learnt and incorporated into the new defences. As with the original Séré de Rivières concept fifty years before, some of the existing border fortifications of the Séré de Rivières period were incorporated into '*la Ligne Maginot*', some of which were reconstructed to bring them up to date with the new 1930's concepts.

Although not part of *le camp retranché de Verdun*, the defences around the town of Maubeuge on the Franco-Belgian border, the *camp retranché de Maubeuge* of the *groupe Nord*, had a number of the forts and fortlets incorporated into '*la Ligne Maginot*'. The *fort de Boussois*, the *fort de Sarts*, the *ouvrage de Bresilles* and the *ouvrage de la Salmagne* were all

---

[23] Figures as quoted in Horne's The Price of Glory ibid.

[24] André Maginot (1877-1932), a pre-war lawyer and parliamentarian was the elected *député de Bar-le-Duc* (Representative for Bar-le-Duc in Lorraine – 56km south-west of Verdun). In August 1914, as a 37 year old, Maginot volunteered for army service as a private and joined the *44ᵉ régiment d'infanterie territoriale* in Verdun. Promoted to sergeant in September 1914, he was then wounded just below his left knee on the night of 9 November 1914. The resulting wound lead to his leg being amputated and him being invalided out of the army. He returned to the French Parliament after a year of convalescing and after the war served in several ministerial roles; first as *la ministre des colonies* and then from 1929 as *la Ministre de Guerre*. On 14 January 1930 Maginot pushed through the law that saw the construction of the new fortification program on the Franco-German border that bore his name.

totally reconstructed to the standard of the other Maginot fortifications; however the *Fort de Leveau* was left un-modernised.

On 22 May 1940, during the Battle of France, the Germans using Junkers JU 87 Skukas dive-bombers bombed the *fort de Sarts*, destroying much of the defensive structures. Today nothing much remains of the fort apart from the shattered wreck of the concrete blockhouse within the centre.

***

Today, almost all of the major fortifications remain in some form or another. Only a few of the fortifications have been demolished: for example *la batterie de Damloup*, which was severely damaged during the battle, has been demolished – the site is now just a piece of flat scrub.

The condition of the fortifications that have survived varies considerably, mainly as a result of their locations - those in the *1er secteur* understandably showing the scars of battle to a much greater degree than those in the other two *secteurs*, with the fortifications in the rear (south west) showing little or no damage. Nevertheless, most of the *retranchment* that were in the battle zone were totally destroyed. The *batteries* that were sited on farmland have mostly been demolished and returned to farmland.

Also the type of construction has a bearing on the present day condition of the fortifications, the earlier masonry structures being more prone to ageing and damage by natural causes.

As a general guide to the damage inflicted on the forts, between the capture of the *fort de Douaumont* on 26th February 1916 by the Germans and it's recapture by the French on 24th October of the same year (almost eight months later), it has been estimated that the French hit the fort with about 120,000 shells, of which 3,300 were of 155 millimetre up to 305 millimetre calibre and 400 of 370 millimetre or 420 millimetre calibre. As can be imagined the superstructure of this fort is totally pock marked, however the internals are still in remarkably good condition, although the basement is subject to flooding. It has also been stated that during the 2nd June 1916 German attack on the *fort de Vaux*, the German artillery fired approximately two thousand shells per hour at the fort, of which about three quarters of them found their target. Again, like the *fort de Douaumont,* the internal structure of the *fort de Vaux* is still in fine shape. To give an appreciation of how much damage was actually done to the ground and especially the soil during the Battle of Verdun, the hill on the left (west) bank of the River Meuse known as Cote 304, the name deriding from the 1914 map reference of its summit's elevation above mean sea level (304 metre above m.s.l.) - is now 295 metre above m.s.l.! The French and the German artillery between them blowing off about nine metres of ground from the summit – all the topsoil down to the bedrock was shot away.

To repair the damage done to the topsoil over the whole battlefield area by the shelling during the battle, the French Government in the early 1920's planted forests of deciduous trees to naturally regenerate the soil. Since the 1990's these trees are being replaced, with the result that a number of the smaller fortifications are now being "rediscovered".

The *fort de Douaumont* and the *fort de Vaux* are now national memorials. A number of the fortifications within close proximity to the *fort de Douaumont* and the *fort de Vaux* have had their grounds cleared of the adjacent woodlands allowing easy access for visitors. The clearance work now being carried out is by the *Association Nationale du Souvenir de la Bataille de Verdun* (A.N.S.B.V.). They include the *ouvrage de Froideterre* and the *ouvrage de Thiaumont*.

With the passing of every year the A.N.S.B.V. clears more of the woodland away so that more battlefield sites are 'rediscovered'. Other 'forts' are now in private hands, one is a stud farm (the *ouvrage de Charny*), and two (I believe) are mushroom farms (the *ouvrage de Saint-Symphorien* and the *fort d'Haudainville*) and finally the *redoute de Belrupt* is now used as a 'paint-ball' ground! The rest of the 'forts' still belong to the French Army, with a small number still in use by them as assault courses (for example, the group of 'forts' within the 3e *secteur* - the *ouvrage de Fromeréville* - the *poste des Sartelles* - the *poste de Chana* - the *poste de Choisel* - *redoute de La Chaume*.) Officially all those army 'forts' are off limits to the public, however access to the 'forts' not in common use by the army, are viewed by them with a blind eye with regards to visitors, although permission should still be sought from the authorities before entering one.

Most visitors to the battle area are generally more interested to see the fortifications that took the brunt of the battle in the 1er *secteur*, on the right (east) bank, and naturally therefore, those that received the most damage. A number, but not all, of the fortifications in the 1er *secteur* are signposted, however almost all are located on the *Institut Géographique Nationales* (*IGN*) maps of the area. The *fort de Douaumont* and the *fort de Vaux* are open to the public, with guided tours - the more dangerous areas within them, the *galleries souterraines* to the *coffres* and the *sortie lointaine*, are closed to the public. Of the newer fortifications in the 1er *secteur*, the *ouvrage de Thiaumont* (just behind the rear north west corner of the *Ossuary*) remains as a shattered heap of concrete with no way to enter, while the *ouvrage de Froideterre* (just down the road and well sign posted) and the *ouvrage de La Laufée* (just to the south of the *fort de Vaux* and not signposted at all!) survived the battle in relatively good condition, and at the time of writing (2005), the buildings were safe enough to enter and view.

The older fortifications that were within the firing line all fared quite badly over the years, with some becoming extremely dangerous – the *fort de Tavannes*, the *redoute de Belleville*, the *redoute de Saint-Michel* and the *redoute de Souville* of masonry construction with an earthen cover have become very fertile grounds for trees, and so have receded back into the woods. The tree roots have grown into the masonry thereby forcing the masonry apart and hence weakening the structures. This is causing the ceilings of the rooms to collapse. The underground *caserne* of the *redoute de Souville* was still passable until the winter of 1997 when the roof finally caved in.

Another problem within these forts is the holes in the floors. Steel manhole covers in the rooms and corridors have been removed (presumably for scrap), leaving very deep holes, some of which are over rooms or cisterns that have filled with water. As mentioned earlier, the design of the forts follows a logical pattern, however the *sortie lointaines* were dug to no set pattern and can be found in any location and of any size - the *sortie lointaine* in the *fort de Tavannes* is particularly dangerous, being in a small room with a window at the far end opposite the long pitch black corridor from which you enter; temporarily blinded by the sun light streaming through the window, you find yourself in front of a hole the size of three quarters of the room's floor and with about a 50m straight drop! The *fort de Bois-Bourrus*, of the 3^e secteur, has a *sortie lointaine* with two entrances: the first is to the right-hand side of the fort; the second is to the left-hand side of the fort, and is located just after a bend in the corridor.

The forts that are officially open to the public have a few areas closed off as a safety measure - the basement of the *ouvrage de Froideterre* has been sealed off by steel shutters over the ladder shaft entrances. Of the forts that are not officially open to the public, some have now been totally sealed – the *fort de Vacherauville* has had a steel door welded across its entrance, again for safety. The *redoute de Souville* has had a barred gate placed across the main entrance to its underground *magasin* because of a European Union directive to protect the bats that have made their home within!

One of the largest of the fortified sites within the Verdun area is the *tunnel fortifié de Tavannes*. The tunnel was taken out of service in 1936 when a replacement tunnel was completed a few metres to the north side of the original. This was due to the movement inwards of the walls in the original tunnel, which had been weakened by the explosion and the following fires in 1916. The original tunnel today has concrete buttresses and tie beams cast in at the spots where the walls are at their weakest. The track has been lifted, but the *Corps de garde* on the south side of the eastern portal is still in place, the northern one being demolished at the time of the construction of the replacement tunnel. Access to the tunnel can still be gained from either portal, but care should be taken since the railway line is still in use. Once inside one can walk quite safely through to the other end and observe the glazed brick lining melted by the heat of the fire.

On all battlefields there is still a degree of danger, mainly from unexploded munitions, however the forts, as noted before, are somewhat more dangerous. If anyone is keen to tour the forts, it is best to be taken around initially by an experienced guide, to learn where the pitfalls are. Even on the smaller *abris*, there are dangers to be wary of. A powerful torch or flashlight is a must; use it to keep an eye on both the ceiling, for potential cave-ins, and the floors for uncovered holes. Be very wary of water on the floor, since in the pitch darkness under floodlight, the water will cause you to see the reflection of the light and not the potential flooded hole under the surface. Always enter a fortification in numbers, if you are on your own and fall down a hole, you might never be found!

The area to the north and north east of Verdun is the site of a horrendous battle that officially cost the lives of 262,308 [25] men and as such the ground should be regarded as a memorial. The tragic losses in the *fort de Douaumont* by the Germans and in the *tunnel de Tavannes* by the French are well known, however there were other examples just as tragic: the *abri de combat 'VLL1'* between the *fort de Vaux* and the *ouvrage de La Laufée*, for instance, received a direct hit from a German heavy shell just after a company of French infantry had entered looking for shelter. Their remains (about 120 men) are still there within the collapsed structure of this concrete shelter. For notes on the names and designations, see Appendix 4B.

One final point to bear in mind when viewing the forts today is that the French are not adverse to the use of some 'artistic licence' with regards to their history and their historical monuments. As already mentioned above, concerning Driant's bunker; it appears to be a 'later addition' to the battlefield. Recently, the local French authorities (presumably within the A.N.S.B.V.) have taken the decision to 'renovate' the *fort de Douaumont* by adding a reconstruction of the ad hoc structure to the front of the *fort*. This structure is based on the 1917 reconstruction, but unfortunately does not shows the scars of battle or the work that was done to the *fort* later on! Therefore when viewing the forts today, be aware that all might not be as it seems!

---

[25] The official figures for the Battle of Verdun of 162,308 French and approximately 100,000 German dead are probably an underestimate, I feel that a more likely figure to be in the region totalling 500,000 dead.

1. The *redoute de Regret* (*Le camp retranché de Verdun*) looking south obliquely, taken from an USA Airforce Reconnaissance Aircraft, summer 1918. The *fort de Regret* as it was reclassified was up-graded and modernised. From this photograph the overall shape of the fort as outlined by the *fossé* can be clearly seen, and with the *caserne* (barracks for the 132 officers and men) located in the middle, its size can be gauged. Of note is the ground contours making up the *glacis* in front of the *fossé* and the *talus extérieur*, the *plongée* and the *baquette d'artillerie* behind. Cut into the nearest *baquette d'artillerie* is a *casemate Bourges* and located on top of the *baquette d'artillerie* above the corners of the fort are a number of *tourelles*. On the corner of the *fossé* to the right of the *casemate Bourges* a new masonry corner can be seen built into the *escarpe* (showing up lighter than the neighbouring masonry) where the original *caponnière simple* has been demolished and replaced by a *coffres simple* which is located out of sight on the *contrescarpe* opposite. At the next corner of the *fossé* to the right of the photograph can be seen a *coffres double* cut into the *contrescarpe*. Finally on the concave corner of the *fossé* to the left of the photograph a *caponnière de gorge* can be seen protruding out from the rear *escarpe* protecting the rear *fossé* and the *entrée* which is seen just to the far side of the *caponnière de gorge*.

2. The *fort de Douaumont* (*Le camp retranché de Verdun*) looking east obliquely. No date, but probably taken pre war. Like the *fort de Regret* the *fort de Douaumont* was modernised before the war Again from this photograph the overall shape of the fort as outlined by the *fossé* can be clearly seen, and with the *caserne* (barracks for the 648 officiers and men) located in the middle, its size can be gauged. The *batterie 3.6* can be clearly seen to the south of the fort (on the right hand side) as can a number of *bâtiments extérieur* namely building for the officers' quarters, the pump house for water supplies and engineers storerooms. (No copyright)

3. The *fort de bois borrus* taken on 14 May 1916. (Bibliotheque Municipale de Verdun MS819-39)

4. The *fort de Marre* taken on 9 April 1916. (Bibliotheque Municipale de Verdun MS819-40)

5. The *Entrée* to the *batterie des Ayville*, no date circa 1914, (Bayerisches Hauptstaatsarchiv - Abt. IV Kriegsarchiv BS-IIf59)

6. The *caserne* and *cour* to the *fort des Ayville*, no date circa 1914, (Bayerisches Hauptstaatsarchiv - Abt. IV Kriegsarchiv BS-II1f60)

7. Photograph taken within a *fossé*, (fort unknown - *Le camp retranché de Verdun*) showing the *escarpe* on the left, the *contrescarpe* on the right and a *caponnières* built onto the corner of the *escarpe*, no date, pre-war

8. View of the *fossé* of the *fort de Bondues* (*Le camp retranché de Lille*) showing the *escarpe* on the left, the *contrescarpe* on the right and a *coffres simple* located at the corner in the *contrescarpe*. Above the *contrescarpe* can be clearly seen the *glacis* and above the *escarpe* the *talus extérieur* and the *plongée*. The *grille* has been removed but would have been located above the *contrescarpe*, no date (IWM Q37114)

9. A *canon de 'Lahitolle' 95 mm modèle 1888* shown in position upon an unknown fort's *baquette d'artillerie,* also showing some details of the *caserne* (Note: The small structure to the left within the *cour* was a mobile *latrine* with four cubicles and a void underneath for the buckets), (*Le camp retranché de Verdun*), no date pre-war

10. A *canon de 'De Bange' 120mm longue modèle 1878* shown in position upon an unknown fort's *baquette d'artillerie* (probably the same fort as photograph 5), no date pre-war

11. A *batteries*/gun enplacement believed to have been Toul Hill, no date, post-war (American Official Photograph via IWM Am O 23355)

12. The *Réduit central – la Citadelle* (*Le camp retranché de Verdun*), looking north taken with the city of Verdun in the background. An *Entrée* can be seen just to the left of the bastion at the foot of the wall leading to the corner. Note wartime damage to a number of the buildings from German long-range artillery. Photograph taken from an USA Airforce Reconnaissance Aircraft, summer 1918

13. The *Réduit central – la Citadelle* (*Le camp retranché de Verdun*) photograph taken on the eastern wall from street level with *bâtiments extérieur* in the foreground, pre war photograph, no date, pre-war

14. The *entrée* to *Ecoute Nº 1* of the *Réduit central – la Citadelle*, (*Le camp retranché de Verdun*) wartime photograph – c1916

15. The *fort de Tavannes* (top left) the *abri du Projecteur* (centre right) and the *Batterie 6.8 - Batterie du Mardi-Gras* (bottom right) on 28 April 1916. (Bibliotheque Municipale de Verdun MS812-191)

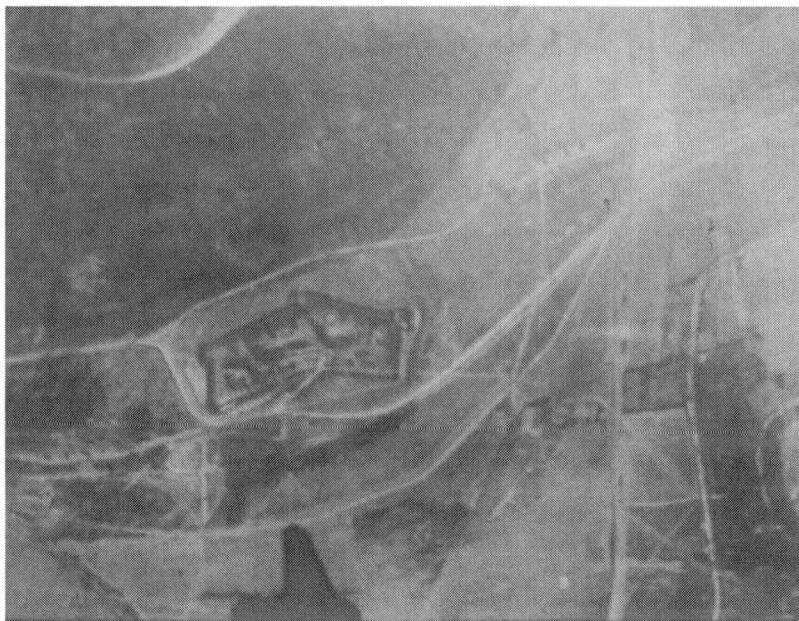

16. The *fort de Michel* taken on 30 March 1916 with the *Batterie 7.9* (top right) and the *Batterie 7.7* (bottom left). (Bibliotheque Municipale de Verdun MS812-222)

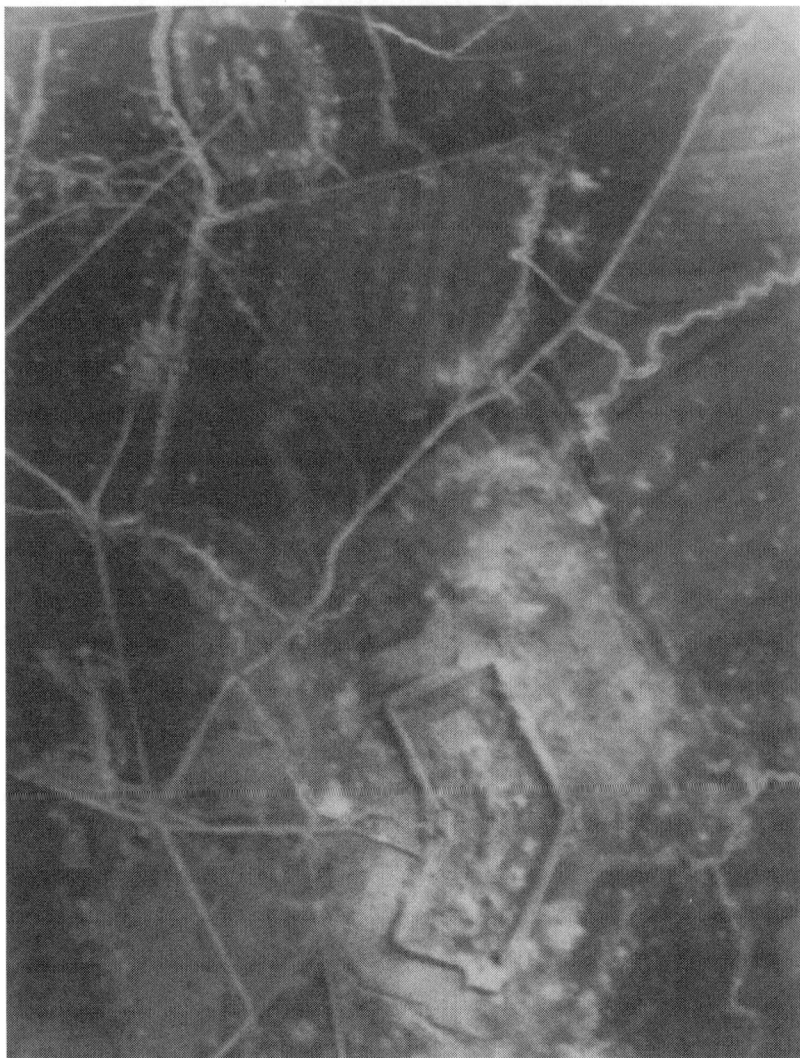

17. The *fort de Moulainville* (bottom centre) and the *ouvrage d'Eix* (top left) on 9 April 1916. The batterie 1.2 can be seen (centre left) and the *abri de combat* LLM2 (centre) (Bibliotheque Municipale de Verdun MS812-180)

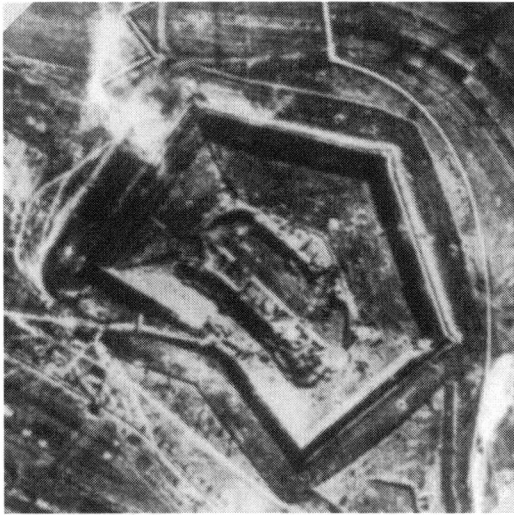

18. The *fort de Douaumont* taken before the Battle of Verdun c1915. (Bayerisches Hauptstaats-archiv - Abt. IV Kriegsarchiv BS-II1g644)

19. The *fort de Douaumont* taken on 7 May 1916. Most of the shell damage seen here was inflicted by French artillery after the Germans captured the fort. (Bibliotheque Municipale de Verdun MS812-116)

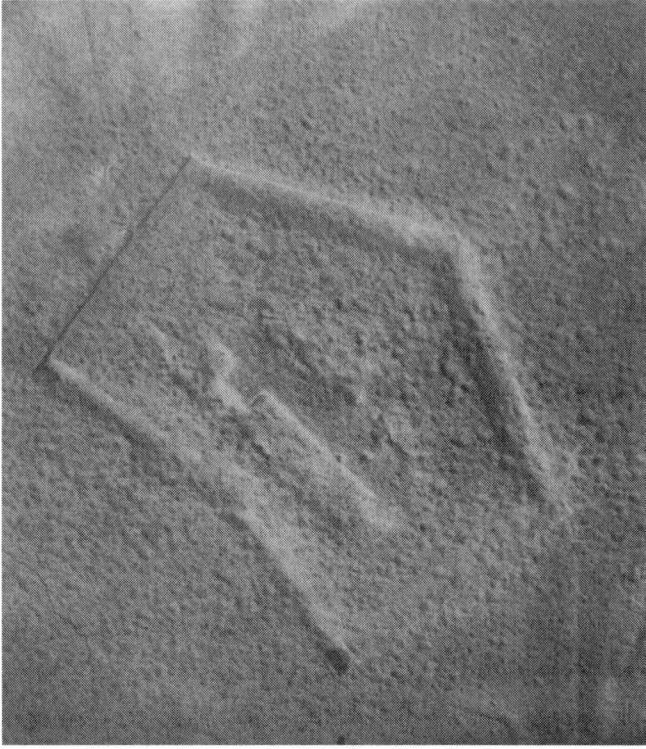

20. Later photograph of the *fort de Douaumont* taken during the Battle of Verdun. 1 October 1916. (Bibliothèque Municipale de Verdun MS812-149)

21. Oblique photograph of the *fort de Douaumont* taken during the Battle of Verdun. 10 October 1916. (Bibliotheque Municipale de Verdun MS812-118)

22. The *Redoute de Souville* (with the *Redoute de Saint-Michel* in the middle-ground and the city of Verdun in the background), looking west taken from a German Airforce Reconnaissance Aircraft, (*Le camp retranché de Verdun*) 22 May 1916.

23. The *fort de Vaux* (*Le camp retranché de Verdun*) looking north-east, taken after the battle and showing damage from shellfire, from an USA Airforce Reconnaissance Aircraft, summer 1918. Note that the *route militaire* has been reconstructed through the shell-pocked terrain of the old battlefield.

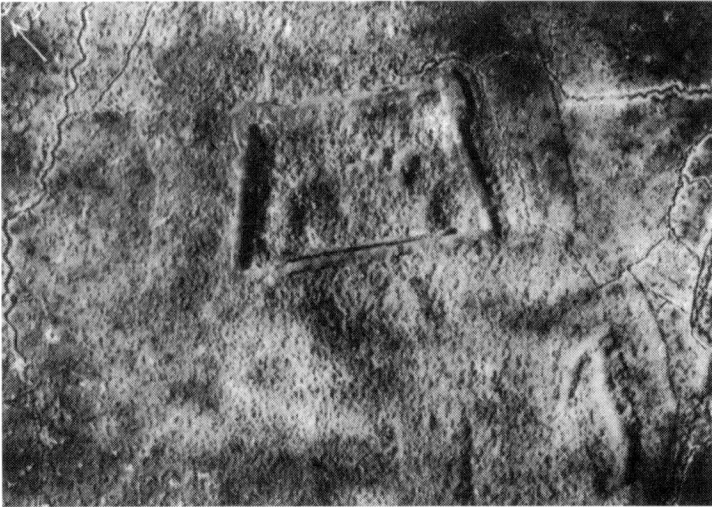

24. The *fort de Vaux* taken during the Battle of Verdun. Most of the shell damage seen here was inflicted by both the French and the German artillery. No date c.1916. (Bayerisches Hauptstaatsarchiv - Abt. IV Kriegsarchiv BS-II1g648)

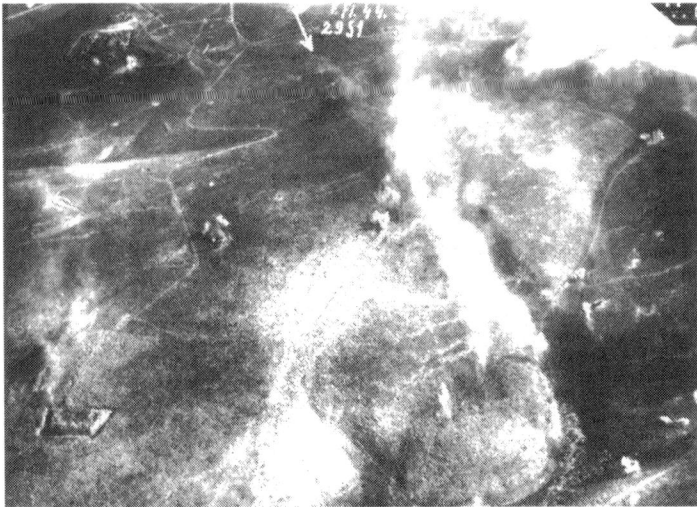

25. The *fort de Vaux* (lower left) and the *fort de Tavannes* (upper left) taken during the Battle of Verdun. Shells can be seen exploding on the right of the photograph. 5 August 1916. (Bayerisches Hauptstaatsarchiv - Abt. IV Kriegsarchiv BS-II1g643)

26. The barrack of the *fort de Vaux* (*Le camp retranché de Verdun*) taken after the battle probably in the winter of 1917 and showing damage from shellfire. As the barracks faced to the rear of the fort, the damage was probably caused by French artillery whilst the Germans held the fort during the course of the battle. Of note is that the exterior rear wall of the barrack had a layer of *bétonné special* added, which although had taken heavy damage, had not been breached. It can be clearly seen that the French had added a number of wartime repairs and modifications. (IWM Q81472)

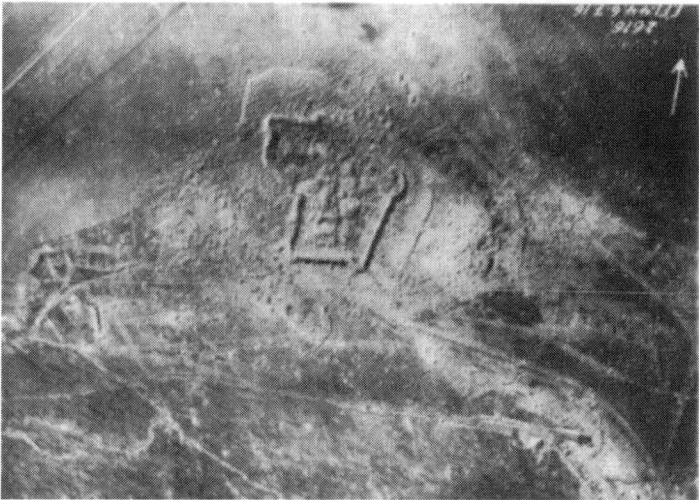

27. The *fort de Souville*. No date circa mid 1916. (Bayerisches Hauptstaatsarchiv - Abt. IV Kriegsarchiv BS-II1g647)

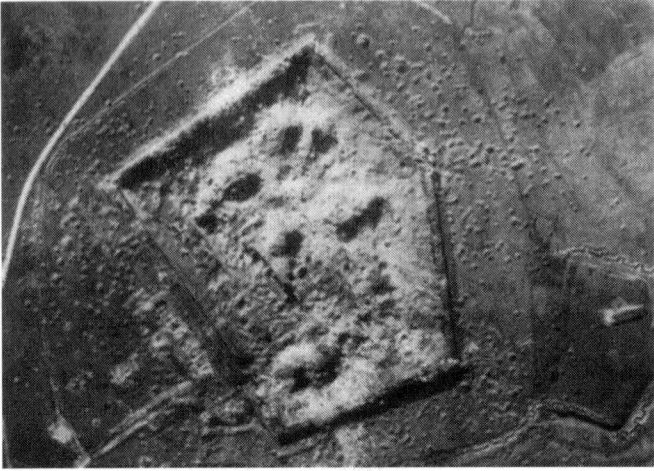

28. The *fort de Manonviller* taken during the Battle of Lorriane. Most of the shell damage seen here was inflicted by the German artillery. No date c.1914. (Bayerisches Hauptstaatsarchiv - Abt. IV Kriegs-archiv BS-II1g249)

29. Photograph of the *fort de Manonviller* after its capture by the Germans. This view was taken from the *fossé* showing the *entrée*, the *pont* and the *pont mobile*. No date c.1914. (Bayerisches Hauptstaatsarchiv - Abt. IV Kriegs-archiv BS-II1g250)

30. The *fort de Manonviller* after its capture on 27 August 1914 by the Germans. This view shows a *Tourelle de mitrailleuses (GF4)* in its firing position August/September 1914. (Bayerisches Hauptstaatsarchiv - Abt. IV Kriegsarchiv BS-II1g255)

31. The *fort de Manonviller* after its capture by the Germans. This view shows a *Tourelle de 75mm (T75) Galopin* in its raised firing position and shows damage to the *avant-cuirasse* caused by German shelling. General der Infanterie Dr. Ing. Karl Ritter von Brug, seated, was responsible for planning the artillery bombardment of this fort. August/September 1914. (Bayerisches Hauptstaatsarchiv - Abt. IV Kriegsarchiv BS-II1g260)

32. The *fort de Manonviller* (*Forts d'arrêt - en avant de Toul*) showing the bombardment damage to the fort. In the foreground is the *baquette d'artillerie* with an artillery piece, which is possibly a *canon de 'De Bange' 155mm longue S.P. modèle 1888*. no date, circa September 1914

33. The *fossé* of the *fort de Manonviller* (*Forts d'arrêt - en avant de Toul*) showing the bombardment severe damage to the *Bétonné spécial* of this reinforced structure. In the foreground is a *grille*. 28 August 1914.

34. The *fort de Manonviller* (*Forts d'arrêt - en avant de Toul*) taken by the German Air Service, and also showing the clear outline of the fort a long with bombardment damage to the outer surface. No date, possibly early war.

35. View of the *fossé* of the *fort de Boussios* (*Le camp retranché de Maubeuge*) showing the *escarpe* on the left with the *pont* leading into the *entrée* and the *contrescarpe* on the right. This photograph was taken from the top of the *caponnière de gorge* which has been badly damaged by the German bombardment during the Battle of the Frontiers August 1914 – c1914. (IWM Q57542)

36. Damage by shellfire to the *fort de Malmaison* (*Frontière du nord - le groupe Nord/ Deuxième ligne /Forts d'arrêt – Soissons*). It should be noted that most of the damage here was inflicted by French artillery both before and during the Great War – this fort was used in trials using modern high explosive shells in the mid 1880's. It was captured by the Germans in 1914 and used by them until recaptured by the French late in 1917. No date, post-war. (IWM Q44751)

38. A *Locomotive Péchot-Bourdon modèle 1888* of the military *Voie ferré de 0.6m* (600mm military railway) – pre-war / no date

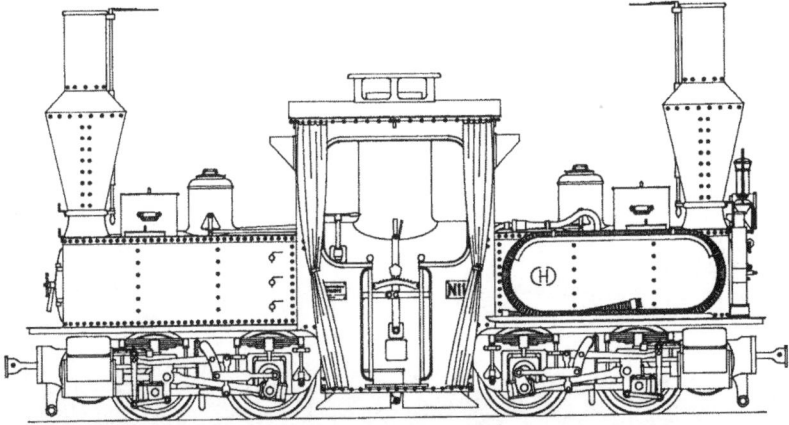

Section 7. Side Elevation of the *Locomotive Péchot-Bourdon modèle 1888* (After Christian Cénac Copyright ©1991)

39. Three quarter front view of a *Locomotive Péchot-Bourdon modèle 1888* with artillery officiers and men including the locomotive crew, no date, pre-war

40. A *Plate-Forme du Tablier de Truck modèle 1883* transporting a *Canon de 'De Bange' 155mm longue S.P. modèle 1888*, no date, pre-war

41. Two *Affûts Trucks du général Peigne* mounting *Canon de 'De Bange' 120 mm court modèle 1878* and a *Plate-Forme du Tablier de Truck modèle 1883* loaded with shells being hauled by a *Locomotive Péchot-Bourdon modèle 1888*. Note the shell wagon is not a *Transport d'Obus*, which was designed to carry shells of a heavier calibre, no date, pre-war

42. Three *Affûts Trucks du général Peigne* mounting *Canon de 'De Bange' 120 mm court modèle 1878* during peacetime manoeuvres, no date, pre-war

43. An *Affûts Trucks du général Peigne* mounting a *canons de 155mm Court modèle* 1912, no date, wartime, (French Official Photograph via IWM FO W674)

44. Locally recruited infantry (regiment unknown, but possibly from either the *164ᵉ*, *165ᵉ* or *166ᵉ régiments d'infanterie*) marching through a village in the Verdun area (*Le camp retranché de Verdun*), no date, pre-war

45. Locally recruited cavalry (regiment unknown, but possibly from either the *2ᵉ*, *4ᵉ* or *5ᵉ divisions de cavalerie*) marching through a village in the Verdun area (*Le camp retranché de Verdun*), no date, pre-war

Plan 1: Roof and Floor Plans of The *Fort de Vaux* as built in 1884. (Based upon German Intelligence Report.)

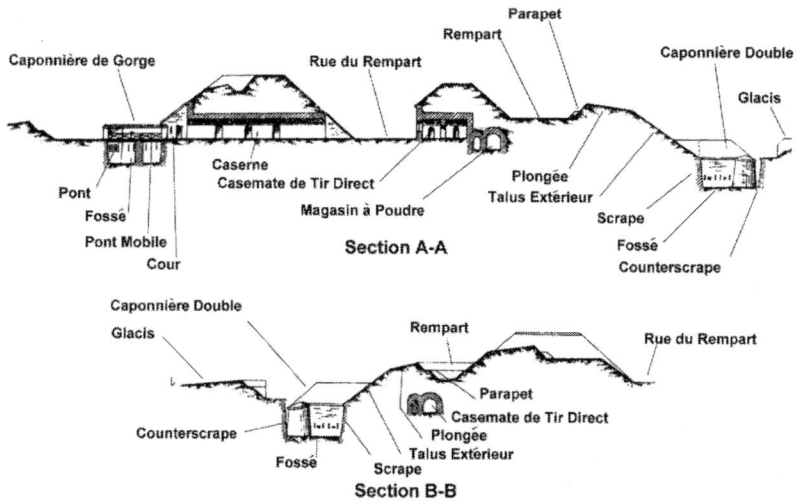

Section 1: Cross-Section of The *Fort de Vaux* as built in 1884. (Based upon German Intelligence Report.)

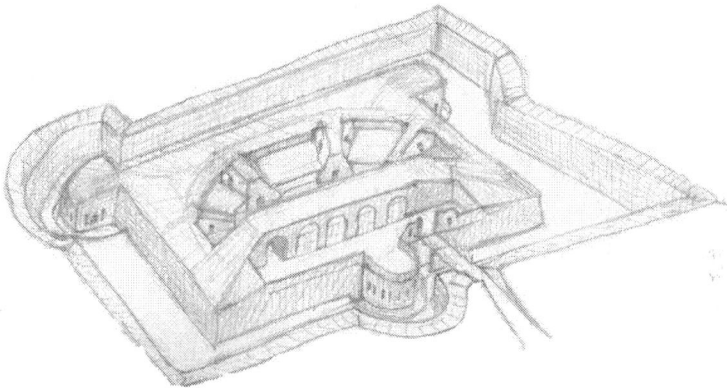

Sketch 1: Artist's impression of the *Fort de Vaux* as built in 1884. (Veiw Looking to the South East.)

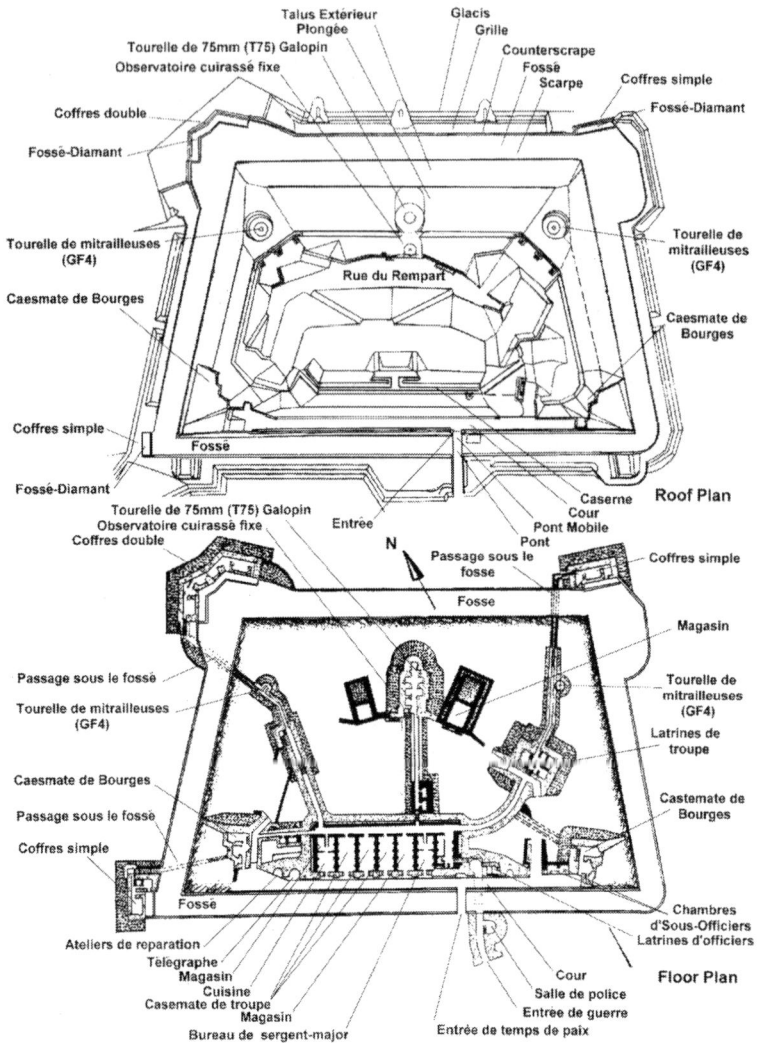

Roof Plan

Talus Extérieur
Plongée

Glacis
Grille

Tourelle de 75mm (T75) Galopin
Observatoire cuirassé fixe

Counterscrape
Fossé
Scarpe

Coffres simple

Coffres double

Fossé-Diamant

Fossé-Diamant

Tourelle de mitrailleuses
(GF4)

Rue du Rempart

Tourelle de
mitrailleuses
(GF4)

Caesmate de Bourges

Caesmate de
Bourges

Coffres simple

Fossé

Fossé-Diamant

Tourelle de 75mm (T75) Galopin
Observatoire cuirassé fixe
Coffres double

Entrée

Caserne
Cour
Pont Mobile
Pont

N

Passage sous le
fosse

Coffres simple

Fossé

Magasin

Passage sous le fossé

Tourelle de mitrailleuses
(GF4)

Tourelle de
mitrailleuses
(GF4)

Latrines de
troupe

Caesmate de Bourges

Passage sous le fossé

Coffres simple

Castemate de
Bourges

Fossé

Chambres
d'Sous-Officiers
Latrines d'officiers

Ateliers de reparation
Télégraphe
Magasin
Cuisine
Casemate de troupe
Magasin
Bureau de sergent-major

Cour
Salle de police
Entree de guerre
Entrée de temps de paix

Floor Plan

(The uses of the rooms shown here are that which were designated before the war hence the
commander was foreseen to be of the rank of sergeant major and not a commissioned officer.)

Plan 2: Roof and Floor Plans of The *Fort de Vaux* after modification in 1906. (Based upon French Army Engineers Drawings.)

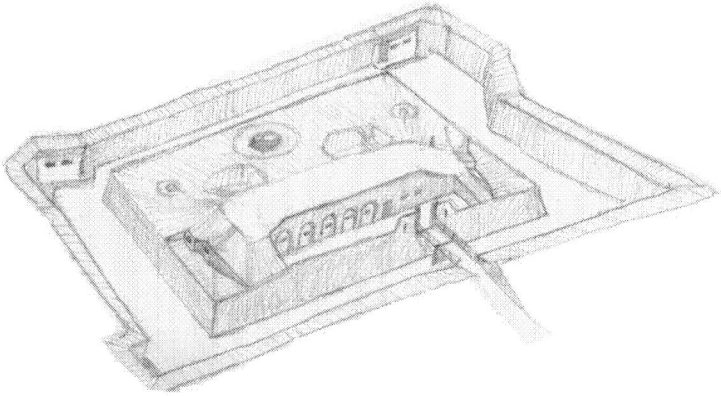

Sketch 2: Artist's impression of the *Fort de Vaux* after modification in 1906. (Veiw Looking to the South East.)

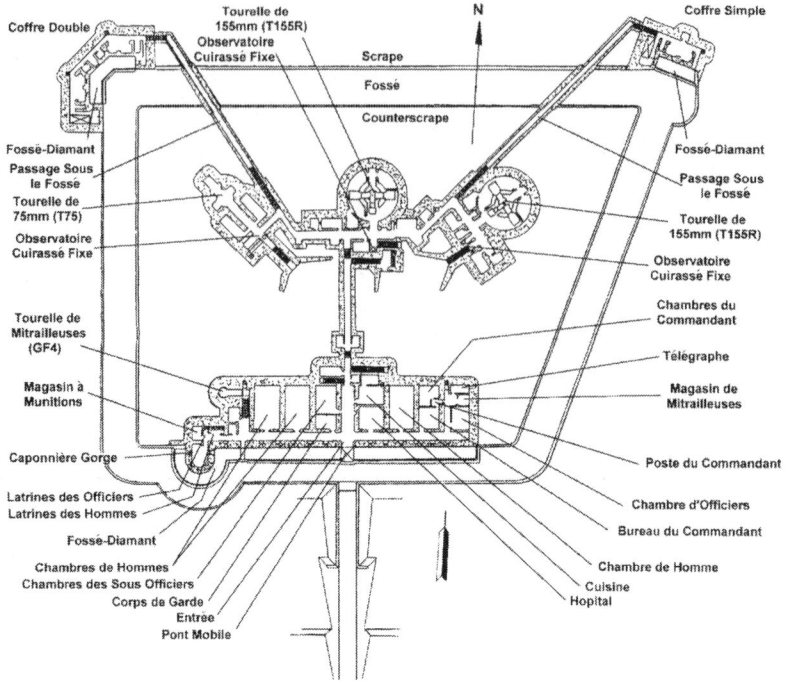

Plan 3: Roof and Floor Plans of The *fort de Vacherauville* as built in 1910. (Based upon French Army Engineers' Drawings.)

37. The *fort de Vacherauville*, 4 June 1916 (Bibliotheque Municipale de Verdun MS812-47)

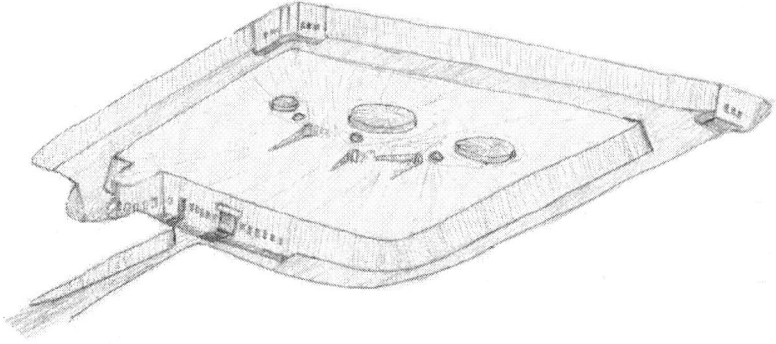

3: My impression of the *fort de Vacherauville* as built in 1910. (Veiw Looking to the North West.)

Gun Chamber
Gun Mountings (connons not shown)
Armoured Plate Roof
Re-inforced Concrete
Sheel Hoist within Central Support Column
Working Chamber
Entrance Passageway
Canterlever Arm
.mmunition Store
Counter Weight

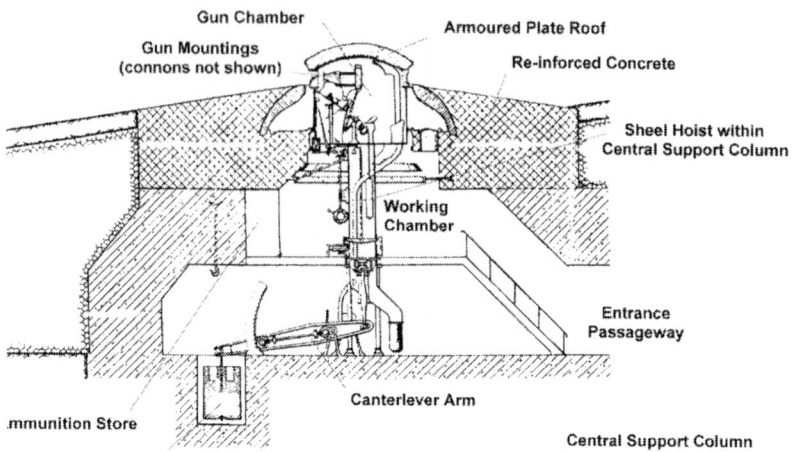

Section of through Turret showing Gun and Working Chambers.

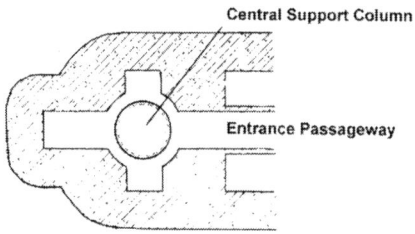

Central Support Column
Entrance Passageway

Plan of Lower Chamber

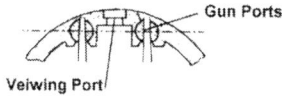

Gun Ports
Veiwing Port

Gun Ports
Veiwing Port

Plan of Turret Front Plate

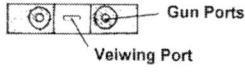

Front View of Turret Front Plate

Section 2: Cross-Section of a 'tourelle de 75mm (T75)'.(Based upon German Intelligence Report.)

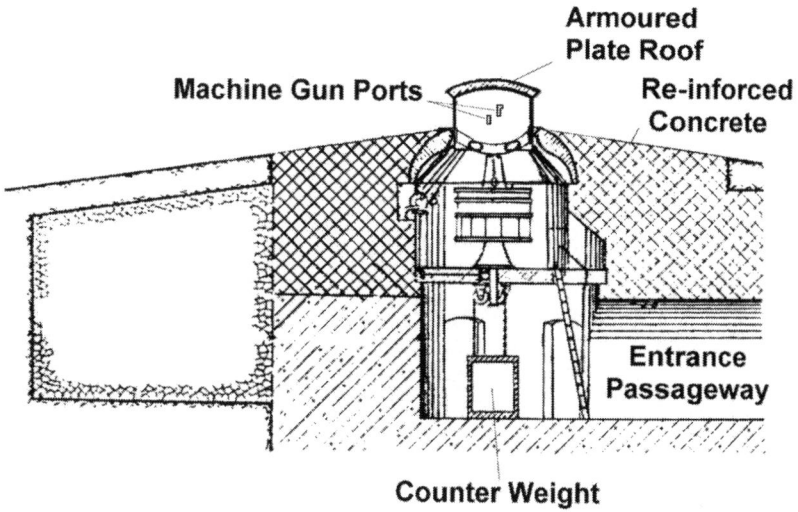

Section 3: Cross-Section of a *Tourelle de Mitrailleuses (GF4)*.(Based upon German Intelligence Report.)

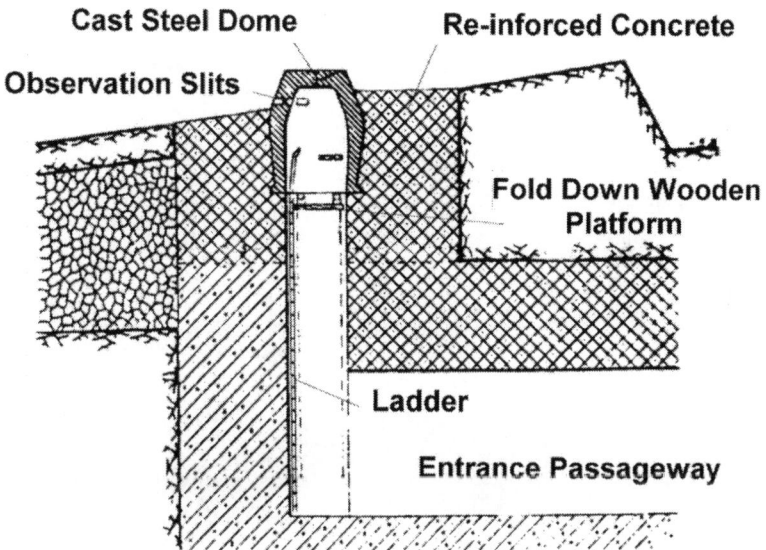

Section 4: Cross-Section of an *Observatoire Cuirasse Fixe*. (Based upon German Intelligence Report.)

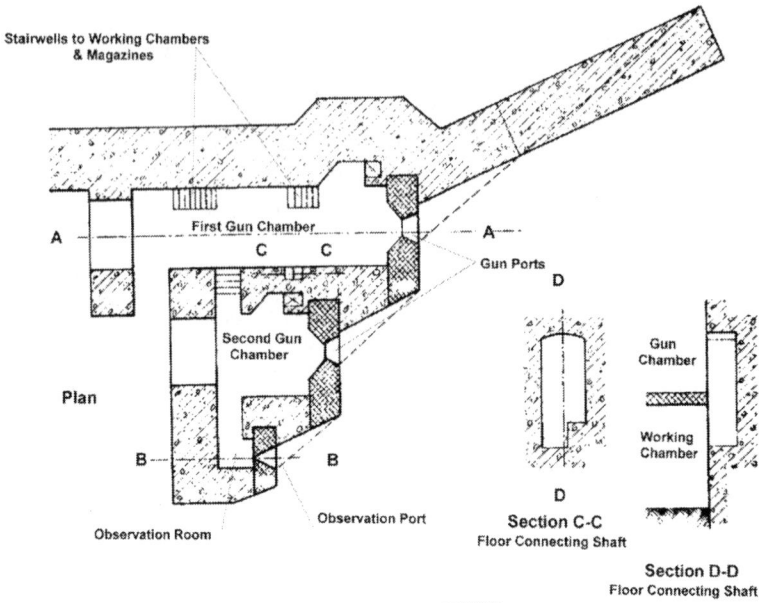

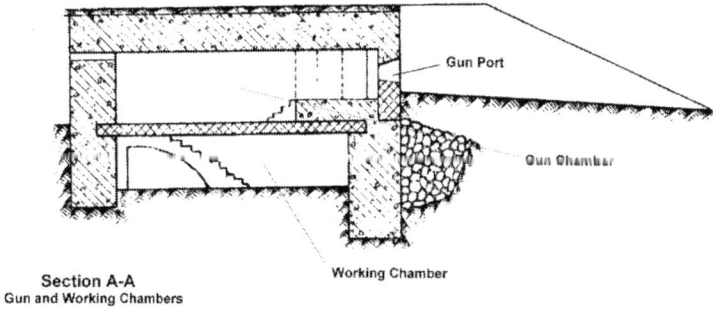

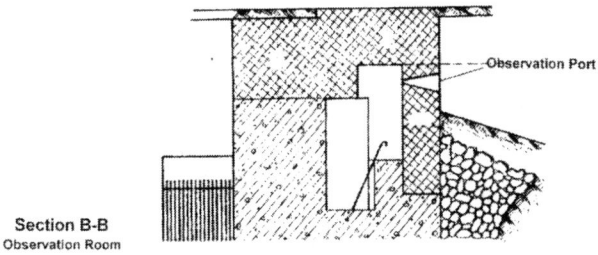

Section 5: Plan and Section of a 'Casemate Bourges'. (Based upon French Army Engineers' Drawings.)

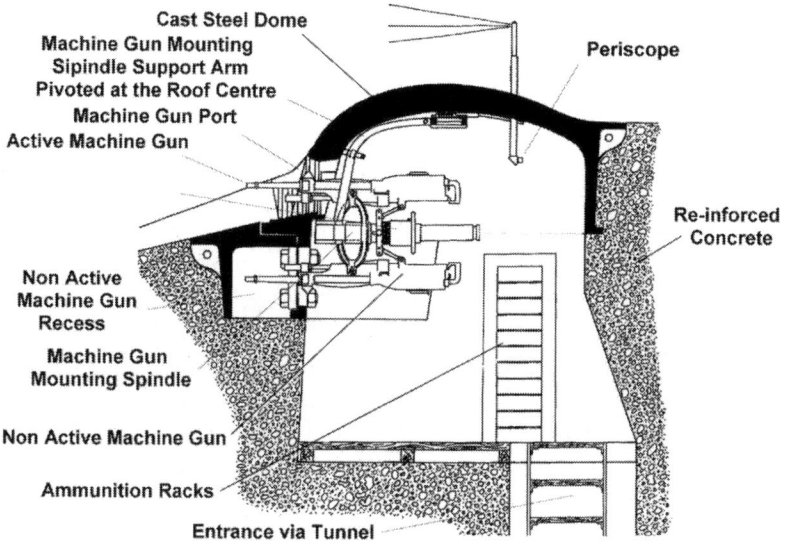

Cast Steel Dome
Machine Gun Mounting
Sipindle Support Arm
Pivoted at the Roof Centre
Machine Gun Port
Active Machine Gun

Periscope

Re-inforced Concrete

Non Active Machine Gun Recess

Machine Gun Mounting Spindle

Non Active Machine Gun

Ammunition Racks

Entrance via Tunnel

Section 6: Section through a *'Casemate Pamards'*. (After M. & J. Barro's sketch Copyright © 1995)

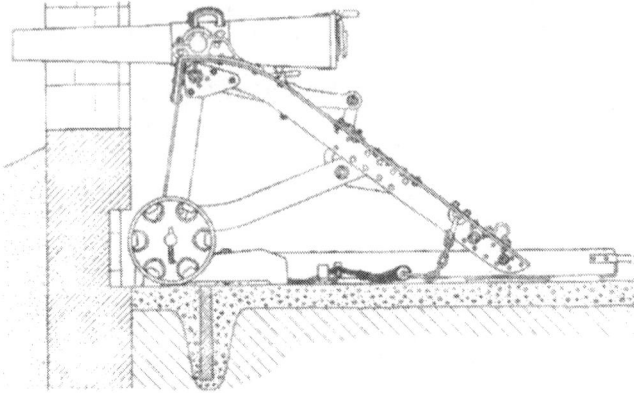

Section 7: Section of a 'Canon de 12-culasse modèle 1858 modifiée 1880'.

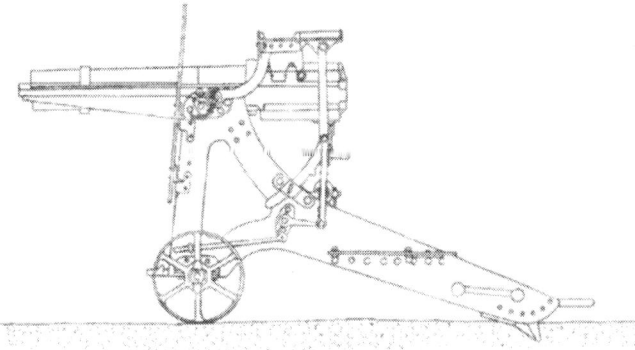

Section 8: Section of an 'Canon revolver de 40mm Hotchkiss modèle 1877'.

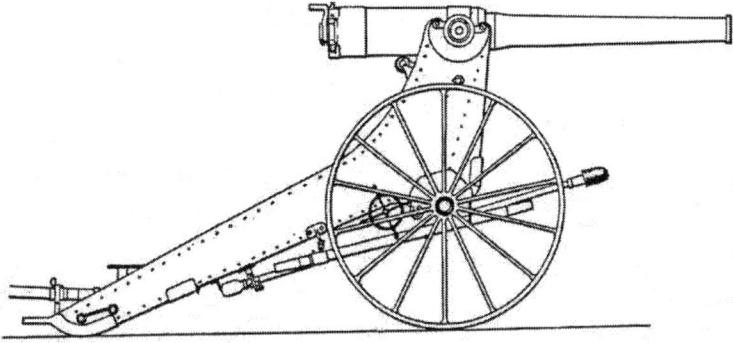

Section 9: Section of a 'Canon de 'Lahitolle' 95 mm modèle 1888'. (Note the wheels shown are of the all steel type for employment in fortresses.)

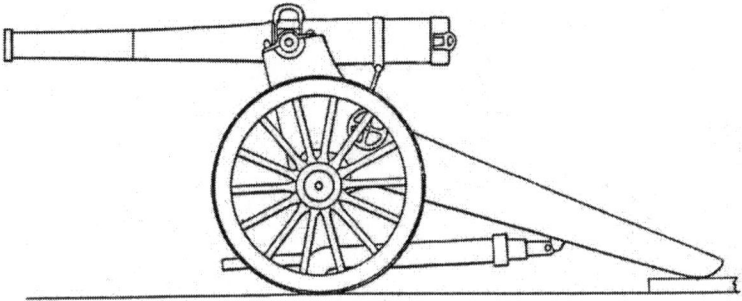

Section 10: Section of a 'Canon de 'De Bange' 120 mm longue modèle 1878'. (Note the wheels shown are the wooden with steel tyres type for employment in the field.)

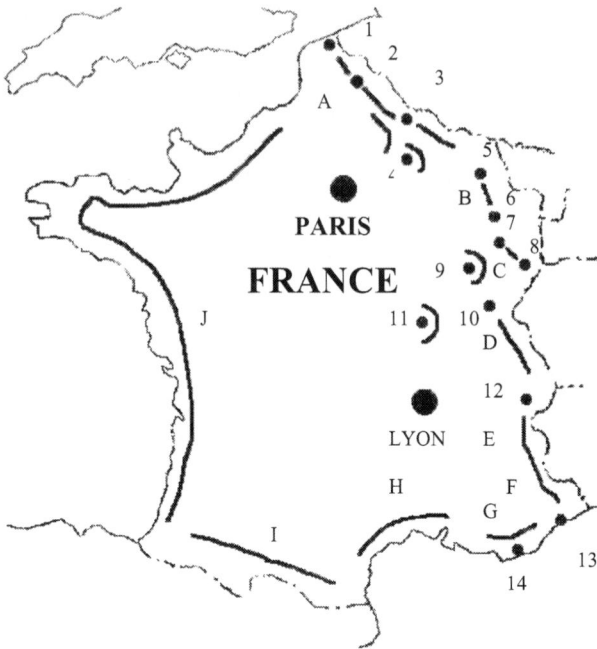

Map 1: France's Frontier Defences Regions (Groups) as defined by *général* Séré de Rivières

PARIS	*Le camp retranché de Paris*
LYON	*Le camp retranché de Lyon*
A	*la frontière du nord - le groupe Nord.*
B	*la frontière du nord-est (hauts de Meuse) - le groupe de la Meuse.*
C	*la frontière de l'est (côte de Moselle) - le groupe Vosges.*
D	*la frontière jurassienne (Besançon) – le groupe Jura.*
E	*la frontière italienne – premier ensemble (d'Albertville à Briançon).*
E	*la frontière italienne – deuxième ensemble (de Briançon au Barbonnet).*
G	*les côtes méditerranéennes.*
H	*la Corse.*
I	*la frontière pyrénéenne.*
J	*défense des côtes de la façade ouest de la France (côte atlantique).*
1	*Le camp retranché de Dunkerque*
2	*Le camp retranché de Lille*
3	*Le camp retranché de Maubeuge*
4	*Le camp retranché de Reims*
5	*Le camp retranché de Verdun*
6	*Le camp retranché de Toul*
7	*Le camp retranché de Épinal*
8	*Le camp retranché de Belfort*
9	*Le camp retranché de Langres*
10	*Le camp retranché de Besançon*
11	*Le camp retranché de Dijon*
12	*Ensemble fortifiés de Grenoble*
13	*la place forte de Nice (Alpes Maritimes).*
14	*la place forte de Toulon (Var).*

Map 2: The First two Groups of Fortifications;
le groupe de la Meuse **and** *le groupe Vosges*
(Names of city within Brackets are the German Names.)

A	*la frontière du nord-est (hauts de Meuse)* - *le groupe de la Meuse.*
B	*la frontière de l'est (côte de Moselle)* - *le groupe Vosges.*
C	Franco-German Border 1872-1919
D	Present Day Franco-German Border
E	Trouée de Stenay
F	Trouée de Charmes
G	Trouée de Belfort
H	German Fortified Zone 1875-1919

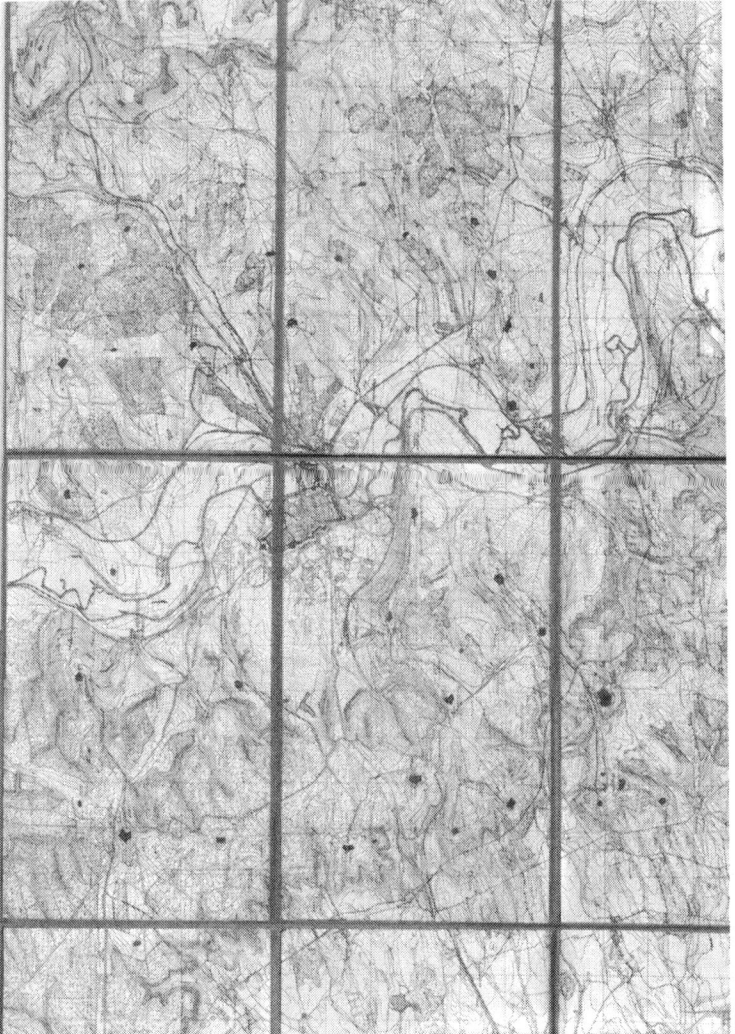

Map 3: German Army Trench Map of the Verdun Sector dated
October 1915

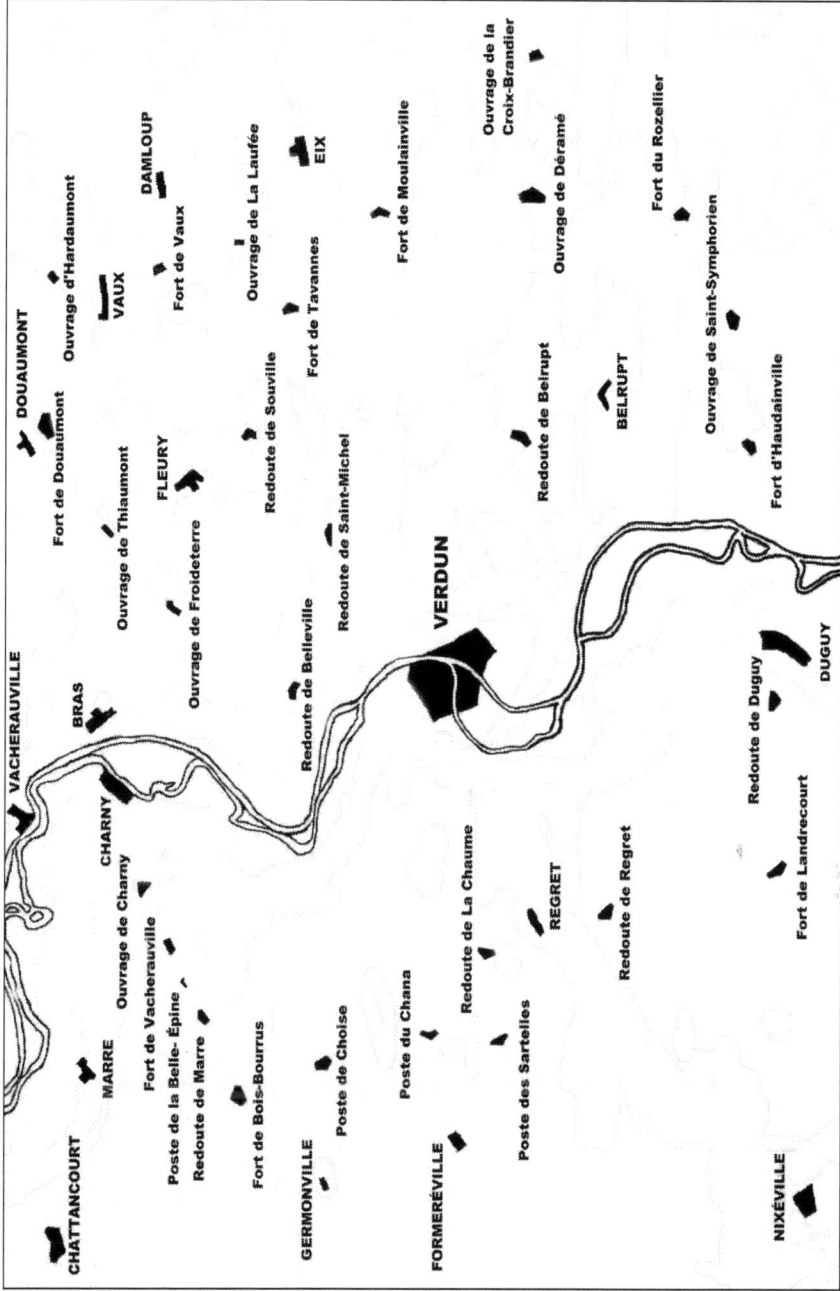

Map 4: The Main Fortifications of Verdun – *Le camp retranché de Verdun.* (Based on *Les Armée Françaises dans la Grande Guerre, Tome IV, Volume 1, Carte 13*)

Map 5: The Fortifications within the 1st Sector of the Verdun defences. (Based on *Les Armée Françaises dans la Grande Guerre, Tome IV, Volume 1, Cartes 14 & 26*)

Chronology

1567-1591	Construction of Verdun's first citadel – started by *Marechal* de Tavannes and finished by *Marechal* de Marillac
1699	Completion of the total Reconstruction of Verdun's first citadel by *Marechal* de Vauban creating the second Verdun citadel
1862	*Général* Séré de Rivières works on the defences of Nice
1864-70	Séré de Rivières works on the defences of Metz
1870-1871	The Franco-Prussian War
1870	Fall of the French fortified city of Metz
1871	Séré de Rivières plans attacks against Parisian forts
1871	The Treaty of Frankfurt signed between France and Germany ending the Franco-Prussian War
1872	The *Comité de Défense* by Adolphe Thiers under the chairmanship of *Maréchal* de MacMahon
1873-1878	The *Dreikaiserbund* of 1873 formed (the League of the Three Emperors) between Germany, Austro-Hungary and Russia, causing France to be isolated from the other Great Powers
1873	Séré de Rivières writes his third study *'Considérations sur la reconstitution de la frontière de l'Est'*
1873	Maréchal Canrobert replaced de MacMahon as chairman of the Comité de Défense
1874-1884	The first period of French fortification construction
1874	Construction of the Séré de Rivières' fortifications on the north-eastern and eastern boundaries begins
1874	The *Chambre des Députés* vote in the first instalment of 29 million *Francs d'Or* to construct the defences
1874	The *Commission des Cuirassements* formed under the chairmanship of *Général* Cadart. Within the first year, Cadart hands over the chairmanship to *Général* Secrétain
1875	The first *redoutes* (forts) were built at Verdun, along with supporting infrastructures such as *routes militaire* and *casernes*
1875	Outbreak of political tension between France and Germany
1875	The *Caves à Canon* constructed as an emergency measure
1876	Acceptance of the *casemates de Mougin, modèle 1876*
1876	Séré de Rivières developed plans for the fortifications of the northern border
1877	Séré de Rivières developed plans for the fortifications of the eastern Swiss border
1878	The *parc d'Artillerie* and its *arsenal* built in the Verdun suburb of Jardin Fontaine

1879	The *Zweibund* (the Dual Alliance) of 1879 signed between Germany and Austro-Hungary
1880	The *Plan Nr. I*: the first of the series of French army contingency war plans was published. This mobilisation plan was based on Séré de Rivières defensive strategy
1881	First batteries were built at Verdun
1881-1886	The League of 1881 – the *Dreikaiserbund* resurrected and renewed
1882	The *Dreibund* (the Triple Alliance) of 1882 signed between Germany, Austro-Hungary and Italy
1885-1891	The second period of French fortification construction
c1885	Eugene Turpin developed the first picric acid high explosive known as *mélinite* in France
1885	Acceptance of the *tourelle de 155mm Mougin, modèle 1885* along with the supporting *observatoires cuirassé fixe* (the *cloche Digoin* and the *petites cloches Digoin*)
1886	The *fort de la Malmaison* was used in experiments to determine the impact of the modern new explosive
1887-1890	The *Rückrersicherungsrertrag* (Reinsurance Treaty) of 1887 signed between Germany and Russia
1887	The *Plan Nr. VIII* linking in the defence of Nancy into the overall scheme of the defence of France was published
1887	The first *ouvrages intermediare d'infanterie* were built at Verdun
1887	Work started on the *galeries souterraines* under the citadel at Verdun
1887	Construction of the *voie ferré de 0.6m* begins
1888	The *Plan Nr. IX* was published. Although a defensive plan, it was less static due to the shell crisis cause by the development of the *mélinite* high explosive. The plan foresaw offensive operations to prevent the enemy's artillery from being positioned in range of the fortifications
1888	Testing and acceptance of the *tourelle de 155mm (T155L) Bussière modèle 1888*
1888	Testing and acceptance of the *coupole de 155mm Châtillon-Commentry, modèle 1888*
1888	Testing and acceptance of the *coupole de 155mm de Saint Chamond, modèle 1888*
1889	Acceptance of the *tourelle de 57mm (T57CF) modèle 1889*
1889	The first *abris cavernes* and *magasins à poudre* were built at Verdun
c1890	The *parc à dirigeables* was built at Verdun

1891-1905	*Generalfeldmarschall* von Schlieffen tenancy as German Chief of Staff during which time he developed his contingency plans
1892	The first *dépôts intermédiaire* were built at Verdun
1892	The Franco-Russian Alliance of 1892 signed – France was no longer isolated
1892-1914	The third period of French fortification construction
1894	*Generalfeldmarschall* von Schlieffen suggested a plan to attack France via Nancy
1895	The acceptance of the *tourelle de mitrailleuses (GF3) modèle*
1896	*Général* Miribel's mobilisation and deployment *Plan Nr. XIII* foresees using the forts as a springboard to attack the Germans
1898	The *Plan Nr. XIV* was a defensive/offensive Plan: Much more offensive, envisaged the positioning of the French forces in front of defensive curtains to support their fortified positions
1899	The first *casemates de Bourges* built at Verdun
1899	The first *abris du projecteur* built at Verdun
1900	The first *ouvrages intermediare d'infanterie* rebuilt as *ouvrages modernisée* built at Verdun
1900	The first *abris de combat* built at Verdun
1900	The first *retranchements d'infanterie* and the *ouvrages en terre de infanterie* built at Verdun
1900	Acceptance of the *tourelle de mitrailleuses (GF4) modèle 1900*
1902	Acceptance of the *tourelle de 75mm (T75) Galopin modèle 1902*
1903	Acceptance of the *tourelle de 155mm (T155R) Galopin modèle 1903*
1903	*Général* Brugère's the *Plan Nr. XV* was a modification of the *Plan Nr. XIV*. It was based on a general offensive eastward into Lorraine and northward towards Belgium but left Verdun un-defended
1904	The agreement of 1904 – The Anglo-French Entente Cordiale agreed
1906	*Generalfeldmarschall* von Schlieffen publishes his final memorandum, which forms the basis of the German contingency plan that became known as The Schlieffen Plan
1906	The only *ouvrages moderne* to be constructed in the Verdun (the *ouvrage de La Falouse*) was completed
1907	The Anglo-Russian Alliance signed leaded to the Triple Entente
1907	The agreement of 1907 – the Triple Entente agreed between Britain, France and Russia

1907	*Général* Hagron's modification of the *Plan Nr. XV*, became known as the *Plan Nr. XV* Variant. This modified plan foresaw the same offensives as required by the *Plan Nr. XV*, but that Verdun was now to be defended
c1908	The *terrain d'aviation* was built at Verdun
1908	The acceptance of the *projecteur à éclipse*
1908	*Général* Michel's French mobilisation and deployment *Plan Nr. XVI* incorporating the British forces into the overall French war plans
1910	The only *fort moderne* to be constructed in the Verdun defences (the fort de Vacherauville) was completed
1914	*Général* Joseph Joffre French's mobilisation and deployment scheme the *Plan Nr. XVII* – the final French war plan before the Great War
1914-1918	The Great War
1914	Germany invades Belgium and France
1914	German Artillery batters the Belgian forts into submission. The Battle of the Frontiers including German attacks on French fortifications
1915	The *Grand Quartier Général* orders the decommissioning, dismantling (especially of the weapons) and demolition of the forts. Order rescinded once the Battle of Verdun starts
1916	The Battle of Verdun is fought 21 February to 18 December. The fortifications play a major role during the course of the battle
1916	The first of the *casemates Pamards* constructed at Verdun
1918	The *Blockhaus bétonné* constructed at Verdun

Glossary

A

Abris	Shelters
Abris bétonne	Concrete shelters
Abris caverns	Underground shelters
Abris de combat	Combat shelters
Abris d'intervalle	Interval shelters
Abris du projecteur	Projector or searchlight shelters – same as a *Poste Photo-Électrique*
Affûts	Mounting (for a gun)
Affûts trucks	Rail mounted artillery wagons
Ambulance	Field hospital or anything relating to one, however in this case, the fort's first aid post
Arsenal	Arsenal
Ateliers de reparation	Repair shops
Avant-cuirasse	Armoured front face or collar

B

Baquette d'artillerie	Artillery ramparts.
Bâtiments extérieur	Exterior ancillary buildings
Batteries	Battery positions - gunnery emplacements
Bétonné	Concrete
Bétonné spécial	Special concrete - extra hard concrete developed for the up grading of the *forts*, in later years reinforced with steel bars for greater strength
Blockhaus bétonné	Concrete blockhouse
Boucherie	Butcher's shop
Bouclier mobile	Movable armoured shield
Boyau	Communication trench
Bureau(x)	Office(s)
Bureau du commandant	Commanding officer's office

Camps retranché	Entrenched camps (fortified towns)
Canon de 75mm tir rapide modèle 1897	75mm calibre quick firing model 1897 field gun
Canon de 155C modèle 1912	155mm calibre short barrelled gun model 1912
Canon de 'De Bange' 90 mm longue modèle 1877	90mm calibre gun model 1877 invented by the army engineer Col. de Bange
Canons de 'De Bange' 120 mm court modèle 1878	155mm calibre short barrelled cannons model 1878 invented by the army engineer Col. de Bange
Canon de 'De Bange' 120 mm longue modèle 1878	120mm calibre gun model 1878 invented by the army engineer Col. de Bange
Canon de 'De Bange' 155 mm longue modèle 1877	155mm calibre gun model 1877 invented by the army engineer Col. de Bange
Canon de 'De Bange' 155mm court modèle 1881	155mm calibre howitzer model 1881 invented by the army engineer Col. de Bange
Canon de 'De Bange 155mm longue S.F. modèle 1888	155mm calibre gun model 1888 invented by the army engineer Col. de Bange
Canon de 'De Bange' 155mm raccourci modèle 1902	155mm calibre shortened gun model 1902 invented by the army engineer Col. de Bange
Canon de 'Lahitolle' 95 mm modèle 1888	95mm calibre gun model 1888 invented by the army engineer Col. de Lahitolle
Canon de Nordenfelt 57mm CF modèle 1889	57mm calibre gun invented at the *Nordenfelt* factory
Canon de rapide modèle 75-02	Quick firing model 1902, a shortened barrel version of the *75mm TR modèle 1897* field gun

Canon revolver de 40mm Hotchkiss modèle 1877	40mm calibre cannon revolver model 1877
	the *Hotchkiss* Company of St. Denis
Canon de 12-culasse modèle 1858 modifiée 1880	Cannon firing a projectile with 12 lugs model 1858 and modified in 1880
Caponnières	Caponiers or bastions located on the corner of the *escarpe* to cover the *fossé(s)*
Caponnières simple	Individual bastion covering the line of a single *fossé*
Caponnières double	Paired bastions covering the lines of two *fossés*
Caponnière de gorge	Gorge's caponier – bastion covering the entrance
Casemates de Bourges	Type of *casemate de Flanquement* – flank casemates – proof tested at the Bourges firing ranges
Casemates à canons	Gun casemates
Casemates de flanquement	Flanking casemates
Casemates de flanquement du fossé	Flanking casemates covering the *fossé*
Casemate de tir direct	Primary magazine rooms
Casemate de tir indirect	Secondary magazine rooms
Casemates de Mougin	Early type of *casemate* designed by Cmdt. Mougin.
Casemate de troupe	Chambers – living accommodation
Casemates Pamards	Wartime-built machine gun(s) shelter designed by Capt. Pamards
Casemates Pamards simple	*Casemates Pamards* with one machine gun port
Casemates Pamards double	*Casemates Pamards* with two machine gun ports
Caserne	Barrack block
Cave à canon	Cellar with a cannon
Centres de résistance	Centres of resistance
Chambres de hommes	Chambers for the men/other ranks dormitories
Chambres aux lampes	Lamp recesses

Chambres d'officiers	Chambers for officers dormitories
Chambres d'sous-officiers	Chambers for N.C.O's dormitories
Chambre de tir	Gun chamber
Chapelle	Chapel
Chargeur	Gun loader
Chef de pièce	Gun commander – normally a N.C.O.
Cisternes	Water cisterns
Cloches Digoin	Digoin's bell – an armoured observation post for *forts*
Coffres	Coffers or casemates set in the *contrescarpe* at a corner to cover the *fossé(s)*
Coffres simple	Individual casemate covering the line of a single *fossé*
Coffres double	Paired casemates covering the lines of two *fossés*
Corps de garde	Guardhouse
Coupole	Cupolas
Cour	Courtyard
Couchages	Sleeping dormitories
Contrescarpe	Outer *fossé* wall
Cuisine	Kitchen

D

Dépôts intermédiaire	Intermediate depots
Deuxième ligne	Second line (of fortifications)

E

Echappatoires	Loopholes – a small slot shaped opening for defenders to fire small arms through for close defence
Ecoutes	Underground corridors
Entrée	Main gate or entrance
Entrée de Guerre	War entrance
Entrée de Temps de Paix	Peacetime entrance
Escarpe	Inner *fossé* wall

114

F

Forts	Forts
Forts d'arrêt	Arresting or blocking forts (individual forts).
Forts isolé	Isolated forts (individual forts)
Forts de liaison	Linking forts
Forts moderne	Modern forts
Forts de rideau	Curtain forts – another name for *Forts de liaison*
Fossé(s)	Ditch(es) or dry moat(s).
Fossé-diamant	Diamond ditch (secondary ditch) within the *fossé*

G

Galeries	Underground galleries
Galeries souterraine	Underground galleries or tunnels
Glacis	Bank sloping downwards away from the fort to the top of the *contrescarpe*
Grille	Iron-railing fence, was also applied to barbed wire obstacles
Grand Quartier Général	General Headquarters
Groupes	Groups

H

Haha	Ha-ha – deep slab sided pit
Hangar Bessonneau	Wooden framed linen covered aircraft hanger designed Julien Bessonneau
Hôpital	Hospital

L

La Citadelle	The Citadel - see *Réduit central*
Latrines	Latrine – the toilet block
Latrines de troupes	Other ranks' toilet block
Latrines d'officiers	Officers' toilet block

Lignes de défense	Defensive lines (of fortifications)
Ligne principale de résistance	Main line of resistance (of Fortifications)
Ligne de soutien	Support line or support line (of fortifications)
Ligne intérieure de	Inner line – same as *Ligne soutien*
Locomotive Péchot-Bourdon modèle1888	Péchot-Bourdon Locomotive model 1888 (Steam Locomotive designed by Capitaine P. Péchot and engineer Ch. Bourdon)
Logements d'Officiers	Officers' quarters

M

Magasin	Storerooms
Magasin à poudre	Gunpowder storerooms
Magasin à poudre et à munitions	Powder and munitions magazines
Magasin du génie	Engineers storerooms
Magasin de secteur	Sector magazine
Matériel	Materials – guns, munitions,
Matériel Artillerie 1888	Official name for the *voie ferré de 0.6m* – it was generally referred to as the *système Péchot*
Mitrailleur	Machine gunner
Mitrailleuses Hotchkiss modèle 1899	Machine guns model 1899 developed by the *Hotchkiss* Company of St. Denis
Mitrailleuse Modèle 1907 transformée	Converted Machine guns model 1907 developed by the *Saint Étienne* armaments factory – commonly known as the *Mitrailleuse dit Saint Étienne*
Modèle	Model – normally the year of acceptance or sometimes introduction

N

Niches à munitions	Ammunition niches

P

Parapet	Parapet
Parc d'Artillerie	Artillery Park
Parc à dirigeables	Dirigible balloon enclosure
Passages sous le fossé	Passageways or tunnels under the *fossé*
Petites cloches Digoin	Digoin's small bell – an armoured observation post for use in the field or artillery positions
Pharmacie	Pharmacy
Place fortifiée	Fortified place or Strongholds
Places fortes de l'Est	Strongholds of the East
Plongée	Almost flat sloping bank downwards in front of the *parapet*
Pompe et lavabos	Pump and basins – washroom
Pont	Bridge
Pont mobile	Drawbridge
Pont roulant latéral intérieure	Type of *pont mobile*
Pont roulant longitudinal extérieur	Type of *pont mobile*
Postes	Posts - pre-built defensive positions for artillery
Poste de commandement	Command post
Poste Photo-Électrique	Electric searchlight post – same as an *abris du projecteur*
Poste de secours	First aid post
Postes de ravelin	Ravelin bastions
Pourvoyeurs	Gun ammunition carriers.
Première ligne	First line (of fortifications)
Projecteur Électrique de 90cm	90-centimetre diameter searchlight
Puits d'eau	Water wells

O

Observateur	Observer
Observatoire	Observation post for fire control
Observatoire cuirassé fixe	Armoured observation post for fire control set low to the ground level
Ouvrages infanterie	Infantry field works – pre-built defensive positions for infantry
Ouvrages en terre de infanterie	Infantry earth works –again, pre-built defensive positions for infantry
Ouvrages modernisée	Modernized *ouvrages* – upgrading the *ouvrages infanterie* to fort status

Q

Quartier Général	Headquarters

R

Rampe	Gun ramp
Redoutes	Redoubt – a small fort
Réduit central	Central storage 'structure' or shelter - the tunnels additions to *La Citadelle*.
Refectoire des officiers	Officers' mess
Rempart	Rampart – artillery platforms
Région fortifiée	Fortified Region
Retranchement	A recess within a trench – a dugout
Retranchements de campagne	Field trenches – pre-built defensive positions for infantry
Retranchements d'infanterie	Infantry trenches – as above pre-built defensive positions for infantry
Routes	Metalled tracks or roads
Route militaire	Military road – *fort* entrance track

Rue du rempart	Rampart's supply road

S

Sabord	Gun port
Salle de lecture	Lecture hall
Salle de recreation	Recreation room
Secteur	Sector
Sortie lointaine	Underground tunnel leading to a remote exit - an 'escape or supply tunnel'
Station électrique	Electrical power station
Système Péchot	Generally used, but unofficial name give to the *voie ferré de 0.6m*
Système Poncelet longitudinal	Type of *pont mobile extérieur*
Système Tripier latéral intérieur	Type of *pont mobile*
Système Tripier longitudinal extérieur	Type of *pont mobile*

T

Talus extérieur	Gently sloping bank upwards from the *escarpe* to the *plongée*
Télégraphe	Communications or telegraphy room
Téléphonique	Telephone exchange
Terrain d'aviation	Aircraft flying ground
Tireur	Gun layer
Tourelle à éclipse	'Disappearing' or retractable turret
Tourelle à fixes	'Non-retractable' or permanent fixed turret
Tourelle de mitrailleuses (GF4)	Twin machine gun retractable turret
Tourelle de 57mm (T57CF)	Twin 57mm guns retractable turret
Tourelle de 75mm (T75) Galopin	Twin 75mm guns 'retractable' turret designed by Cmdt. Galopin

Tourelle de 155mm (T155L) Bussière	Twin 155mm guns 'retractable' turret designed by Col. Bussière
Tourelles de 155mm (T155R)	Single or twin 155mm gun(s) *Galopin* 'retractable' turret designed by Cmdt. Galopin
Tourelle de 155mm Mougin	Twin 155mm guns *fixes* (non-retractable) turret designed by Cmdt. Mougin
Tranchée	Front line or fighting trench
Tranchées bétonné	Concrete lined trenches
Tunnel fortifié	Fortified tunnel

V

Vieux fort	Old fort (that was included into the new defensives system)
Vivan-Bessière	Rifle grenades designed by the engineers M. Vivan and M. Bessières
Voie ferré de 0.6m	600mm narrow gauge railway

Z

Zone de défense	Defensive Zone

Appendices

Appendix 1
Regional Grouping of the Fortified Zones

The original four *groupes* were as follows:
la frontière du nord - le groupe Nord.
la frontière du nord-est (hauts de Meuse) - le groupe de la Meuse.
la frontière de l'est (côte de Moselle) - le groupe Vosges.
la frontière jurassienne (Besançon) – le groupe Jura.

Other defensives *groupes*, which were added later to cover the remaining uncovered frontiers, were:
la frontière italienne – premier ensemble (d'Albertville à Briançon).
la frontière italienne – deuxième ensemble (de Briançon au Barbonnet).
la place forte de Nice (Alpes Maritimes).
la place forte de Toulon (Var).
les côtes méditerranéennes.
la Corse.
la frontière pyrénéenne.
défense des côtes de la façade ouest de la France (côte atlantique).

Finally there were two fortified cities within France:
la place de Paris.
la place de Lyon.

Appendix 2
All the Fortifications as Originally Planned as Built by *général* Séré de Rivières (listed by regional group then alphabetically)[26]

Frontière du nord - le groupe Nord:

Première ligne
Le camp retranché de Dunkerque (1878-1880):
    Fort des Dunes
    Batterie des Côtes
    Ouvrage de Petite Synthe (added in 1908)
    Ouvrage de Ouest (added in 1911)

Le camp retranché de Lille (1878-1893):
    Fort de Bondues
    Fort d'Englos
    Fort de Mons-en-Baroeul
    Fort de Sainghin
    Fort de Séclin
    Fort du Vert Galant
    Ouvrage de la Croix de Vallers
    Ouvrage d'Énchemont
    Ouvrage d'Entrepôt
    Ouvrage d'Épinoy (later renamed *Babylone*)
    Ouvrage de Flers (later renamed *Marchenelles*)
    Ouvrage de Hallemes (later renamed *Moulin Neuf*)
    Ouvrage de Houplin
    Ouvrage de La Jonchère
    Ouvrage de Lompret
    Ouvrage de Noyelles
    Ouvrage de Sart (later renamed *Haut-Vinage*)
    Ouvrage de Vendeville
    Ouvrage de Wambrechies
    Batterie de Lezennes
    Batterie de Premesques

---

[26] Appendix 2 is based on information mainly from the book "Le Systeme Séré de Rivières" by Guy Le Hallé.

Forts d'arrêt - Ligne Lille-Maubeuge (1880):
  Fort de Curgies
  Fort de Flines
  Fort de Maulde

Le camp retranché de Maubeuge (1878-1897):
  Fort de Boussois
  Fort de Cerfontaine (or *Colleret*)
  Fort d'Hautmont
  Fort de Leveau
  Fort de Sarts
  Ouvrage de Bourdiau
  Ouvrage de Bresilles
  Ouvrage de Feignies
  Ouvrage de Ferrière-la-Petite
  Ouvrage de Grevaux
  Ouvrage de Héron Fontaine
  Ouvrage de la Salmagne
  Ouvrage de Rocq (or *Lorme*)
  Batteries des Foyaux
  Batteries d'Ostergnies
  Batterie de Recquignies

Forts d'arrêt - Ligne Maubeuge-Longwy (1877-1880):
  Fort des Ayvelles
  Fort du Bois (later renamed *Hirson*)
  Batterie Ayvelles

Deuxième ligne
Forts d'arrêt – La Fère (1877-1881):
  Fort de Liez
  Fort de Mayot
  Fort de Vendeuil
  Batterie de Renansart

Forts d'arrêt – Laon (1876-1882):
  Fort de Montérault
  Batterie de Classon
  Batterie de Laniscourt (3 gunnery positions)
  Batterie de Manège
  Batterie de Marlot
  Batterie de Russe
  Batterie de Saint-Martin (2 gunnery positions)
  Batterie de Saint-Vincent (2 gunnery positions)

Batterie de Vinox

Forts d'arrêt – Soissons (1874-1882):
  Fort de Condé-sur-Aisne
  Fort de la Malmaison

Frontière du nord-est (hauts de Meuse) - le groupe de la Meuse:

Première ligne
Le camp retranché de Verdun (1878-1912):
  Fort de Bois-Bourrus
  Fort de Douaumont
  Fort d'Haudainville
  Fort de Landrecourt
  Fort de Moulainville
  Fort du Rozellier
  Fort de Tavannes
  Fort de Vaux
  Fort de Vacherauville
  Redoute de Belleville
  Redoute de Belrupt
  Redoute de Duguy
  Redoute de La Chaume
  Redoute de Marre
  Redoute de Regret
  Redoute de Saint-Michel
  Redoute de Souville
  Poste des Sartelles
  Poste de la Belle- Épine
  Poste du Chana
  Poste de Choise
  Ouvrage de Baleycourt
  Ouvrage de Bezonvaux
  Ouvrage du Bois du Chapitre
  Ouvrage du Bois Saint-Maure
  Ouvrage du Bois-Réunis
  Ouvrage de Bois-Rogé
  Ouvrage de Bruyères
  Ouvrage de la Croix-Brandier
  Ouvrage de Charny
  Ouvrage de Châtillon
  Ouvrage de Déramé

Ouvrage d'Eix
Ouvrage de Froideterre
Ouvrage de Fromeréville
Ouvrage de Germonville
Ouvrage d'Hardaumont
Ouvrage de Jaulny
Ouvrage de Josémont
Ouvrage de La Falouse
Ouvrage de La Laufée
Ouvrage de Manesel
Ouvrage du Maubois
Ouvrage de Thiaumont
Ouvrage de Thierville
Ouvrage du Trimard
Ouvrage de Saint-Symphorien
Batterie de Belle- Épine
    (Batteries 9.1 & 9.2)[27]
Batterie de Belleville (Batteries 7.2, 7.3, 7.4, 7.5 & 7.6)
Batterie de Bois-Bourrus (Batteries 7.1, 7.2 & 7.3)
Batterie de Bourvaux (Batteries 6.2 & 6.3)
Batterie de Charny (rebuilt as *fort de Vacherauville*)
Batterie de Choisel (Batteries 6.2 & 6.3)
Batterie de Côte-du-Chêve (Batteries 5.6 & 5.7)
Batterie de La Chaume (Batterie 4.1, 4.2 & 4.3)
Batterie de Damloup (Batterie 6.1)
Batterie de Douaumont (Batteries 3.1, 3.2 & 3.4)
Batterie de Dugny (Batteries 1.2, 1.3, 1.4, 1.5 & 1.6)
Batterie d'Eix (Batterie 1.1)
Batterie du ravin de la Fausse- Côte (Batterie 5.1)
Batterie de la Folie (Batterie ?)
Batterie de Froideterre (Batteries 1.3 & 1.4)
Batterie d'Haudainville (Batterie 6.1 & 6.3)
Batterie de l'Hôpital (Batterie 8.5)
Batterie de Landrecourt (Batteries 2.3, 2.4, 2.5 & 2.6)
Batterie du Mardi-Gras (Batterie 6.8)
Batterie de Marre (Batteries 8.1, 8.2, 8.4 & 8.5)
Batterie du Maubois (Batterie 3.1 & 3.2)
Batterie de Montgrignon (Batterie 7.1)
Batterie de Moulainville (Batterie 1.2, 1.4 & 1.5)
Batterie du Moulin (Batterie 2.1)
Batterie de l'Ollier (Batterie 6.6)

---

[27] Neither the wartime *Batteries* have been included, nor the ones that were planned and given numbers but not built – hence the gaps within the sequence numbers.

Batterie de Regret (Batteries 3.4, 3.5, 3.6 & 3.7)
Batterie du Rozellier (Batterie 3.3 & 4.1)
Batterie de Saint-Michel (Batteries 7.7, 7.8 & 7.9)
Batterie de Saint-Symphorien (Batterie 5.1 & 5.4)
Batterie des Sartelles (Batterie 5.5)
Batterie de Souville (Batterie 8.3 & 8.4)
Batterie de Tavannes (Batterie 6.9)
Batterie de Thiaumont (Batteries 2.1, 2.2, 2.6, 2.7 & 2.8)
Batterie de Torcy (Batterie 8.1)
Batterie Tourelle de Souville (Batterie 8.2)
Batterie du Tunnel (Batterie 8.6)
Batterie de Vaux (Batteries 5.2, 5.3 & 5.5)

Forts de Redeau – Ligne Verdun-Toul (1875-1885):
    Fort du Camp-des-Romains
    Fort de Génicourt
    Fort de Gironville
    Fort de Jouy-sous-les-Côtes
    Fort de Liouville
    Fort des Paroches
    Fort de Troyon
    Batterie de Saint-Aignan (abandoned)

Le camp retranché de Toul (1874-1910):
    Fort de Blenod
    Fort de Bruley
    Fort de Domgermain
    Fort d'Ecrouves
    Fort de Gondreville
    Fort de Le Chanot
    Fort de Lucey
    Fort de Saint-Michel
    Fort du Tillot
    Fort de Trondes
    Fort de Vieux-Canton
    Redoute de Chaudeney
    Redoute de Dommartin
    Redoute de la Justice
    Ouvrage du Bas-du-Chêve
    Ouvrage du Bouvron
    Ouvrage de Charmes
    Ouvrage de la Cloche
    Ouvrage d'Est-Vieux-Canton
    Ouvrage de Fays

Ouvrage de Francheville
Ouvrage de Haut-des-Champs
Ouvrage du Mordant
Ouvrage d'Ouest-Vieux-Canton
Ouvrage de Ropage

Forts d'arrêt - en avant de Toul (1874-1910):
    Fort de Frouard
    Fort de Manonvillers
    Fort de Pont-Saint-Vincent
    Batterie de l'Éperon
    Village fortifié de Villey-le- Sec (consisting of the *fort de Villey-le-Sec* and two *Batteries*)

Forts d'arrêt - entre Toul-Langres sur la Meuse (1874 -1910):
    Fort de Bourlemont
    Fort de Pagny-la-Blanche-Côtes

Deuxième ligne
    Le camp retranché de Reims (1875-1883):
    Fort de Brimont
    Fort de Fresnes
    Fort de Herbillon (renamed *Fort de Pompelle*)
    Fort de Montbré
    Fort de Nogent-l'Abbesse
    Fort de Saint-Thierry
    Fort de Witry-lès-Reims
    Batterie de Berru
    Batterie de Chenay
    Batterie de Le Cran
    Batterie de Loivre
    Batterie de la Vigie de Berru

Frontière de l'est (côte de Moselle) - le groupe Vosges:

Première ligne
Le camp retranché de Épinal (1876-1885):
    Fort des Adelphes
    Fort de Bambois
    Fort de Bois l'Abbé
    Fort de Dogeneville
    Fort des Friches
    Fort de Girancourt
    Fort de la Grande Haye

Fort de Longchamp
Fort de la Mouche
Fort de Razimont
Fort du Roulon
Fort du Sanchey
Fort de Thiera
Fort d'Uxegney
Fort de la Voivre
Ouvrage du Bois d'Arches
Ouvrage de Deyvillers
Batterie des Friches
Batterie du Sanchey
Batterie du Thiera

Forts de Redeau – Ligne Épinal-Belfort (1874-1876):
Fort d'Arches
Fort de Parmont
Fort de Rupt
Ouvrage de Château-Lambert
Ouvrage de Giromagny
Batterie de Ballon de Servance
Batterie de la Tête des Planches

Le camp retranché de Belfort (1869-1914):
Fort de Basses Perches
Fort de Bessoncourt
Fort du Bois d'Oye
Fort de Chevremont
Fort de Harty (renamed *Fort des Barres*)
Fort des Hautes
Fort de Mont Vaudois
Fort de Roppe
Fort de Salbert
Fort de Vezelois
Ouvrage du Bas-du-Mont
Ouvrage du Bois-des-Essert
Ouvrage de Bosmont
Ouvrage de Bourogne
Ouvrage de Côte d'Essert
Ouvrage de Denney
Ouvrage de Dorans
Ouvrage de la Forêt
Ouvrage de Fougerais
Ouvrage des Grands Bois

Ouvrage du Haut-du-Bois
Ouvrage du Haut d'Evette
Ouvrage de l'Étang Neuf
Ouvrage de Monceau
Ouvrage de Moval
Ouvrage du Piton d'Éloi
Ouvrage du Rondot
Batterie de Meroux
Batterie du Mont Rudolphe
Batterie du Piton-Lagace
Batterie de Sevénans
Batterie d'Urcerey
Batterie de la Verpilliere

Deuxième ligne
Le camp retranché de Langres (1869-1891):
Fort du Cognelot (renamed *Fort de Vercingétorix*)
Fort de Dampierre
Fort de La Bonnelle
Fort de Peigney
Fort de Plesnoy
Fort de la Pointe de Diamant
Fort de Montlandon
Fort de Saint-Menge
Ouvrage du Bois de la Montagne
Ouvrage de Brévoines
Ouvrage de Buzon
Ouvrage de Champigny
Ouvrage de la Croix d'Arles
Ouvrage du Fays
Ouvrage des Fourches
Ouvrage de Jorquenay
Ouvrage de la Marnotte
Ouvrage de Montrouge
Ouvrage de Noirdant
Ouvrage de Noirdant-le-Rocheux
Ouvrage de Perrancey
Ouvrage de Vieux Moulin
Batterie de Brévoines
Batterie de Buzon
Batterie de Corlée
Batterie des Franchises
Batterie de la Gare
Batterie de la Marnotte

Batterie du Mont

Frontière jurassienne (Besançon) – le groupe Jura:

Première ligne
Forts de Redeau – le secteur de Pont-de-Roide (1874 - 1880):
  Fort de La Chaux
  Fort du Lomont
  Fort de Mont Bart
  Batterie des Roches
  Batterie des Établons

Le camp retranché de Besançon (1870-1880):
  Fort de l'est des Buis
  Fort de l'ouest des Buis
  Fort de Châtillon-le-Duc
  Fort de la Dame Blanche (renamed *Fort de Chailluz*)
  Fort de Fontain
  Fort des Justices
  Fort de Montboucons
  Fort Neuf-de-Montfaucon
  Fort de la Planoise
  Fort de Pugey
  Redoute de Montfaucon
  Ouvrage Au Bois
  Ouvrage Pouilley-les-Vignes
  Batterie de Benoît
  Batterie du Calvaire
  Batterie des Épesses
  Batterie de la Ferme de l'Hôpital
  Batterie de Planoise
  Batterie des Rattes
  Batterie de Rolland
  Batterie de Rosemont

Énsemble fortifié de Pontarlier (1879-1883):
  Fort du Larmont Supérieur (renamed *Fort de Catinat*)
  Fort de Saint-Antoine
  Fort des Risoux
  Vieux fort des Bancs
  Vieux fort de l'Écluse
  Vieux fort de Joux
  Vieux fort du Larmont Inférieur

Vieux fort des Rousses
Batterie de Pierre Chatel

Deuxième ligne
Le camp retranché de Dijon (1879-1883):
    Fort de Beauregard
    Fort Brûlé
    Fort de Hauteville
    Fort de la Motte Giron
    Fort Saint-Apollinaire
    Fort de Sennecey
    Fort de Varois
    Redoute de Norges-la-Ville
    Réduit de Mont Afrique
    Batterie d'Asnières

La frontière italienne – premier ensemble (d'Albertville à Briançon):

Première ligne
Ensemble de Bourg-Saint-Maurice (1890-1913):
    Fort du Truc
    Ouvrage de la Redoute Ruinée
    Batterie de Courtbâton
    Batterie du Roc Noir
    Batterie des Têtes
    Batterie de Vulmix
    Blockhaus de la Platte

Fortification du Mont-Cenis (1890-1898):
    Fort de la Turra
    Ouvrage des Arcellins
    Ouvrage de la Beccia
    Ouvrage du Mont-Froid
    Ouvrage de Tomba
    Batterie de La Loza
    Batterie de Sardières

Ensemble fortifiés de Modane et de l'Esseillon(1885 - 1908):
    Fort du Replaton
    Fort du Sappey
    Fort du Télégraphe
    Redoute du Sappey

Batterie du Télégraphe

Deuxième ligne
Ensemble d'Albertville (1875-1883):
    Fort de Lestal
    Fort du Mont
    Fort de Tamié
    Fort de Villard
    Ouvrage de l'Alpettaz
    Blockhaus de Laitelet
    Blockhaus des Têtes
    Batterie de Conflans
    Batterie de Granges
    Batterie de Lançon

Ensemble Aiton-Chamousset (1875-1884):
    Fort d'Aiton
    Fort de Montgilbert
    Fort de Montperché
    Blockhaus de Crepas
    Blockhaus de Foyatier
    Blockhaus de Rochebrune
    Blockhaus de Sainte-Lucie
    Blockhaus de Tête-Lasse
    Batterie de Frepertuis
    Batterie de Plachaux
    Batterie de la Tête Noire

Ensemble fortifiés de Grenoble (1875-1889):
    Fort du Bourcet
    Fort de Comboire
    Fort de Montavié
    Fort du Mûrier
    Fort des Quatre Seigneurs
    Fort de Saint-Eynard
    Batterie du Néron
    Batterie du Quichat

La frontière italienne – deuxième ensemble (de Briançon au Barbonnet):

Ensemble fortifiés de Briançon (1875-1906):

L'épi defénsif de l'Infernet (1875-1906):
  Fort de l'Infernet
  Fort du Janus
  Ouvrage A
  Ouvrage B
  Ouvrage C (known as Fort du Gondran)
  Ouvrage D
  Blockhaus du Janus

L'épi defénsif de la Croix de Bretagne (1876-1890):
  Fort de la Croix de Bretagne
  Fort de la Grande Maye
  Fort de la Lauzette
  Blockhaus de la Grande Maye A
  Blockhaus de la Grande Maye B
  Batterie d'Ayes
  Batterie du Col
  Batterie de Gafouille
  Batterie de la Lauze
  Batterie de la Lauzette
  Batterie de la Roche Noire
  Batterie de la Trois-Mélèzes
  Batterie de la Tour

L'épi defénsif de l'Olive-Granon (1881-1904):
  Fort de l'Olive
  Blockhaus des Acles
  Blockhaus de Lenlon (position de Lenlon)
  Blockhaus de Mallfosse (position de la Croix de Toulouse)
  Batterie de la Croix de Toulouse
  Position d'artillerie du col de Barteaux (position du Granon)

Ensemble fortifiés de la vallée de l'Ubaye (1880-1893):
  Fortin de surveillance de Cuguret
  Fortin de surveillance de la Duyère
  Fortin de surveillance de Serre de Laut
  Redoute du Chaudron (position de Sainte-Vincent)
  Poste du ravin de la Tour (position de Sainte-Vincent)
  Batterie du Châtelard (position de Sainte-Vincent)
  Batterie de Colbas (position de Sainte-Vincent)
  Batterie du Cuguret
  Batterie de Les Caurres
  Batterie de Malemort
  Batterie Séré de Rivières

Batterie de la Roche La Croix
Batterie de position de Tournoux
Batterie de Vallon Claus
Batterie de Viraysse
Casernement défensif de Viraysse

Position du col de Restefond
Fortin de la Pelousette
Blockhaus des Fourches
Position d'artillerie Las Planas
Position d'artillerie de la Tête de Vinaigre

Position avancée de Provence
Fort de surveillance de la Forca(l'ensemble de l'Authion)
Fort de surveillance des Mille Fourches (l'ensemble de l'Authion)
Redoute de surveillance de la Pointe des Trois-Communes
Fort du Chiuses de Bauma Negra
Fort du Pic Charvet
Fort de Saint-Jean de la Rivière

Ensemble fortifiés de Barbonnet (1883-1898):
Fort Suchet
Ouvrage du Mont-Ours
Ouvrage de Siricoca

La place forte de Nice (Alpes Maritimes):

Front de terre de Provence (1885-1893):
Fort d'avant la Drette
Fort d'avant la Revère
Fort d'avant la Tête du Chein
Fort d'après le Mont Agel
Fort d'avant le Mont Chauve d'Aspremont
Fort d'après le Mont Chauve de Tourette
Batterie des Cabanes

Front de mer de Provence (1885-1892):
Batterie d'après du Cap Ferrat
Batterie d'après du Cimetière Russe
Batterie d'après des Mont Boron
Batterie de la Maure

Défenses de golfe de Saint-Tropez (1874):

Batterie du cimetière de Sainte-
Maxime

La places forte de Toulon (Var):

Défenses terrestres, d'ouest en est (1872-1907):
   Hauteurs de la Seyne
   Fort du Pipaudon
   Fort de la Six-Four
   Gande Forte de Peyras (batterie de bombardement)
   Ouvrages de la Chaîne du Gros Cerveaus
      (2 batteries de bombardement)

Évenos
   Fort du Pipaudon
   Ouvrages du Mont-Caumes est (batterie de bombardement)
   Ouvrages du Mont-Caumes ouest(batterie de bombardement)

Défenses du Faron
   Fort de la Croix-Faron
   Vieux fort Faron
   Crémaillère du Faron

Défenses du Coudon
   *Fort du Coudon (*also known as *Fort de l'Est* or *Fort du lieutenant*
                                          Girardon)
   Fortin du Bau-Pointu
   Batterie du Gros-Rocher

Défenses de Carqueyranne
   Fort de la Colle-Noire
   Fortin de la Gavaresse

La rade et le littoral, d'ouest en est (1877-1913):
   Presqu'île de Saint-Mandrier
   Fort de Cepet
   Batterie de la Croix des Signaux(batterie de bombardement)
   Batterie du Gros Bau
   Batterie de Lazaret Haut (batterie de bombardement)
   Batterie de Saint-Elme

Presqu'île de Gien
   Fort de la Badine

Rade d'Hyères
  Batterie Mauvanne
  Batterie de Brégançon

Porquerolle
  Fort de la Repentance

Les côtes méditerranéennes. (c1880):

  Fort Séré de Rivières du Cap

La Corse:

  Corse du nord (c1880):
    Fort Lacroix

  Corse du sud (1872-1891):
    Batterie de Bonifacio
    Batterie de Porticcio

La frontière pyrénéenne. (1885):

    Fort Bear
    Fort le Serrat de la Tausse
    Fort le Serrat d'En Vaquer

Défense des côtes de la façade ouest de la France (côte atlantique):

  En Gironde (1652-1689/1877-1880):
    Défenses de l'embouchure de la Gironde à la pointe de Grave
    Fort du Verdon
    Vieux Fort Médoc
    Vieux Fort Pâté

  En Charente-Maritime (1625-1845):
    Défenses de Rocheford
    Vieux Fort de la Pointe
    Vieux Fort de l'Enet

  Ile Madame
    Vieux Fort ile Madame

Ile d'Aix
 Vieux Fort Liédot
 Batterie de Coudepont
 Batterie de la Rade
 Batterie de la Force

Ile d'Oléron
 Vieux Fort Chapus
 Vieux Fort des Saumonards

Ile d'Ré
 Vieux Fort de la Prée
 Batterie de Sablanceaux

Loire-Atlantique (1890-1899):
 Défenses de la rade de la Loire
 Fort de l'Ève
 Batterie de Ville-ès-Martin

Dans le Morbihan (1846-1903):
 Presqu'île de Quiberon
 Fort de Kernevest
 Fort Saint-Julien
 Fort de Penthièvre

Défenses de Lorient
 Fort Bloqué
 Fort de Locqueltas
 Fort du Talud
 Batterie de Port-Puce

A Belle-Ile
 Batterie du Gros-Rocher
 Batterie de Taillefer
 Batterie de Ramonet

Ile de Groix
 Fort du Haut-Grognon
 Vieux Fort Surville
 Batterie du Bas-Grognon
 Batterie du Méné

Dans le Finistère (1694-1997/1876-1899):
 Fort de Bertaume

Fort de Crozon
Fort de Landaoudec
Fort de Toulbroc'h
Vieux Fort de l'Armorique
Vieux Fort des Capucins
Vieux Fort du Corbeau
Vieux Fort du Minou
Batterie de Cornouailles
Batterie du Tourlinguet
Batterie Kerbronn
Batterie Kervinou
Batterie Robert

Dans les Côtes d'Armor (1873-1874):
Fort réduit de Bréhat

Dans la rade de Cherbourg
(1787-1859/1878-1895):
Vieux Fort Central de la Digue
Vieux Fort de Chavagnac
Vieux Fort de l'Ile Pelée
Vieux Fort de Querueville
Batterie de la Digue

Les côtes de chaque côté de la rade de Cherbourg à l'ouest
Batterie d'Équeurdreville
Batterie celle de Naqueville-Bas
Batterie celle de Naqueville-Haut
Batterie Nouvelle de Couplets
Batterie de Sainte-Anne

Les côtes de chaque côté de la rade de Cherbourg à l'est
Batterie du Capelain
Batterie de Bretteville Bas
Batterie de Bretteville Haut
Batterie de Grenneville
Batterie de la Mare de Tourlaville

En Seine- Maritime, Le Havre (1453-1859/1892):
Vieux Fort de Tourneville
Vieux Fort de Sainte-Adresse
Batterie de la Havre
Château de Dieppe (upgraded to modern standards)

La place de Paris, Le camp retranché de Paris:

Position du nord (1874-1879):
Première secteur
    Fort de Cormeilles
    Fort de Domont
    Fort de Montlignon
    Fort de Montmorency
    Redoute de Franconville
    Batterie A du Moulin de Risq
    Batterie B de la Borne de M.
    Batterie C de l'Étang
    Batterie D du Rond-Point
    Batterie E du Chateau Rouge

Deuxième secteur
    Fort de Stains
    Fort d'Écouen
    Redoute du Moulin
    Moulin de la Butte Pinçon
    Batterie A de Pierrefitte
    Batterie B de Stains
    Batterie de Blémur
    Batterie des Sablons

Position de l'est (1874-1881):
Troisième secteur
    Fort de Chelles
    Fort de Vaujours
    Batterie Nord
    Batterie Sud

Quatrième secteur
    Fort de Champigny
    Fort de Villiers

Cinquième secteur
    Fort de Sucy
    Fort de Villeneuve-Saint-Georges
    Redoute des Hautes Bruyères
    Batterie de Limeil

Position du sud-ouest (1874-1881):
Sixième secteur
    Fort de Châtillon
    Réduit de Verrière
    Coupure de Châtillon
    Fort de Palaiseau
    Fort de Villeras
    Batterie de Bièvres
    Batterie de la Châtaigneraie
    Batterie des Gâtines
    Batterie d'Igny
    Batterie de la Pointe
    Batterie du Terrier
    Batterie de l'Yvette

Septième secteur
    Fort de Saint-Cyr
    Fort de Haut-Buc
    Ouvrages des Docks
    Batterie de Bois d'Arcy
    Batterie de Bouviers
    Batterie de Porte du Désert
    Batterie du Ravin des Bouviers
    Batterie de Saint-Cyr
    Batterie de la Station

Huitième secteur
    Fort du Trou d'Enfer
    Groupe d'ouvrages de Marly
    Batterie des Arches (Louveciennes)
    Batterie de l'Auberderie
    Batterie de Chapelle-Saint Jean (Fonternay-le-Fleury)
    Batterie de Champ de Mars
    Batterie de Marly
    Batterie de Noisy
    Batterie des Réservoirs

La place de Lyon, Le camp retranché de Lyon (1875-1893):

Fort de Bron
Fort de Bruissin
Fort de Champvillars
Fort de Chapoly
Fort Corbas
Fort de Feyzin
Fort de Genas
Fort de Meyzieu
Fort de Montcorin
Fort du Mont Verdun
Fort du Paillet
Fort de Saint Genis
Fort de Saint Priest
Fort de Vancia
Batterie de Bruissin
Batterie des Carrière
Batterie de Décines
Batterie de la Freta
Batterie de Lassignas
Batterie du Montoux
Batterie du Narcel
Batterie de Neyron
Batterie de Parilly
Batterie de Sathonay
Batterie de Sermenaz

Appendix 3
Organization of *Le camp retranché de Verdun*

Originally the fortified zone of Verdun had been divided up into seven *secteurs*, however by 1914, the number of *secteurs* had been reduced to three. They were numbered clockwise, starting in the north from the River Meuse, the *1er secteur* followed by the *2e secteur* both being on the right (east) bank and with the *3e secteur* being the remaining area on the left (west) bank. The *secteurs* were then sub-divided into *groupes* based around the forts and the larger *ouvrages modernisée*. The *groupes*, again passing clockwise from the River Meuse in the north, were:

1er secteur, ligne principale de résistance
consisted of:
> groupe ouvrage de Froideterre
> groupe ouvrage de Thiaumont
> groupe fort de Douaumont
> groupe ouvrage d'Hardaumont
> groupe fort de Vaux
> groupe ouvrage de La Laufée & fort de Tavannes

1er secteur, ligne de soutien ou ligne intérieure
consisted of:
> groupe redoute de Belleville & redoute de Saint-Michel
> groupe redoute de Souville

2e secteur, ligne principale de résistance
consisted of:
> groupe fort de Moulainville
> groupe ouvrage de la Croix-Brandier & ouvrage de Déramé
> groupe ouvrage du Maubois
> groupe fort du Rozellier
> groupe ouvrage de Saint-Symphorien
> groupe fort d'Haudainville

2e secteur, ligne de soutien ou ligne intérieure
consisted of:
> groupe redoute de Belrupt

3e secteur, ligne principale de résistance

consisted of:

> *groupe ouvrage de La Falouse - redoutes de Duguy*
> *groupe fort de Landrecourt*
> *groupe redoute de Regret*
> *groupe ouvrage de Fromeréville – poste des Sartelles – poste de Chana*
>
> *groupe poste de Choisel*
> *groupe fort de Bois-Bourrus*
> *groupe redoute de Marre*
> *groupe poste de la Belle- Épine*
> *groupe ouvrage de Charny*[28]

3e secteur, ligne de soutien ou ligne intérieure

consisted of:

> *groupe redoute de La Chaume*

---

[28] As mentioned above the *fort de Vacherauville* was built upon the site of the *batterie de Charny* that was part of the *groupe ouvrage de Charny*. Therefore since the *groupe* name was already in existence before the *fort de Vacherauville* was built, the original name was kept.

Appendix 4A
Types of Fortifications

Forts	Forts
Forts d'arrêt	Arresting forts
Forts isolé	Isolated forts
Forts de liaison	Linking forts
Forts moderne	Modern forts
Forts de rideau	Curtain forts.
Vieux forts	Old forts
Redoutes	Redoubts
Ouvrages	Works
Ouvrages infanterie	Infantry field works
Ouvrages en terre de infanterie	Infantry earth works
Ouvrages modernisée	Modernized *ouvrages*
Abris	Shelters
Abris caverns	Underground shelters
Abris de combat	Combat shelters
Abris d'intervalle	Interval shelters
Abris du projecteur	Projector shelters
Batteries	Battery positions
Postes	Artillery posts
Poste Photo-Électrique	Electric searchlight post
Retranchements	Trenches
Retranchements de campagne	Field trenches
Retranchements d'infanterie	Infantry trenches

Appendix 4B
Designation of the Fortifications

The *forts, redoubts, ouvrages, postes,* and *abris cavernes* were all named after local geographical locations and features, for example villages and woods, whereas the *casernes* were also named after individuals, for example, the *fort de Vaux*, and the *Casernes Marceau* respectively. Key *ouvrages* were also given a letter designation in addition to their name for example, the *ouvrage de Froideterre* was designated '*ouvrage A*' and the *ouvrage de Eix* was '*ouvrage E*' – the sequence started at the *ouvrage de Froideterre* and went clockwise around the fortified zone. There were however a couple of *ouvrages* that were given designation letters later, and therefore were out of sequence with the others, as per the *ouvrage de Bezonvaux* which is positioned between the above mentioned *ouvrages* was '*ouvrage O*'. For the names and designations of the *ouvrages* see Appendix 6.

Originally the *batteries* where generally given names, often the same name as the fort that they were supporting or covering, and often with a added prefix sequence number or letter if there was more than one. Sometimes where the *batteries* were located independently of a fort they, like the forts, were given the name of a local feature. As examples, the *batterie n° 1 de Vaux* and the *batterie n° 2 de Vaux* covered the *fort de Vaux*, whilst the *batterie de Damloup* close by, covered the *ravin de Damloup*.

However, in 1908 all the *batteries* were given a number designation in addition to their names. The *batterie de Damloup*, for instance, was given the designation *batterie 6.1*. The *batteries*' designation numbers, within a *secteur*, consisted of a *Centres de résistance* number (normally a major fortifications such as the *ouvrage de Froideterre*) followed by an individual sequence number. As an example, in the *1er secteur*, the *batterie 1.1* and the *batterie 1.2* were positioned to cover the *ouvrage de Froideterre*. The *batteries* designation numbers would therefore be repeated in each *Secteur*. So that in the *2e secteur*, there were also the *batterie 1.1* and the *batterie 1.2* positioned to cover the *fort de Moulainville*.

Newer *batteries* built after 1908 (including the ad hoc wartime built *batterie* positions) were given the next sequence number in line with the 1908 numbering system or in some cases during the war years given the same number as a related *batterie* with the suffix *bis* (repetition or replica). The wartime built *batteries 2.7, 2.8* and *2.9* in the *2e secteur* or the *batteries 2.3bis* and *2.5bis* in the *1er secteur* are examples of the later numbering system, none of which were given official names.

To add to the confusion over *batteries* numbers, during the course of the Great War plans for new defence layouts that included planned *batteries* positions (most of which were never built) were made and often used a simplified sequence numbering system without reference to the *Centres de résistance*, but still grouping them within the *secteurs*. The *batterie de Damloup*, for instance, was referred to as number 34 in the 1915 plans, as well as its original number *batterie 6.1*.

All the *magasin à poudre de secteurs* were named like the *forts* after nearby local features. They were also given a sequence number, prefixed with the letter 'M' for example *Magasin à Poudre de Secteur de Fleury* being designated '*M8*'. Like the *batteries*, there was yet more confusion over the naming of the *Magasin à Poudre de Secteur* – some had been given common names, which became to be used officially on maps etc. an example of which is the above mentioned *Magasin à Poudre de Secteur de Fleury* '*M8*' being commonly known as '*la Poudrière*' and was shown as such on wartime trench maps. For names and designation of the *magasins à poudre de secteur* see Appendix 7.

The *dépôts intermédiaire* were simply given a lower case letter (the *dépôt* behind the *fort de Souville*, located on the opposite side of the *route militaire*, being designated '*b*' and that located on the other side of the road from the *batterie du Tunnel* being ' *i*'.)

The *abris de combat* (being late additions to the fortified zones) were given alphanumeric designation in 1909, made up of the initial letters of the principle fortifications that they were positioned between, followed by a sequence number, hence the four *abris de combat* between the *fort de Douaumont* and the *fort de Vaux* were designated '*DV1*', '*DV2*', '*DV3*' and '*DV4*', '*DV1*' being the closest to the *fort de Douaumont*.

The wartime *Postes de Commandement* (Command Posts) were normally established just behind the front lines. These were situated in ad hoc locations where existing shelters could be utilized or new dugouts could be built without too much interference from the Germans. The *abri de combat* were often utilised in this way and were given a wartime sequence number preceded by *PC*. For example '*PC118*' was established in the *abri de combat* '*FT3*'; '*PC119*' in the *abri de combat* '*FT2*' and '*PC120*' in the *abri de combat* '*FT1*'.

The *retranchements d'infanterie* appear not to have been assigned official designations before the war, presumably being seen as part of an existing fortification (a fort or an *abri de combat*) and therefore coming under the designation of the said fortification. However when the war stagnated and they became occupied by the infantry, they were given designations by the local commanders, who followed no set pattern. Like the wartime ad hoc trenches all along the western front there was no real set pattern for their designations; they were given names, sequence numbers or letters, sometime with the prefix 'R' (*retranchements*) – for examples: the pre-war built *retranchements* were given names such as '*Retranchement*

'*R2*'[29] (located in front of the *abri de combat 'DV3'*) and '*Retranchement X*' (covering the *abri de combat FT1*), however the wartime built (1917) trench in front of the *abri de combat MF1* was known as '*Retranchement Roi de Prusse*'.

The *ouvrages en terre de infanterie*, like all other *ouvrages*, were given names based on their geographical location. For example: the *ouvrage d'Hardaumont* had three new *ouvrages en terre de infanterie* (the only ones to be constructed at Verdun) to supplement it and these were given the names - the *ouvrage de Lorient,* the *ouvrage de Josémont* and the *ouvrage du Muguet.* In the case of these three *ouvrages*, they were not given a supplemental letter designation.

The defensive structures built during the war to supplement the forts (the *casemates Pamards* and the *Blockhaus bétonné*) were grouped together, based on the fort that they were built to defend, and given the fort name followed by the designation 'M' with a sequence number, for example '*fort de Tavannes* M1'. Out of interest, the *fort de Tavannes* was due to have five defensive structures built in 1918 numbered 'M1' to 'M5', however, the war finished before 'M2' and 'M3' could be constructed, but the original planned numbering sequence was not changed, so that the two *casemates Pamards* carried the numbers 'M1' and 'M4' whilst the *Blockhaus bétonné* 'M5'.

---

[29] Note that *Colonel* Driant's wartime-built *Poste de commandement* in the *Bois des Caures* well to the north of *Le camp retranché de Verdun*, was also known as '*R2*' - being the second of a group of five - '*R1*' to '*R5*'.

Appendix 5
Dates of Construction and Modifications of the Principal Fortifications of *Le camp retranché de Verdun*

(in chronological order - The *cote* (altitude) of the principal fortification is shown in metres above mean sea level)

Redoute de Belleville (cote 299) .... 1875-9 (not modernized)

Redoute de Belrupt (cote 347) .... 1875-7 (not modernized)

Redoutes de Duguy (cote 290) .... 1875-7 modernized 1901-2 & 1908

Redoute de La Chaume (cote 320.5) .... 1875-7 (not modernized)

Redoute de Marre (cote 297.9) .... 1875-8 modernized 1888-9& 1905-6

Redoute de Regret (cote 318) .... 1875-7 modernized 1906-1909

Redoute de Saint-Michel (cote 351) .... 1875-7 (not modernized)

Fort d'Haudainville (cote 344) .... 1876-9 modernized 1900-1902

Fort du Rozellier (cote 393) .... 1877-9 modernized 1890, 1902, 1904 & 1913

Fort de Bois-Bourrus (cote 310.3) .... 1881-7 modernized 1892-1894, 1904-7 & 1913-4

Fort de Vaux (cote 350) .... 1881-4 modernized 1888-1895, 1904-6 & 1910-2

Poste des Sartelles (cote 315) .... 1881-4 modernized 1894-7& 1904-6

Fort de Landrecourt (cote 330) .... 1883-6 modernized 1891 & 1904-6

Fort de Moulainville (cote 372) .... 1883-5 modernized 1889-1891 & 1905-9

Poste de la Belle- Épine (cote 298) .... 1883-6 (not modernized)

Poste du Chana (cote 285.5) .... 1883-4 modernized 1906-1911

Poste de Choisel (cote 288.6) .... 1883-5 modernized 1891-7 & 1906-12

Ouvrage de la Croix-Brandier (cote 358) .. 1883 (not modernized)

Fort de Tavannes (cote 369) .... 1884-93 modernized 1902

Fort de Douaumont (cote 395.5) .... 1885-91 modernized 1897-1899, 1901-3,1907-9 & 1911-3

Redoute de Souville (cote 388) ....1885-9 modernized 1888-
1889[30]

Batterie de Charny/fort de Vacherauville. 1887; rebuilt as a fort 1908-10
(*cote* 260)

Ouvrage de Charny (cote 245) ....1887-8 modernized 1902-1904

Ouvrage de Déramé (cote 374) ....1887-8 modernized 1902-1903

Ouvrage de Froideterre (cote 345) ....1887-8 modernized 1902-1905

Ouvrage de Fromeréville (cote 280) ....1887-8 modernized 1900

Ouvrage d'Hardaumont (cote 339)............1887-93 (not modernized)

Ouvrage de La Laufée (cote 336) ....1887-8 modernized 1904-6 &
1913-4

Ouvrage de Thiaumont (cote 320)..............1887-93 modernized 1902-1905

Ouvrage de Saint-Symphorien (cote 357)..1888-9 modernized 1900 &
1902

Ouvrage du Maubois (cote 380).................1889-90 (not modernized)

Ouvrage de La Falouse (cote 237).............1906 (built as modern type)

Réduit central – la Citadelle 1887

---

[30] The external *tourelle de 155mm (T155L) Bussière* was added in 1890-1 and was
given the designation *Batterie 8.2.*

Appendix 6
Ouvrages of *Le camp retranché de Verdun*

(listed clockwise from the *Ouvrage de Froideterre* and showing their
designated letters and if they were modernized or not)

Ouvrage de Froideterre	*Ouvrage A*	(modernized)
Ouvrage de Thiaumont	*Ouvrage B*	(modernized)
Ouvrage de Bezonvaux	*Ouvrage O*	(non-modernized)
Ouvrage de Lorient	*not designated*	(built c1912)[31]
Ouvrage de Josémont	*not designated*	(built c1912)[31]
Ouvrage du Muguet	*not designated*	(built c1912)[31]
Ouvrage d'Hardaumont	*Ouvrage C*	(non-modernized)
Ouvrage de La Laufée	*Ouvrage D*	(modernized)
Ouvrage d'Eix	*Ouvrage E*	(non-modernized)
Ouvrage de la Croix-Brandier	not designated	(non-modernized)
Ouvrage de Manesel	*Ouvrage F*	(non-modernized)
Ouvrage de Déramé	not designated	(modernized)
Ouvrage de Châtillon	*Ouvrage G*	(non-modernized)
Ouvrage du Maubois	not designated	(non-modernized)
Ouvrage de Jaulny	*Ouvrage P*	(non-modernized)
Ouvrage du Bois-Réunis	not designated	(non-modernized)
Ouvrage de Saint-Symphorien	*Ouvrage H*	(modernized)
Ouvrage de La Falouse	not designated	(built 1906)
Ouvrage du Trimard	not designated	(Abandoned 1910)
Ouvrage de Bois-Rogé	not designated	(Abandoned 1910)
Ouvrage de Thierville	not designated	(non-modernized)
Ouvrage du Bois du Chapitre	*Ouvrage I*	(non-modernized)
Ouvrage du Bois Saint-Maure	not designated	(non-modernized)
Ouvrage de Baleycourt	*Ouvrage J*	(non-modernized)
Ouvrage de Fromeréville	*Ouvrage K*	(non-modernized)
Ouvrage de Germonville	*Ouvrage L*	(non-modernized)
Ouvrage de Bruyères	*Ouvrage M*	(non-modernized)
Ouvrage de Charny	*Ouvrage N*	(modernized)

---

[31] These three *ouvrages* – the *ouvrage de Lorient*, the *ouvrage de Josémont* and the *ouvrage du Muguet* - were built as *ouvrages en terre de infanterie*.

Appendix 7
Names and Designation of the *Magasins à Poudre de Secteur* of *Le camp retranché de Verdun*

(numerically by designation)

Magasin à Poudre de Secteur de Madeleine *M1*
Built 1892 modified 1898
Magasin à Poudre de Secteur de la Renarderie *M2*
Built 1888 modified 1906
Magasin à Poudre de Secteur de la Renarderie *M3*
Built 1889 modified 1906
Magasin à Poudre de Secteur de la Beholle *M4*
Built 1889 modified 1897
Magasin à Poudre de Secteur du Champ de la Gaille *M5*
Built 1890 modified 1898
Magasin à Poudre de Secteur de Lombut *M6*
Built 1890 modified 1906
Magasin à Poudre de Secteur de Saint-Michel *M7*
Built 1888 modified 1906
Magasin à Poudre de Secteur de Fleury [32] *M8*
Built 1910

---

[32] Commonly known as the '*la Poudrière*'.

Appendix 8
Abris de Combat Designations of *Le camp retranché de Verdun*
(listed clockwise from the Meuse)

Meuse-Froideterre: .... *MF 1* and *MF 2*
Froideterre-Thiaumont: .... *FT 1*, *FT 2* and *FT 3*
Thiaumont-Douaumont: .... *TD 1*, *TD 2* and *TD 3*
Douaumont-Vaux: .... *DV 1*, *DV 2*, *DV 3* and *DV 4*
Vaux-La Laufée: .... *VLL 1*
La Laufée-Moulainville: .... *LLM 1* and *LLM 2*
Moulainville-Déramé: .... *MD 1* and *MD 2*
Déramé-Rozelier: .... *DR 1*
Rozelier-St. Symphorien: .... *RSS 1* and *RSS 2*
St. Symphorien-Haudainville: .... *SSH 1*
Haudainville-La Falouse: .... *HLF 1*
La Falouse-Dugny: .... *LFD 1* and *LFD 2*
Dugny-Landrecourt: .... *DL 1* and *DL 2*
Landrecourt-Regret: .... *LR 1* and *LR 2*
Regret-Les Sartelles: .... *RS 1* and *RS 2*
Choisel-Bois Bourrus: .... *CBB 1* and *CBB 2*
Bois Bourrus-Marre: .... *BBM 1*
Marre-Belle Epine: .... *MBE 1*

Appendix 9
Total Costs of the Principal Fortifications of
Le camp retranché de Verdun
(land acquisition, original construction costs, modification costs and
armaments, but excluding wartime modifications) in order of cost

Fort de Douaumont ....6,100,000 *Francs d'Or*[33]
Fort du Rozellier ....4,500,000 *Francs d'Or*
Ouvrage de Saint-Symphorien ....4,000,000 *Francs d'Or*
Fort de Moulainville ....3,650,000 *Francs d'Or*
Fort de Bois-Bourrus ....2,950,000 *Francs d'Or*
Fort de Vaux ....2,900,000 *Francs d'Or*
Fort de Landrecourt ....2,750,000 *Francs d'Or*
Redoute de Souville ....2,650,000 *Francs d'Or*
Redoute de Regret ....2,600,000 *Francs d'Or*
Fort de Tavannes ....2,500,000 *Francs d'Or*
Redoute de Marre ....2,500,000 *Francs d'Or*
Fort d'Haudainville ....2,400,000 *Francs d'Or*
Fort de Vacherauville ....2,400,000 *Francs d'Or*
Redoutes de Duguy ....2,200,000 *Francs d'Or*
Redoute de Belrupt ....1,600,000 *Francs d'Or*
Redoute de La Chaume ....1,300,000 *Francs d'Or*
Poste de Choisel ....1,300,000 *Francs d'Or*
Poste du Chana ....1,150,000 *Francs d'Or*
Ouvrage de Froideterre ....1,100,000 *Francs d'Or*
Poste des Sartelles ....1,100,000 *Francs d'Or*
Ouvrage de Déramé ....1,000,000 *Francs d'Or*
Ouvrage de Charny ....935,000 *Francs d'Or*
Ouvrage de La Laufée ....900,000 *Francs d'Or*

---

[33] For a breakdown in the costs of typical *forts*:

Fort de Douaumont
Original Cost ....4,100,000 *Francs d'Or*
Cost of Modifications ....2,000,000 *Francs d'Or*

Total Cost ....6,100,000 *Francs d'Or*

Redoute de Souville
Original Cost ....1,100,000 *Francs d'Or*
Cost of Modifications ....1,550,000 *Francs d'Or*

Total Cost ....2,650,000 *Francs d'Or*

Ouvrage de La Falouse ....550,000 *Francs d'Or*
Redoute de Belleville ....450,000 *Francs d'Or*
Redoute de Saint-Michel ....450,000 *Francs d'Or*
Ouvrage de Thiaumont ....410,000 *Francs d'Or*
Poste de la Belle-Épine ....400,000 *Francs d'Or*
Ouvrage de la Croix-Brandier ....(approx) 302,000 *Francs d'Or*
Ouvrage de Fromeréville ....(approx) 302,000 *Francs d'Or*
Ouvrage d'Hardaumont ....(approx) 302,000 *Francs d'Or*
Ouvrage du Maubois ....(approx) 302,000 *Francs d'Or*

Réduit central – la Citadelle ....1,900,000 *Francs d'Or*

Appendix 10
Manpower Requirements for the Principal Fortifications of *Le camp retranché de Verdun*

(total garrison sizes, officers and other ranks, as originally planned followed by the 1917 garrison sizes - in wartime garrison size order)

	Planned	2 August 1914	Mid War[34]
Fort de Douaumont	484	648	320
Fort de Vaux	157	157	270
Fort de Moulainville	334	171	230
Fort du Rozellier	127	257	200
Fort de Tavannes	761	160	160
Fort de Bois-Bourrus	198	197	150
Redoute de La Chaume	208	150	150
Redoute de Marre	416	224	150
Redoute de Souville	314	213	150
Fort de Vacherauville	250	202	150
Fort de Landrecourt	263	169	140
Redoute de Belrupt	298	130	130
Ouvrage de La Laufée	100	81	120
Poste de la Belle- Épine	89	100	100
Ouvrage de Charny	122	140	100
Ouvrage de Déramé	100	148	100
Poste des Sartelles	116	86	100
Ouvrage de Froideterre	100	77	90
Redoute de Saint-Michel	160	90	90
Redoute de Belleville	164	80	80
Redoute de Regret	132	237	80
Poste de Choisel	158	74	70
Redoutes de Duguy	252	217	70
Ouvrage de La Falouse	110	68	70
Poste du Chana	105	104	50
Fort d'Haudainville	233	159	50
Ouvrage de Saint-Symphorien	100	50	50
Ouvrage de Thiaumont	100	76	76

---

[34] Wartime garrison sizes varied based on the then current G.Q.G. thinking. For example at the time of the capture of the fort *de Douaumont* on 26th February 1916, the garrison consisted of *Maréchal des Logis-Chef* (sergeant major) Chenot in command along with his 56 elderly territorials.

Ouvrage de la Croix-Brandier............ 100................(1/2 infantry company)
Ouvrage de Fromeréville .... 100................(1/2 infantry company)
Ouvrage d'Hardaumont .... 100................(1/2 infantry company)
Ouvrage du Maubois .... 100................(1/2 infantry company)

Réduit central – la Citadelle .... 71,000 [35].......2000................ 2000+

---

[35] The *Réduit central – la Citadelle* as noted above was designed and built as a huge underground barracks large enough to give shelter to 71,000 men plus the entire civil population of Verdun.

Appendix 11A
Types of Armament Used within the
Fortifications[36]

Initially the fortifications were armed with standard French Army field weapons that were in service during that period, for example. The cannons being those in use with the heavy and medium artillery regiments. However, with time special fortress weapons were developed and were incorporated into the fortifications.[37]

The main armament of the fortifications up to circa 1900 (i.e. pre-turrets) consisted mainly of the following weapon types:

Canon de 'De Bange'[38] 90mm modèle 1877....................range 6,900m[39]
Canon de 'Lahitolle' 95mm modèle 1888 ....range 9,800m
Canon de 'De Bange' 120mm longue modèle 1878 ....range 8,200m[40]
Canon de 'De Bange' 155mm longue[41] modèle 1877......range 9,000m[42]

---

[36] Not all of the armaments listed in this appendix were used at Verdun, see Appendix 10B and 10C: Main Armament for the Principal Fortifications of *Le camp retranché de Verdun.*

[37] Before the advent of specialised fortress cannons the field cannons in use in the forts were modified simply by having their wooden wheels with steel tyres replaced with non-wooden, steel tired wheels, since the fortress guns were to be used upon prepared gunnery platforms.

[38] The cannon designations often included the name of the designer – Baquet; De Bange; Lahitolle; Reffye and Rimailho. However the designer of the *Canon de 75mm Tir Rapide,* Colonel Albert Deport's name was not included in the designation of his cannon probably since he was working for the government armaments factory at Puteaux. In the case of the *Canon de 'Schneider' 150mm* the designation derived from the name of the manufacturer *Schneider et Compagnie.* Finally the *Canon revolver de 40mm Hotchkiss* and the *Mitrailleuse de 8mm Hotchkiss* had their designation derived from the manufacturer *Société Anonyme des Anciens Établissements Hotchkiss et Compagnie.*

[39] The range of the *De Bange 90 mm* was the initial range, however with the use of modern propellants developed towards the end of the nineteenth century the range was increased to 9,700m.

[40] The initial range of the *De Bange 120mm longue* could be increased to a maximum of 9,000m by artificially increasing the elevation to 33°. With the use of modern propellants developed towards the end of the nineteenth century the range was increase still further to 11,200m.

[41] The French Army during this period did not use the term 'Howitzer'; instead they used the generic term '*Canon*' for all artillery pieces. To differentiate between a gun and a howitzer, the terms '*longue*' (long) and '*court*' (short) were used with regard to the barrel length – the shorter barrel weapon being the howitzer.

Canon de 'De Bange' 150mm court[41] *modèle 1881* ....range 6,300m
Mortier de 'De Bange' 220mm modèle 1880 [43] ....range 5,260m

In addition to the above weapons there were a whole diversity of older cannons and mortars (some of which were modified) with calibres up to 320mm, the following being the most commonly used:

Canon de 'Reffye' 138 mm court modèle 1816
                     modifiée 1874.................range 7,770m
Canon de 220 mm court modèle 1827 modifiée 1864......range 4,800m
Canon de 240 mm modèle 1876 ....range 13,450m
Canon de 270 mm modèle 1870 ....range 11,200m

The secondary armaments for the defence of the forts, which relied on the *fossés*, were initially protected by small arms (rifles) and early machine guns of the Gatlin gun type along with some old breach loading cannons of 45mm and 70mm calibres. However from 1880 the following two special weapons were developed and assigned, which replaced the earlier breach loading cannons:

Canon revolver de 40mm Hotchkiss modèle 1879 ....range 500m
Canon de 12-culasse modèle 1858 modifiée 1880...........range 300m

With the introduction from 1885 of the turrets and casemates including the *coffres–* the *following* weapons were introduced as follows:

Mitrailleuse de 8mm Hotchkiss modèle1899...................range 2,000m[44]
Mitrailleuse de 8mm modèle 1907 transformée..............range 2,400m[45]
Canon de 'Maxim-Nordenfelt' 57mm CF
                     modèle 1889........... Range not known
[46]

Canon de 75mm tir rapide modèle 1897 on an *affût à pivot*
                     modèle 1900.................range 11,300m[47]
Canon de 75mm rapide modèle 75-02 ....range 8,200m[48]

---

[42] The initial range of the *De Bange 155mm longue* could be increased to a maximum of 12,700m with the use of modern propellants.

[43] *Mortier* translates as mortar.

[44] Used in the *tourelle de Mitrailleuse (GF4) modèle 1900*, the *caponnières* and the *coffres*.

[45] Used in the *casemate Pamard*. This weapon was commonly known as the *Mitrailleuse dit Saint Étienne*.

[46] Used in the *tourelle de 57mm (T57C) Galopin modèle 1889*.

[47] Used in the *casemate de Bourges*.

[48] Used in the *tourelle de 75mm (T75) Galopin modèle 1902*.

Canon de 'De Bange' 155mm longue modèle 1877 ....range 9,000m[49]
Canon de 'De Bange' 155mm longue S.P. modèle 1888. range 5,500m[50]
Canon de 'De Bange' 155mm raccourci modèle 1902.... range 9,800m[51]

From circa 1900, the *batteries* used the *'Lahitolle'* and *'De Bange'* weapons mention above as well as the following:

Canon de 75mm tir rapide modèle 1897 ....range 11,300m
Canon de 'Baquet' 120mm court modèle 1890.................range 5,800m
Canon de 'Schneider' 155mm longue modèle 1877 ....range 13,600m
Canon de 'Baquet' 155mm court modèle 1890.................range 6,300m
Canon de 'Rimailho' 155mm court tir rapide
                    modèle 1904 ....range 6,285m

Finally the following weapons were used on the *affûts trucks* of the *voie ferré de 0.6m*:

Canon de 'De Bange' 120mm court modèle 1878 ....range 5,800m
Canon de 'De Bange' 155mm court modèle 1881
                    modifiée 1912.................range 6,300m

---

[49] Used in the *casemate de Mougin* and the *tourelle de 155mm Mougin modèle 1885.*
[50] Used in the *tourelle de 155mm (T155L) Bussière modèle 1888.*
[51] Used in the *tourelle de 155mm (T155R) Galopin modèle 1907.*

Appendix 11B
Comparison of the Main Armament for the Principal Fortifications of *Le camp retranché de Verdun* as per the original design requirements

Ouvrage de Froideterre...Infantry small arms

Ouvrage de Thiaumont ....Infantry small arms

Fort de Douaumont ....8 x 120mm
2 x 95mm
2 mortars

Ouvrage de Bezonvaux ....Infantry small arms

Ouvrage d'Hardaumont ....Infantry small arms

Fort de Vaux...5 x 95mm cannons

Ouvrage d'Eix ....Infantry small arms

Ouvrage de La Laufee ....Infantry small arms

Fort de Tavannes ....2 x 155mm
4 x 120mm

Redoute de Belleville ....2 x 155mm
2 x 120mm
2 x 95mm

Redoute de Saint-Michel ....3 x 155mm
2 x 120mm

Redoute de Souville ....9 x 155mm
7 x 120mm
4 x 95mm

Fort de Moulainville...8 x 95mm

Ouvrage de Manesel ....Infantry small arms

Ouvrage de la Croix-Brandier ....Infantry small arms

Ouvrage de Châtillon ....Infantry small arms

Ouvrage de Déramé ....Infantry small arms

Ouvrage du Maubois ....Infantry small arms

Ouvrage de Jaulny ....Infantry small arms

Fort du Rozellier ....4 x 120mm
4 x 95mm

Ouvrage du Bois-Réunis ....Infantry small arms

Ouvrage de Saint-Symphorien ....Infantry small arms

Ouvrage du Trimard ....Infantry small arms
(Abandoned 1910)

Fort d'Haudainville ....1 x 155mm

Ouvrage de Bois-Rogé ....Infantry small arms
(Abandoned 1910)

Redoute de Belrupt ....5 x 120mm

Redoutes de Duguy ....unknown

Ouvrage de Thierville ....Infantry small arms

Fort de Landrecourt ....unknown

Ouvrage du Bois du Chapitre ....Infantry small arms

Ouvrage du Bois Saint- Maure ....Infantry small arms

Ouvrage de Baleycourt ....Infantry small arms

Redoute de Regret ....unknown

Ouvrage de Fromeréville ....Infantry small arms

Poste des Sartelles .... unknown

Poste du Chana .... unknown

Ouvrage de Germonville .... Infantry small arms

Poste de Choisel .... unknown

Ouvrage de Bruyères .... Infantry small arms

Fort de Bois-Bourrus .... unknown

Redoute de Marre .... 4 x 120mm
                                                                                          2 x 95mm

Poste de la Belle- Épine .... 8 x 120mm

Ouvrage de Charny .... Infantry small arms

Redoute de La Chaume .... unknown

Réduit central – la Citadelle .... 4 x 120mm

Appendix 11C
Comparison of the Main Armament for the Principal Fortifications of *Le camp retranché de Verdun* as required for the period just before the war
(as listed in 1912)

Ouvrage de Froideterre....................................2 x 75mm
(1 tourelle T75)
2 x 75mm
(1 Casemates de Bourges)
4 x mitrailleuse
(2 tourelles GF4)

Ouvrage de Thiaumont....................................2 x 75mm
(1 Casemates de Bourges)
2 x mitrailleuse
(1 Tourelle GF4)

Fort de Douaumont ....1 x 155mm
(1 tourelles T155R)
2 x 75mm
(1 tourelle T75)
2 x 75mm
(1 Casemates de Bourges)
4 x mitrailleuse
(2 tourelles GF4)

Ouvrage de Bezonvaux ....Infantry small arms

Ouvrage de Lorient [52] ....Infantry small arms

Ouvrage de Josémont[52]..................................Infantry small arms

Ouvrage du Muguet [52] ....Infantry small arms

Ouvrage d'Hardaumont ....Infantry small arms

---

[52] The *ouvrage de Lorient,* the ouvrage *de Josémont* and the *ouvrage du Muguet* were all built as *ouvrages en terre de infanterie* in 1912.

Fort de Vaux..2 x 75mm
(1 tourelle T75)
4 x 75mm
(2 Casemates de Bourges)
4 x mitrailleuse
(2 tourelles GF4)

Ouvrage d'Eix ....Infantry small arms

Ouvrage de La Laufée ....2 x 75mm
(1 tourelle T75)

Fort de Tavannes ....10 x 90mm

Redoute de Belleville ....6 x 90mm

Redoute de Saint-Michel ....6 x 90mm

Redoute de Souville ....6 x 90mm[53]

Fort de Moulainville.......................................1 x 155mm
(1 tourelles T155R)
2 x 75mm
(1 tourelle T75)
2 x 75mm
(1 Casemates de Bourges)
4 x mitrailleuse
(2 tourelles GF4)

Ouvrage de Manesel ....Infantry small arms

Ouvrage de la Croix-Brandier.......................Infantry small arms

Ouvrage de Déramé.......................................4 x 75mm
(2 Casemates de Bourges)
2 x mitrailleuse
(1 tourelles GF4)

Ouvrage de Châtillon ....Infantry small arms

[53] The *Batterie 8.2* that had the *Redoute de Souville's* external *tourelle de 155mm (T155L) Bussière* (2 x 155mm) is not included here, although it was grouped in with the same modernization program as for the rest of the fort and formed an integral part of the fort defences it was regarded as independent.

Ouvrage du Maubois ....Infantry small arms

Ouvrage de Jaulny ....Infantry small arms

Fort du Rozellier...1 x 155mm
(1 tourelles T155R)
4 x 75mm
(2 Casemates de Bourges)
4 x mitrailleuse
(2 tourelles GF4)

Ouvrage du Bois-Réunis ....Infantry small arms

Ouvrage de Saint-Symphorien........................2 x 75mm
(1 Casemates de Bourges)

Fort d'Haudainville..4 x 95mm
(2 Casemates de Bourges)
4 x mitrailleuse
(2 tourelles GF4)

Redoute de Belrupt ....4 x 90mm
4 x 120mm

Ouvrage de La Falouse[54] ....2 x 75mm
(1 tourelles T75)
2 x mitrailleuse
(1 tourelles GF4)

Redoutes de Duguy ....2 x 75mm
(1 tourelles T75)
2 x 75mm
(1 Casemates de Bourges)
4 x mitrailleuse
(2 tourelles GF4)

Ouvrage de Thierville ....Infantry small arms

---

[54] The *Ouvrage de La Falouse* being completed in 1906 had its designed armaments in keeping with later concepts as seen in the later fort modifications.

Fort de Landrecourt ....2 x 75mm
(1 tourelles T75)
2 x 75mm
(1 Casemates de Bourges)
4 x mitrailleuse
(2 tourelles GF4)

Ouvrage du Bois du Chapitre ....Infantry small arms

Ouvrage du Bois Saint- Maure ....Infantry small arms

Ouvrage de Baleycourt ....Infantry small arms

Redoute de Regret..4 x 75mm
(2 tourelles T75)
2 x 75mm
(1 Casemates de Bourges)
4 x mitrailleuse
(2 tourelles GF4)

Ouvrage de Fromeréville ....Infantry small arms

Poste des Sartelles ....4 x 75mm
(2 Casemates de Bourges)
4 x mitrailleuse
(2 tourelles GF4)

Poste du Chana..2 x 75mm
(1 tourelles T75)

Ouvrage de Germonville ....Infantry small arms

Poste de Choisel..4 x 75mm
(2 tourelles T75)
2 x 75mm
(1 Casemates de Bourges)
4 x mitrailleuse
(2 tourelles GF4)

Ouvrage de Bruyères ....Infantry small arms

Fort de Bois-Bourrus..2 x 75mm
(1 tourelles T75)
4 x 75mm
(2 Casemates de Bourges)
6 x mitrailleuse
(3 tourelles GF4)

Redoute de Marre ....2 x 75mm
(1 tourelles T75)

Poste de la Belle- Épine ....Infantry small arms

Fort de Vacherauville[55] 2 x155mm
(2 tourelle T155R)
2 x 75mm
(1 tourelles T75)
2 x mitrailleuse
(1 tourelle GF4)

Ouvrage de Charny ....2 x 75mm
(1 Casemates de Bourges)
2 x mitrailleuse
(1 tourelles GF4)

Redoute de La Chaume....................................2 x 95mm

Réduit central – la Citadelle ....4 x 120mm

---

[55] The *Fort de Vacherauville* being completed in 1912 had its designed armaments in keeping with later concepts as seen in the later fort modifications.

Appendix 12A
The Costs of the *Tourelles Fixes, Tourelles à Éclipse* and *Casemates de Bourges*[56]

Observatoires cuirassé: fixe- cloche Digoin .... 7,000 *Francs d'Or*

Tourelle de mitrailleuses (GF4), modèle 1900 .... 22,000 *Francs d'Or*

Tourelle de 57mm (T57CF) Galopin, modèle 1890[57] ...200,000 *Francs d'Or*

Tourelle de 75mm (T75) Galopin, modèle 1902 ....140,000 *Francs d'Or*

Tourelle de 155mm Mougin, modèle 1885[58] ....205,000 *Francs d'Or*

Coupole de 155mm Châtillon-Commentry, modèle 1888[57]
.... unknown

Coupole de 155mm de Saint Chamond, modèle 1888[57]
.....................................103,380 *Francs d'Or*

Tourelle de 155mm (T155L) Bussière, modèle 1888 ....260,000 *Francs d'Or*

Tourelle de 155mm (T155R) Galopin, modèle 1903[58] .800,000 *Francs d'Or*

Tourelle de 155mm (T155R) Galopin, modèle 1907 ....500,000 *Francs d'Or*

Cave à Canon [57] .... unknown

Casemate de Mougin, modèle 1876[57] .... unknown

Casemate de Bourges, modèle 1895 .... 50,000 *Francs d'Or*

Cloche Digoin (*Observatoire cuirassé fixe*) .... 1,500 *Francs d'Or*

---

[56] Prices are based on the cost at the time of construction.
[57] Not use in la *camp retranché de Verdun.*
[58] Only the cost of the turret is shown here. The cost of the structure that it sat was another 60,000 *Francs d'Or* - a total of 265,000 *Francs d'Or.*

Appendix 12B
Total Costs of the *Tourelles à Éclipse* and *Casemates de Bourges* for the *camp retranché de Verdun*

Total Cost for all the *Tourelles à Éclipse*...................5,450,000 *Francs d'Or*

Total Cost for all the *Casemates de Bourges*.............1,150,000 *Francs d'Or*

Total Cost for all the *Tourelles* and *Casemates*.... <u>6,600,000 *Francs d'Or*</u>

Appendix 13
The Principle Manufacturers of all the Fortifications and the Associated Equipment 1874 – 1914

(factory location within brackets)

Ateliers et Chantiers de la Loire (Saint Denis sur Seine, Paris)

Ateliers de Puteaux (Puteaux, Paris)

Compagnie des Fives-Lille pour Construction Mécaniques et Entreprises (Lille, Norde Pas de Calais)

Compagnie des Forges et Aciéries de Marine et d'Homécourt (Saint Chamond, Rhône-Alpes)

Compagnie des Forges de Châtillon, Commentry et Neuves-Maisons (Montluçon, Auvergne)

Établissements Decauville Aîné (Corbeil, Champagne-Ardenne)

Établissements Delaunay–Belleville (Longwy, Lorraine)

Établissements Marrel Frères (Rive de Gier et Saint Etienne, Rhône-Alpes)

Schneider et Compagnie (Le Creusot, Pays de la Loire)

Société Anonyme des Anciens Établissements Hotchkiss et Compagnie (Saint-Denis sur Seine, Paris)

Société de Construction de Batignolles (Nantes, Pays de la Loire)

Société des Établissements Cail (Paris)

Appendix 14
Major Wartime Additions to the Principal Fortifications of *Le camp retranché de Verdun*
(as of November, 1918)

Ouvrage de Froideterre..no wartime additions
Ouvrage de Thiaumont..no wartime additions
Fort de Douaumont ....no wartime additions
Ouvrage d'Hardaumont ....no wartime additions
Fort de Vaux..no wartime additions
Ouvrage de La Laufée ....no wartime additions
Fort de Tavannes ....2 x *Casemates Pamards double*
1 x *Blockhaus bétonné*
Redoute de Belleville ....no wartime additions
Redoute de Saint-Michel ....1 x *Casemates Pamards double*
Redoute de Souville ....3 x *Casemates Pamards double*
Fort de Moulainville...no wartime additions
Ouvrage de la Croix-Brandier....................................no wartime additions
Ouvrage de Déramé..no wartime additions
Ouvrage du Maubois ....no wartime additions
Fort du Rozellier..no wartime additions
Ouvrage de Saint-Symphorien ....no wartime additions
Fort d'Haudainville..no wartime additions
Redoute de Belrupt ....no wartime additions
Ouvrage de La Falouse ....no wartime additions
Redoutes de Duguy ....1 x *Casemates Pamards double*
1 x *Casemates Pamards simple*
Fort de Landrecourt ....1 x *Casemates Pamards simple*
Redoute de Regret..no wartime additions
Ouvrage de Fromeréville ....no wartime additions
Poste des Sartelles ....2 x *Casemates Pamards double*
Poste du Chana..2 x *Casemates*

	Pamards double
Poste de Choisel	2 x *Casemates*
	Pamards double
Fort de Bois-Bourrus	1 x *Casemates*
	Pamards double
Redoute de Marre	1 x *Casemates*
	Pamards double
Poste de la Belle- Épine	1 x *Casemates*
	Pamards double
Fort de Vacherauville	2 x *Casemates*
	Pamards double
Ouvrage de Charny	no wartime additions
Redoute de La Chaume	2 x *Casemates*
	Pamards double

Appendix 15
Summary of *Le camp retranché de Verdun*

In summary, there was within the fortified zone at the beginning of the Great War the following:

Forts and *redoutes* 17
(1 modern, 12 modernized and 4 non-modernized).
Ouvrages and *Postes* (modernized)...10
Ouvrages infanterie and *Postes* (non-modernized)............................17
Ouvrages en terre de infanterie 3
Batteries[59] 114
Abris cavernes – underground shelter (command posts) 3
Abris de combat (1 company) – combat shelter....................................16
Abris de combat (½ company) – combat shelter 18
Retranchements de campagne.. unknown
Abri du projecteur.. 3
Magasin de secteur – sector magazine.. 8
Dépôt intermédiaire - depot...25
Terrain d'aviation - airfield 1
Parc à dirigeables - balloon field... 1

The above included:

Tourelle de 155mm (T155R) – single 155mm gun turret...................... 5
Tourelle de 155mm (T155L) – twin 155mm guns turret 1
Tourelle de 75mm (T75) – twin 75mm guns turret..............................14
Cloches Digoin (Observatoire cuirassé fixe).......................................50
Petites cloches Digoin (Small Observatoire cuirassé fixe)..................42
Tourelle de mitrailleuse (GF4) – twin Hotchkiss mg turret 29
Casemate de Bourges – twin 75mm guns casemate..............................23

However by the end of the war the following had been added:

Casemates Pamards 22
(20 *Pamards double* and 2 *Pamards simple*)
Blockhaus bétonné 1

---

[59] In January 1915 the *batteries* had between them 384 cannons, which had increased to 407 cannons by December 1915. It has been stated that during the height of the battle in 1916, the number of *batteries* increased to 130 with 670 cannons. The figure shown above only includes the pre-war built *batteries*, but does not include the ad hoc positions set up during the war period.

Appendix 16
The *système Péchot* - French Military Railways[60]

The origins of the French military railways, commonly known as *la système Péchot*, dates from 1880 when an artillery officer *Capitaine* Prosper Péchot put forward the suggestion of utilising the *Decauville* commercial narrow gauge railway system for military use. Péchot inspiration came from the German Army who in 1876 had started to use permanent standard gauge railways for military purposes. As an artillery officer, his original scheme was for the transportation of artillery equipment – especially of the heavier calibre cannons, 155mm and larger, as well as the required munitions – into position upon any given battlefield quickly using a field railway. Although the German army had developed a military railway system before the French for the transportation of military personnel and equipment, they did not develop a field railway (*Feldbahn*) using narrow gauge track until 1888.

Péchot's ideas were based on the concept that battles tended to be fought wherever armies meet in the field and not normally on a predetermined, prepared battleground. The Battle of Verdun was unusual in this respect since it was a battle fought on a pre-planned battlefield. Infantry, cavalry and light field artillery could be manoeuvred into position on the field of battle with great ease, unlike the heavy artillery. Therefore he realised that the work of the *Régiments d'Artillerie à Pied* and *Régiments d'Artillerie de Lourde* (Foot Artillery Regiments and Heavy Artillery Regiments) in locating and operating their heavy artillery pieces in a battlefield situation (especially in the case of a siege) would be considerably helped by the use of light field railways. Light railways that could be quickly laid, used and then lifted, to be reused again in a different location.

Railways came in different gauges, so his choice of a *voie etroite* (narrow gauge railways) instead of the *voie normale* (standard gauge) of 1.435m (4 foot 8 ½ inches) for military use, were as follows:

1 Ease of construction, due to the lighter permanent ways thus avoiding the use of heavy construction equipment. Whereas standard gauge required heavier and therefore much more costly permanent ways necessitating the use of heavy construction machinery.

2 Speed of construction, using pre-assembled track pieces which during this period was not available in standard gauge. The lightweight track sections were light enough to be manhandled by the artillery

---

[60] Appendix 16 is based on information mainly from the French railway magazine "Voie Etroite".

personnel, again avoiding the use of heavier and slower transporting machinery.

3   The re-use of the pre-assembled track pieces in different locations, which meant overall flexibility and therefore cost reduction. The re-use of standard gauge track was possible, but was less feasible due to its overall size and weight, again requiring the heavy equipment.

4   Constructability in difficult terrain, especially in hilly or mountainous areas, due to the tighter curves. Narrow gauge locomotives and rolling stock could transverse much tighter radius curves then the larger standard gauge vehicles, which meant that geographical obstacles could be by-passed much more easily, and thus reducing the need for bridging and tunnelling. Whereas in the construction of a standard gauge system that required the use of much larger radius curves, the routing would not be able to avoid geographical obstacles, resulting in extensive bridging and tunnelling.

5   The overall cheapness of the construction of permanent way and the fabrication of rolling stock due to the smaller size.

As can be seen by the concepts above, Péchot's scheme was very much a temporary system – being laid when and where it was required, and then being reused elsewhere at a later date. The laying of a military railway system on a more permanent basis was not part of Péchot's original scheme.

The development of the *camps retranché* by *général* Séré de Rivières and the need to move the heavier artillery equipment between the fortifications and the *parcs d'Artillerie*, *magasins* and *dépôts* led to the idea of utilising *la système Péchot* on a permanent basis.

Péchot concluded that the optimum gauge for military use would be 0.6m (1 foot 11 ½ inches) – incidentally the same gauge as that chosen by the German army later, and although the French Army did use other gauges in a small number of locations, the 0.6m gauge became the standard that was adopted by the French Army. The *voie ferré de 0.6m* (0.6m railway) was officially called *Matériel Artillerie 1888* (Artillery Material 1888), however it was, as mentioned above, more generally referred to as *la système Péchot*.

The engineering firm of *Établissements Decauville Aîné* was one of a small number of companies that had foreseen the need for narrow gauge railways for all of the above reasons, but for civilian use. As such they specialized in the fabrication of narrow gauge railway equipment for the civil market. Their products ranged from steam locomotives and rolling stock, through to pre-assembled track pieces that could be easily transported and assembled on site. In effect their products were similar to an over-sized model train set. They fabricated their railway material to various track gauges starting from 0.4m.

In 1887, Péchot developed, with the aid of the specialist engineer Charles Bourdon, who had worked with *Decauville*, a small double-headed steam locomotive based on the design concept of the British engineer Robert Francis Fairlie. This Fairlie-type locomotive looked liked two locomotives joined back to back with a cabin in the middle and chimneys at each end. It consisted of two chassis each with a set of two pistons (four overall) powering four driving wheels (eight in all). The two chassis were linked together by a carrier frame that supported the two boilers, each one supplying the steam through a flexible pipe only to the pistons set below them. On each side of the boilers were positioned water tanks to supply the required water to produce the steam. The two fireboxes were positioned at the end of the boilers in the centre of the locomotive inside a common cabin, which gave the crew some protection from the elements.

Comparative tests were held on 28 April 1888 at the *fort de Lucey* and the *Ouvrage du Bouvron* (both part of *Le camp retranché de Toul*) between the *Péchot-Bourdon 0220 T* (British and American wheel notation 0-4-4-0T) prototype locomotive and the *Mallet Decauville 0220 T*. Whilst it was found that the *Decauville* product had better traction, the army decided to adopt the Péchot-Bourdon design probably due to the greater cost of the *Decauville* product. It became accepted into the army as the *Locomotive Péchot-Bourdon modèle 1888*.

The company of *Société des Établissements Cail* built the prototype *Locomotive Péchot-Bourdon* in 1887. They were then contracted to build another 19 machines for the army in 1888. In 1889, the army ordered 12 more machines from the firm of *Fives-Lille*, the last of which being delivered in 1890. Finally *Societe des Établissements Cail* was again asked by the army to produced a further 16 machines, which they did over the course of a 14 year period, between 1892 and 1906. Therefore at the start of the Great War the French army had 48 machines.

Once the war had started and with the expansion of the railway system to cover most of the war zones, another 280 machines were found to be required. They were ordered from the American firm of Baldwin Locomotive Works in 1915, the last one being delivered in 1916. There are two *Péchot-Bourdon 0220 T* that have survived. They have been preserved and are on show to the general public, however neither is located in France. The first is in the Museum Pozega, Pozega, Serbia – although built in 1916 it was not used by the French Army. The second was also built in 1916 (by the American Baldwin Locomotive Works) for the French Army and was given the French Army number 215. It is now preserved in the Verkehrsmuseum, Dresden, Germany.

The requirement for locomotives as well as other railway material was foreseen to be large in the even of war and so the French army would requisition compatible equipment from private firms to make up the numbers. In the event, even after the requisitioning, the need for locomotives became so great during the Great War, that other firms other than the original companies were contracted to supply the army with new locomotives. These firms produced locomotives and material to their own designs, which the army purchased through necessity.

The basis of the rolling stock was a series of 4, 6 and 8 wheel wagons that were basically bogies. These bogie wagons had a pivot-mounted platform upon a sprung suspended chassis. When used on their own they could carry 5, 9 and 12 tonnes respectively. However when coupled together, they could carry much greater loads, both in weight and size especially length (when four 8 wheel *wagons* were coupled together with a special coupling chassis they could carry a 48 tonnes cannon barrel, distributing the weight evenly over the 32 wheels which was important on the lightly laid track). There are a number of these bogie wagons that have survived in France; a couple of them can be seen resting on some *Decauville* track pieces located in the car park at the foot of the Butte de Vauquois (10 kilometres west of Verdun).

Apart from carrying small loads individually and the supporting of cannon barrels upon multiple bogie wagons where the barrel formed the connection between the bogies, Péchot designed specialised composite trucks that covered most of the artillery's requirements. These composite tracks utilised one or two bogie wagons with the truck body mounted onto the bogie's platform pivot. The smallest of these composite trucks was the *La Grue à Obus* (Shell Hoist) that consisted of a small crane mounted onto a single 4-wheel bogie wagon. All of the other trucks used two bogies.

The other standard wagons originally available were as follows:

1. The *Grue système Magnard* (Crane type Magnard) was a larger crane than *La Grue à Obus* with a 3.4 metre arm and a lifting capacity of 6 tonnes. It was designed for lifting guns and other heavy artillery equipment.
2. The *Plate-Forme du Tablier de Truck modèle 1883* (Apron Platform truck model 1883), which consisted of a platform with elevated ends, the raised ends to clear the two 4 wheeled bogies that the platform was mounted upon. It could carry up to 8 tonnes, and was often used to carry the 6 tonnes *Canon de 'De Bange' 155mm longue S.P. modèle 1888.*
3. As well as carrying heavy artillery pieces, *général* Peigne came up with the idea of mounting a gun directly onto a truck. The result was the *Affûts Trucks du général Peigne* (Truck Mounting type *général* Peigne). Based upon the *Plate-Forme du Tablier de Truck* it had originally a *Canon de 'De Bange' 120 mm court modèle 1878* mounted upon a naval type stand. It had four stabilising outrigger arms that could be folded out diagonally from the truck to give the platform maximum stability when the gun was in action. The arms were folded

back along the sides of the truck for transportation. The platform itself had fold down platform extensions on either sides of the truck to provide a much greater operating area for the gunners. From 1912 some of the trucks had their *120 mm de 'De Banges'* replaced by the *canons de 'De Bange' 155mm Court modèle 1912* (155mm calibre short barrelled cannons designed by Col. *'De Bange'* model 1912).

At Verdun, the manpower to man the *Affûts Trucks* belonged to a special company of the local *5ᵉ Régiments d'Artillerie à Pied* (5ᵗʰ Foot Artillery Regiment) and consisted in peacetime of 3 officers, 26 non commissioned officers and 174 other ranks. On mobilisation 30 men would be recalled from the 1st class of reservists to increase their numbers initially. However the regiment was to be brought onto a war footing by the addition of more men from the 1ˢᵗ class of the reserve to a compliment of 4, 36 and 264 respectively. They were to be housed in the regimental barrack at the Faubourg de Jardin Fontaine.

A second identical company would be formed by conscripting back into service elderly territorials in the event of war (For a further breakdown of the French Army before and at the start of the Great War see Appendix 17: The Required Manpower To Man The Forts). These Territorial troops were to be lodged in the Buvigner High School.

The *Affûts-trucks* companies were in peacetime organised into three and in wartime six *batteries*, consisting of two (four in wartime) *batteries* of *120mm de 'De Banges'* and one (two in wartime) *batterie* of *canons de 155mm de 'De Banges' Court modèle 1912*. Each *batterie* had a compliment of 33 men.

4. Another special artillery truck was the *Transport d'Obus* (Shell Transporter wagon). It could carry 19 shells of 280mm or 320mm calibre in special notched carrying racks.

5 & 6. Lack of water in the field and especially a battlefield could prove to be a problem for the army. It was especially a problem to the artillery. This problem was resolved by the design of two types of water tanker wagons. The first, *Citerne Prismatique* (Prismatic Tank) was a simple steel box tank, which could hold up to 8 cubic metres of water. The other *Citerne Cylindrique* (Cylindrical Tank) had a maximum capacity of 10 cubic metres.

There were a number of modifications to the *Plate-Forme du Tablier de Truck modèle 1883*, the most common were as follows:

1. The *Voitures de Voyageur* (passenger wagon) with wooden slatted seats for 40 men.
2. The *Wagon Couvert* (Covered Wagon).
3. The *Wagon Tombereau* (Open Wagon).

Although the *système Péchot* was designed for the use of the heavy artillery in the field, it was quickly adopted for the permanent fortifications, the track often paralleling the *routes militaire* and in some cases being built into the metalled roads as tramways. During the war, though necessary, locomotives and rolling stock were either requisitioned from private companies or purchased from different manufacturers giving a much greater range of equipment.

To give an idea of the scale of the French military railway system of the period immediately before the Great War, a report by Verdun's *commandant l'Artillerie* (artillery commander) dated April 1st 1914 gave an inventory of the local military rail network and what he foresaw his requirements would be in case of a war.

The *commandant l'Artillerie*'s report stated that the total length of the 0.6 metre gauge permanent military railway track was 28 kilometres, which he considered to be insufficient, adding that this total did not include the small amount 0.40metre and 0.50metre gauge track (which was mainly located in the *Parc d'Artillerie* and in the workshops of the arsenal).

He went on to state that in November 1913, there were only 15 *Locomotive Péchot-Bourdon*, which he again considered to be quite inadequate for the needs of the artillery, especially for the simultaneous deployment of all the *Affûts Trucks*. Even in the advent of war, when the army would requisition the three 0.6 metre gauge locomotives from the Montgrignon's limekilns works plus another five locomotives of the same gauge belonging to various other local engineering contractors, it would still leave the artillery short of four machines from the 27 machines which he had foreseen would be required. It should be noted that the Montgrignon and contractor's locomotives where not of the *Péchot-Bourdon* type. Incidentally he mentioned that there were six special harnesses and tackle available for horse traction.

As with the available track and locomotives, he forecast that there was not enough rolling stock. He listed 252 bogie wagons, but he added that in 1912 a request for another 100 bogie wagons had been put forward to the high command, but none had been forthcoming. Of the 252 bogie wagons available, 156 were to be used in the makeup of *Plate-Forme du Tablier de Trucks* (i.e. 78 trucks). Another 24 were to be employed for the *Affûts-trucks* (i.e. 12 *Affûts-trucks*), however he then added that there were another 20 canons with mountings available if enough bogie wagons could be found! Continuing on, he remarked that there were two bogie wagons used to support the single *Grue système Magnard* (crane), and finally he noted that there was a requirement for two or four bogie wagons for one or possibly two *Citerne trucks*.

The report concluded that there were approximately 70 bogie wagons remaining that were available for the makeup of 35 *Transport d'Obus* wagons. The Artillery commander then stated that it was his considered opinion that there would be a requirement for 115 *Transport d'Obus* wagons so as to be able to transport the required number of shells to the *forts* and field *batteries*, which meant that there was a short fall of 160 bogie wagons! The *commandant*'s last comment was that, if all the other 'light' wagons that were required for the other types of re-provisioning of the *batteries*, *dépôts*, etc. were to be included, that it was 'obviously insufficient'!

Interestingly, Verdun's *commandant l'Artillerie*'s prediction for the number of *Transport d'Obus* wagon that would be required in a forthcoming war, were based on the existing 909 artillery pieces of all types and calibres assigned for the defence of Verdun (Verdun had 32 different types of cannons which had accrued over the years since 1879). For example, it was anticipated that in the advent of a war each turret mounted *canon 155mm TR modèle 1902* would require 700 shells each and for each turret mounted *canon 75mm R modèle 75-02* 2,000 shells would be required. On their own, the turret guns represented a very large and important tonnage which was to be transported from the *magazines* in the *parc d'Artillerie*, however this did not take into account the shell requirement for the non-turreted guns within the forts nor the field guns located outside the forts in the *batteries*. In hindsight it can be seen that his figures (which were actually far greater than that of the high command's estimates before the war) were still vastly under-estimated when one considers that the French artillery fired off 10 million shells during the first three months of the 1916 Battle of Verdun.

Verdun's *voie ferré de 0.6m* was not connected to the local civilian rural railway system known as the *Chemin de fer de la Woëvre* (built between 1910-1912), which although narrow gauge, used one metre gauge track, hence it's common name of *"la ligne métrique"* (the metre line). Being of different gauges, their locomotives and rolling stock could not be used on the military system. However, in a small number of places the two systems did overlap (for example at Fleury railway station – which was located were the present day memorial museum now stands) and 'dual' tracks were used (where three rails were laid upon the same sleepers using a common rail on one side and the other two being spaced from the first rail to the gauges of the two systems, allowing both systems to use the same track bed).

Finally, as part of Verdun's *voie ferré de 0.6m* infrastructure, there was a small *dépôt des machines* (engine shed) located in the *parc d'Artillerie*, which has now been demolished. There was a number of *point d'eau de la voie de 60* (watering points for the 60cm railway) complete with *reservoir béton* (water tower constructed out of concrete) located next to the track way mainly at various points on the high ground, a good example can be found close to where the *route militaire* for the *Redoute de Souville* crosses the main civilian road running up to the 'Sleeping Lion' Monument.

There were also a small number of bridges, an example is the bridge that carried the standard gauge line to Metz over the *voie ferré de 0.6m* located about half way along the main line between Verdun and the tunnel de Tavannes. There were no tunnels required on the Verdun system, unlike the network at Toul, which required a couple of short tunnels.

Appendix 17
The Required Manpower for *Le camp retranché de Verdun* and the Relating Areas[61]

The French Army immediately before the Great War was divided into the metropolitan army for the defence of the mainland France and the colonial army for the policing and protection of the French Empire.

The colonial army was made up of professional soldiers who had volunteered for overseas service, along with local white colonial conscripts that would serve locally to where they were recruited and native levies again serving locally to where they were raised. There were also a small number of punishment or discipline battalions/companies made up of soldier convicts who also served overseas as part of their punishment.

Based on the above system, the infantry element of the colonial army were organised into three groups; the first group being the *Régiments d'Infanterie Coloniale* (Colonial Infantry Regiments - RIC) and the *Régiments Étranger d'Infanterie* (Foreign Infantry Regiments - RE) which were made up of volunteers recruited in France to serve in the colonies (the former being of all French recruits and the latter being the "Foreign Legion", consisting of anyone of any nationality including Frenchmen who cared to join.) The second group was the *Régiments de Zouaves* (The "Zouaves" Regiments - RZ) which were made up of white colonial conscripts, and finally the third group being made up of native levies who would serve in the *Régiments de Tirailleurs Indigenes* (Indigenous Sharpshooter's Regiments - RT). within this latter group were the *Bataillon d'Infanterie Légère d'Afrique* (African Light Infantry Battalions - BIA), which was the North African native equivalent to the metropolitan army's *Bataillon de Chasseurs à Pied* – rifle or sharpshooter's battalions.

Likewise there were cavalry and artillery arms to support the colonial infantry in the shape of the *Régiments de Chasseurs d'Afrique* (African Light Cavalry Regiments - RCA) made up of colonials, the *Régiments de Spahis* (The "Spahis" Regiments - RS) being North African native light cavalry. The artillery was organised into *Régiments d'Artillerie Coloniale* (Colonial Artillery Regiments - RAC). The native regiments and battalions had a nucleus of volunteered white commissioned and non-commissioned officers as well a few native officers (whose commission was based on long service).

---

[61] Appendix 17 is based on information mainly from "The French Army, 1914" Internet Article by Mark Conrad and *Les Armées Françaises Dans La Grande Guerre Tome X Ordres de Bataille des Grandes Unités Volume 1 and Volume 2.*

Originally, it was felt by the army's planners that it would take too long to mobilise the colonial troops and to deploy them in the north east of France in the case of an outbreak of a European war with Germany. Therefore they were not included in any of the mobilisation plans before the revised *Plan Nr. XVI.* There was also the consideration that the Empire would still need to be policed and that there was a possibility that there might be some native groups that would take the War in Europe as an opportunity for unrest or even an uprising (with or without the European enemy's agitation).

However the manpower problem of 1912 that befell the French army due to the falling birth rate in France before the Great War, along with the improvement of the transport system both railways and steam shipping; the parts of North Africa nearest to mainland France were considered near enough for the colonial troops to be mobilised in such a contingency as a European war. These North African troops were therefore regarded as part of the metropolitan army and not of the colonial army and, as such, were included in the *Plan Nr. XVII.* Once the Great War settled down into stagnant warfare, other units of the colonial army were mobilised and brought to France, as well as to the other parts of the world where the Germans and their allies were active and could be fought – mainly in south Europe and central Africa.

With its primary duty as the defence of mainland France, the metropolitan army was trained to fight an invader along the borders. To this end, metropolitan France (which included the area of North Africa controlled by France as mentioned above) was divided into twenty-one military *régions* (districts), each being given a sequential number. Originally as defined in 1873 there were eighteen *regions* – all eighteen being in mainland France. The nineteenth *région* being French controlled North Africa, which was added when it was decided to include the North African colonial troops in 1912. The *régions* in mainland France were numbered geographically from the north of France starting with the *1re Région* (being centred around Lille in the Pas-de-Calais) to the south where the *18e Région* was located in the south-west (being centred around Bordeaux in Aquitaine). The *19e Région* was the area within North Africa under French control and centred on Algeria, Tunisia and parts of Morocco. However in 1912 the army was reorganisation (the Infantry Cadre Law) and in 1913 the 3 years compulsory service was re-introduced (the Three Year Law) - both laws providing extra manpower, allowing two extra *régions* to be defined within mainland France - the first in 1912, the second in 1913. It was decided that the new *régions* should be in the area most at risk from an attack from the most likely enemy - Germany - and hence the areas were located near to the north-eastern border, the new districts being *Le camp retranché de Toul* which became the *20e Région* and *Le camp retranché de Épinal* becoming the *21e Région.*

Each district was responsible for the recruitment and provisioning of a *Corps d'Armée* (Army Corps - CA); the Corps carrying the same number as the region where it was from - *Ire Corps d'Armée* came from the *Ire Région*.

Based upon the German Army's model, before 1913, a typical Frenchman in his nineteenth year would be liable to complete a two-year or in some cases three-year period of compulsory service in one of the local regiments of the metropolitan army. Specialist or technical regiments (such as the artillery and engineering regiments) where a longer period of training was deemed to be necessary, the period of compulsory service within the active army was three years. To increase the strength of the standing army, the two year period of service for the non-specialist servicemen, such as infantrymen, was increased to three years in 1913, however this only had a limited effect on the size of the army by the time war had broken out in August 1914. The *corps militaire des douanes* (customs' guards) and the Paris Fire Brigade were regarded as part of the French Army and as such men could do their compulsory service within them. Men who lived next to the French coast could do their compulsory service within the French navy, however if a man was deemed to be unfit for active service then he could be required to do his compulsory service in the French civil service.

Men who were deemed to have the right aptitude or potential would be offered a professional career as commissioned officers or as senior non-commissioned officers. However due to political interference, the low pay and the low career prospects of slow promotion, there was a shortage of commissioned officers that had the 'right potential'. This shortage was therefore made up by promoting non-commissioned officers into the ranks of the junior officers, which in turn created a shortage of non-commissioned officers. In theory under the 'Two Year Service Law of 1905', all recruits were assessed within the first six months of their compulsory service. If it was thought that an individual had the right social or educational background to become an officer, he would be interviewed and then offered officer's training. In the event that the individual accepted this officer's training, he would volunteer for an extra three years of service making five years in all including his period of compulsory service. He would complete the rest of his first year as a junior non-commissioned officer. In his second year of service, he would be sent to one of the officer's training schools and was promoted to the rank of *Aspirant* (similar to the old British rank of Ensign – an officer cadet or a candidate for a commission.) There were a number of officer's training schools and colleges in France, the main ones being *Saint Cyr, Saint Maixent*, the *École polytechnique* and the *École navale*. Assuming that he then completed his training and passed his officer's examinations, he would then be promoted to Sous-Lieutenant (Second-Lieutenant) and would join a regiment until his period of service was completed. At which point he could volunteer to stay on within the active army or leave to become a reserve officer.

With the completion of their compulsory service in the active army, a small number of compulsory servicemen could volunteer for a career in the army normally being promoted to non-commissioned officers' rank. These men who did not choose to stay on in the army, were transferred into the reserve. These reservists would then be subject to army call up between the ages of 22 through to 47 in the event of a national emergency such as a war. Before the 'Three Year Service Law of 1913' the period within the reserve of the specialist or technical reservists was decreased by one year compared with the non-specialist regiments (line infantry etc.) so that they would also be released from the army in their forty-seventh year as with all other servicemen. Once in the reserve they would in theory complete periodic training every year. The average reservist was supposed to attend military training camp twice a year, but due to the shortages of funds, it was common that they missed both camps. The trained reservists could then be recalled to the colours at any time in the event of war.

Finally, men over the age of 47 could volunteer for further reservist service as territorials, whose service (due to their advancing years) in the advent of war would be limited to light garrison duties. It was foreseen before the war that the territorials would perform such non-active duties such as guarding lines of communications and guarding prisoners-of-war camps, generally well behind the fighting fronts. However in more than one instance during the war, territorials found themselves in the field and on occasion in the front line actively engaging the Germans. An example of territorials ending up in the front lines was that of the garrison of the *fort de Douaumont*, which as already mentioned was garrisoned by territorials when captured by the Germans on February 26th 1916.

The organisation of the French Army reflected the men that served within it with active, reserve and territorial units from regimental up to divisional level. Taking a typical metropolitan infantry unit as an example: there would be, based on a regional depot, an active *régiment d'infanterie* (Infantry Regiment – RI) was paired with a *régiment d'infanterie de reserve* (Reserve Infantry Regiment - RIR) and if numbers allowed there would be a *régiment d'infanterie territoriale* (Territorial Infantry Regiment – RIT) that was also associated.

Under the law of 1875, all *régiments d'infanterie* were to consist of four *bataillons* (Battalions), but with the new law of 1912 the number of battalions was reduced to three with the exception of eleven regiments. The *régiments d'infanterie* that were left with four battalions were those assigned for the defence of the *camps retranché*. The battalions carried the identification numbers 1 to 3 or to 4 based on the number of battalions. The *régiments d'infanterie de reserve*, which had been created under the law of

1892, had only two battalions that carried the numbers 5 and 6 even when paired with a *régiment d'infanterie* that had had its number of battalions reduced to three. An anomaly to this system was the Corsican regiment– the *173ᵉ régiments d'infanterie (*which had its depot located in Bastia*)* – that, depending on the number of conscripted recruits available in any given year, had from two to five battalions.

The *régiment de Chasseurs à Pied* (Light Infantry Regiment) and the *régiments de Genie* (Regiment of Engineers) were structured differently to the metropolitan infantry regiments in so far as there were only a few regiments, but split into a much great number of battalions. However the battalions had a smaller complement to that of the infantry battalions. The Light Infantry and Engineers had reserve battalions.

The cavalry did not have reserve regiments; however each cavalry regiment had its complement increased in the advent of war, the extra manpower being from the most recently released reservist cavalrymen being recalled to the colours.

At the beginning of the Great War there were two *régiments d'infanterie* that formed a brigade and two brigades that formed an infantry division. A typical infantry division also included a collection of supporting units ranging from artillery and cavalry through to medical services and gendarmes. There were also reserve divisions again consisting of two brigades; however each brigade was made up of six *régiment d'infanterie de reserve* so that the number of infantry battalions remained the same as that of an active infantry division – six battalions in both cases. There were variations on the divisional organisations especially with regards to the *chasseurs à pied*. With its 31 battalions (12 being the specialist *chasseurs alpins* battalions who were trained for use in mountain terrain), the *régiment de chasseurs à pied*'s battalions were used as independent battalions and were often paired when they were incorporated into the higher formations.[62] There were also cavalry divisions made up of cavalry regiments that included a similar array of supporting units as the infantry divisions such as the horse artillery regiments.

Two divisions formed an Army Corps. However by the middle of the Great War the French army was suffering from manpower shortages due to the severe combat losses, forcing the military organisation to be changed. As an example in 1916, the brigade became defunct as a tactical unit and the division lost one of its *régiment d'infanterie* so that there were only three *régiments d'infanterie* in a division.

As can be seen from the make up of the divisions, it was the infantry that made up the bulk of the French army before and during the Great War.

---

[62] For example Colonel Driant was the commander of the *56ᵉ bataillon de chasseurs à pied* and *59ᵉ bataillon de chasseurs à pied* at the start of the Battle of Verdun. Both of these *bataillons de chasseurs à pied* were reserve units.

The infantry was divided up into 173 *régiments d'infanterie* with an equal number of *régiments d'infanterie de reserve*. There were also 145 *régiments d'infanterie territoriale* along with the single *régiments de chasseurs à pied* with its 31 battalions. The *bataillons de chasseurs à pied* also had the same number of reserve and seven *bataillons territorial de chasseurs à pied.*

Unlike the British regiments, which carried the name of the recruitment area, French regiments followed the German practice of being given designation numbers. The active *régiments d'infanterie* were numbered 1 through to 173, with the paired reserve unit, the *régiments d'infanterie de reserve* being designated with the numbers 201 through to 373 (simply by adding 200 to the active regiment's designation number.) Likewise the active *bataillons de chasseurs à pied* were numbered 1 through to 31 and their reserve counterparts numbered 41 through to 71 (by adding 40 to the active battalion's designation number.) Because of this numbering system the 'reserve' description was often dropped from the regimental title in official correspondence. Unlike the reserve regiments numbering system the *régiments d'infanterie territoriale* and the *bataillons territorial de chasseurs à pied* were numbered independently of the active and reserve units; numbered 1 through to 145 and 1 through to 7 respectively. The seven *bataillons territorial de chasseurs à pied* were all *chasseurs alpins* battalions.[63]

Generally, the theoretical wartime strength of a typical three-battalion *régiment d'infanterie* was 3,292 all ranks, however in peacetime this number was reduced to 1,851 all ranks – on the outbreak of war the deficiency of manpower in the *régiment d'infanterie* would be made up to war strength by the recall of the first class of reservists to the colours, namely the most recently released reservists, which had just finished their peacetime military service. Wartime strengths of units in the French Army as in all other national armies during the Great War were almost always under strength due to wartime wastage.

The typical *régiments d'infanterie* had a battalion wartime strength of 1030 officers and men, divided into four fighting companies each having a complement of 203 officers and men - 140 in peacetime - along with a headquarters' company (*compagnie hors rang*) of 218 officers and men. This headquarters' company consisted of the battalion staff, the machine guns sections, the battalion pioneers as well as the non-combatant personnel such as medics, cooks, clerks and messengers. It was common practice for

---

[63] Although the French used the number designation system for their infantry units; the individual units had depots of course. Again using Driant's *56ᵉ bataillon de chasseurs à pied* and *59ᵉ bataillon de chasseurs à pied* as an example, their depots were the same as their active battalions (the *16ᵉ* and the *19ᵉ*) and were located in Conflans-Labry and Verdun respectively.

the regiment to serve as a unit and not to be split up into battalions, as was British practice.

The *régiment d'infanterie de reserve* and the *régiment d'infanterie territoriale* were not to be mobilised until the outbreak of war and as such during peacetime existed on paper only. Their manpower would be made up of the remaining reservists and the territorials that were recalled to the colours respectively. Due to a lack of volunteers for the territorials, there was a smaller number of *régiments d'infanterie territoriale*. The complement of the cavalry and artillery regiments were approximately two thirds the size of a metropolitan infantry regiment of the line.

The above units were under the command of the officers as following:

Army Corps and Divisions .... *Général de Division* (Divisional General)

Brigade.. *Général de Brigade* (Brigadier General)

Regiment.. *Colonel*

Reserve Regiment .... *Lieutenant Colonel*

Battalion.. *Commandant* (Major)

Company.. *Capitaine* (Captain)

An infantry company also had a *Lieutenant* and a *Sous-Lieutenant* (Second Lieutenant) to aid the *Capitaine* in his command.

At each level of command, each commander had a small staff. A good example of these staffs was that of the *régiment d'infanterie*. In peacetime the regimental headquarters was divided into an active staff (*état major du régiment*), and a reserve staff (*cadre complémentaire*.) The *état major du régiment* consisted of the *Colonel* in command, a *Lieutenant Colonel* as his second in command, and a *Commandant* in charge of administration, along with five to seven other officers performing various other duties, including a *Capitaine* who was the regimental adjutant (*Adjoint au Colonel*.) When the regiment was in the field, the *état major* was split into two, with one part staying at the depot, whilst the other part stayed with the rest of the regiment. As can be seen above the peacetime establishment of the *régiments d'infanterie* was well under that of its wartime establishment, however the regiment had a higher ratio of officers to men during peacetime, which were grouped together in the *cadre complémentaire*. The *cadre complémentaire* would be used as the nucleus for the sister *régiments d'infanterie de reserve* in the advent of war, and consisted of a Lieutenant Colonel, two *Commandants* and six *Capitaines*.

The French active army in peacetime totalled around 700,000 men of all ranks. However once all the reservists and territorials had been recalled to the colours on August 1st 1914, the French Army went to war with approximately 4,186,000 men of all ranks and services.

French military planning immediately before the Great War had moved away from the earlier defensive plans that were the basis of the Séré de Rivières fortification programs to the more aggressive plans known as the *Plan Nr. XVI* of 1909/13 and the *Plan Nr. XVII* of 1914.

Based on the final plan - the *Plan Nr. XVII* – the French high command foresaw the metropolitan army taking to the field along the threatened borders well in front of the fortified defensive zones and would launch the massive attack that they hoped would win the war. However there was still the need for troops to be left behind to perform garrison duties that were non-related to the planned attacked and therefore not part of the operations to be carried out by the *Corps d'Armée* that made up the French field army. The units that these troops served were collectively known as *Éléments Non Éndivisionnés* (Non Divisional Elements – ÉNÉ).

In July 1914, Verdun was located within the *6e Région* (6th region), which included the area covered by the *Départements* (areas) of the Ardennes, Marne, Meuse, Meurthe-et-Moselle, Oise, and parts of the Aisne. As such, the troops recruited from Verdun mainly served in the *VIe Corps d'Armée* (6th Army Corp), which had its *Quartier Général* (Headquarters - QG) located in the nearby garrison town of Châlons-sur-Marne[64]. The *VIe Corps d'Armée* consisted of three *divisions d'infanterie* (Infantry Division - DI) along with associated units (cavalry, artillery etc.). The *Éléments Non Éndivisionnés* consisted of three four-battalion *régiments d'infanterie*, along with artillery regiments and an engineering regiment, all of which were required for the running of the fortifications that formed the garrison of Verdun. It was these locally raised regiments that formed the basis of the *Groupe de Verdun* (The Verdun Group) whose duty was the defence of *Le camp retranché de Verdun*.

The pre-war breakdowns of the troops local to Verdun before the start of the Great War were as follows[65]:

---

[64] Châlons-sur-Marne has now been renamed Châlons-en-Champagne.

[65] The translations of the units listed here, but not already given are as follows:

division d'infanterie de réserve	Reserve Infantry Division
division de cavalerie	Cavalry Division
brigade d'infanterie	Infantry Brigade
brigade d'infanterie de reserve	Reserve Infantry Brigade
brigade d'artillerie	Artillery Brigade
bataillon de chasseurs à pied	Light Infantry or Rifle Battalion
régiment de hussars	Hussar (Light Cavalry) Regiment
escadron	Cavalry Squadron
régiment d'artillerie de campagne	Field Artillery Regiment
régiment d'artillerie à pied	Foot (Heavy) Artillery Regiment
régiment de Génie	Regiment of Engineers
bataillon du génie	Engineers Battalion

VIe Corps d'Armée (Châlons-sur-Marne)[66]:

12e divisions d'infanterie (Reims):
   23e brigade d'infanterie (Soissons):
      54e régiments d'infanterie (Compiègne)
      67e régiments d'infanterie (Soissons.
   24e brigade d'infanterie (Reims):
      106e régiments d'infanterie (Chalôns-sur-Marne)
      132e régiments d'infanterie (Reims)

40e divisions d'infanterie (Saint-Mihiel):
   79e brigade d'infanterie (Commercy):
      154e régiments d'infanterie (Lerouville)
      155e régiments d'infanterie (Commercy)
      26e bataillon de chasseurs à pied (Pont-à-Mousson)
   80e brigade d'infanterie (Saint-Mihiel):
      150e régiments d'infanterie (Saint-Mihiel)
      161e régiments d'infanterie (Saint-Mihiel)
      25e bataillons de chasseurs à pied (Saint-Mihiel)
      29e bataillons de chasseurs à pied (Saint-Mihiel)

42e divisions d'infanterie (Perpignan):
   83e brigade d'infanterie (Verdun):
      94e régiments d'infanterie (Bar-le-Duc)
      8e bataillons de chasseurs à pied (Étain)
      19e bataillons de chasseurs à pied (Verdun)
   84e brigade d'infanterie (Verdun):
      151e régiments d'infanterie (Verdun)
      162e régiments d'infanterie (Verdun)

---

bataillon territoriale du génie...................... Territorial Engineers   Battalion
escadron du train des équipages
       militaires.............................. Equipment Train Squadron
secrétaires d'état-major et du
       recrutement............................ Recruitment and Staff Secretaries
commis et ouvriers militaires
       d'administration.................... Administration Commissionaires
                          and Military Assistants
d'infirmiers militaires .... Military Nurses
légion de gendarmerie.................................... Police Force Legion
corps militaire des douanes .... Military Corps of the Customs
groupe des troupes d'aéronautique.............. Aviation Group (Wing)
escadrille.. Aviation Squadron
[66] The *Quartier Général* (Headquarters) for each unit is shown in parenthesis.

192

16e *bataillons de chasseurs à pied (Conflans-Labry)*

6e *brigade d'artillerie*
6e *bataillon du génie, (9e régiment de génie - sapeurs-mineurs)*
6e *escadron du train des équipages militaires*
6e *section de secrétaires d'état-major et du recrutement*
6e *section de commis et ouvriers militaires d'administration*
6e *section d'infirmiers militaries*
6e *légion de gendarmerie.*

Éléments Non Éndivisionnés:

Groupe de Verdun:

164e *régiments d'infanterie (Verdun)* [4 Battalions]
165e *régiments d'infanterie (Verdun)* [4 Battalions]
166e *régiments d'infanterie (Verdun)* [4 Battalions]

Corps militaire des douanes, 4e bataillon
Corps militaire des douanes, 5e bataillon
Corps militaire des douanes, Compagnies de forteresse,
[3 companies]

2e *divisions de cavalerie* [parts]
4e *divisions de cavalerie* [parts]
5e *divisions de cavalerie* [parts]

5e *régiment d'artillerie à pied:*
1re, 2e, 4e, 6e, 7e, 8e, 9e, 10e, 11e et 13e *batteries* and *compagnie*
d'ouvriers
3e *batterie, Verdun*
5e *batterie, Montmédy*
12e *batterie, Longwy*
forts de Lionville, Gironville, Camp des Romains, Troyon

9e *régiment de génie [sapeurs-mineurs]*
25e *bataillon de sapeurs-mineurs de place*
1 compagnie de sapeurs-conducteurs

As mentioned above the French mobilisation and deployment plan, the *'Plan Nr XVII'*, called for the twenty-one Corps to be grouped into five armies. When war came on August 1st 1914, the *VIe Corp d'Armée* was grouped together with the *IVe* and *Ve Corps d'Armée* to form the *IIIe Armée* under the command of *Général* Ruffey. The *IIIe Armée* complete with the

VIe Corp d'Armée moved away from Verdun to their deployment positions. The void at Verdun left by the *VIe Corp d'Armée* when it deployed for war was filled by the *72e division d'infanterie de réserve*, which was part of the general army reserve group of divisions.

Therefore the breakdowns of the troops immediately after the start of the Great War, within the Verdun area were as follows:

Isolée (Isolated - Non Attached Reserve):

> *72e division d'infanterie de réserve (Verdun):*
> > *143e brigade d'infanterie de réserve:*
> > > *351e régiments d'infanterie de réserve (Toul)*
> > > *362e régiments d'infanterie de réserve (Verdun)*
> > > *56e bataillons de chasseurs à pied (Conflans-Labry)*
> > > *59e bataillons de chasseurs à pied (Verdun)*
> > *144e brigade d'infanterie de réserve:*
> > > *356e régiments d'infanterie de réserve (Toul)*
> > > *364e régiments d'infanterie de reserve (Verdun)*
> > > *365e régiments d'infanterie de réserve (Verdun)*

> > *1 escadron du 2e régiment de hussars*
> > *1 escadron du 4e régiment de hussars*

> *1 groupe du 61e régiment d'artillerie de campagne*
> > *[canon de 75mm]*
> *1 groupe du 59e régiment d'artillerie de campagne*
> > *[canon de 75mm]*
> *1 groupe du 11e régiment d'artillerie de campagne*
> > *[canon de 75mm]*
> *1 groupe du 41e régiment d'artillerie de campagne*
> > *[canon de 75mm]*
> *1 groupe du 45e régiment d'artillerie de campagne*
> > *[canon de 75mm]*

> *9e régiment de génie [sapeurs-mineurs]*
> *6e bataillon de sapeurs-mineurs de campagne*

Défense mobile des Place de Verdun

Commandements supérieurs de la défense des places des groupes de Reims
Commandements supérieurs de la défense desplaces des groupes de
> > > > *Verdun*
Commandements supérieurs de la défense des camp de Châlons

Éléments Non Éndivisionnés:

Groupe De Verdun:

164ᵉ régiment d'infanterie (Verdun) [4 Battalions]
165ᵉ régiment d'infanterie (Verdun) [4 Battalions]
166ᵉ régiment d'infanterie (Verdun) [4 Battalions]

2ᵉ divisions de cavalerie [parts]
4ᵉ divisions de cavalerie [parts]
5ᵉ divisions de cavalerie [parts]

5ᵉ régiment d'artillerie à pied
1ʳᵉ, 2ᵉ, 4ᵉ, 6ᵉ, 7ᵉ, 8ᵉ, 9ᵉ, 10ᵉ, 11ᵉ, 13ᵉ batteries and
compagnie d'ouvriers
3ᵉ batterie, Verdun
5ᵉ batterie, Montmédy
12ᵉ batterie, Longwy
forts de Lionville, Gironville, Camp des Romains, Troyon

9ᵉ régiment de génie (sapeurs-mineurs)
25ᵉ bataillon de sapeurs-mineurs de place
1 compagnie de sapeurs-conducteurs

44ᵉ régiment d'infanterie territoriale (Verdun)
6ᵉ bataillon territoriale du genie

2ᵉ groupe des troupes d'aéronautique:
escadrille M.F. 2 (flying Maurice Farman biplanes)
escadrille H.F. 7 (flying Henri Farman biplanes)[67]

Although it was intended that only the *Éléments Non Éndivisionnés* within the *6ᵉ Région* would be used for the defence of Verdun, by the time the war had settle down into trench warfare most of the *VIe Corps d'Armée* had been used in the defence of the area. By the finish of the Battle of Verdun in 1916 it has been estimated that about 90% of the entire French army had past through Verdun in its defence.

---

[67] The French Air Service's *Escadrille* designations before and during the Great War were made up of a sequence number based on all the *Escadrilles* prefixed by an abbreviated code of the aircraft type used by the particular *escadrille*. This meant that an *escadrille* could and did have different designations during the course of the war as new aircraft from a different manufacturer replaced old and out of date types although the sequence number remained the same. For example *escadrille* N103 was re-designated SPA103 when their Neuports 17 fighters were replaced with the later Spad VII fighters.

Appendix 18
List of the *Casemates de Mougin* and *Tourelles de Mougin*

(All were constructed outside of *Le camp retranché de Verdun*)

The *casemates de Mougin* were located near to:
Casemate de Mougin A ....*Fort du Mont Bart*
Casemate de Mougin B ....*Fort de Condé-sur-Aisne*
Casemate de Mougin C ....*Fort de Condé-sur-Aisne*
Casemate de Mougin D .... *Vieux fort de Joux*
Casemate de Mougin E .... *Vieux fort de Joux*
Casemate de Mougin F ....*Fort d'avant la Tête du Chien*
Casemate de Mougin G ....*Fort des Ayvelles*
Casemate de Mougin H ....*Batterie des Ayvelles*
Casemate de Mougin I ....*Batterie de l'Eperon*
Casemate de Mougin J ....*Batterie de l'Eperon*

The *tourelles de Mougin* were located within the following forts of:
Fort deVilley- le-Sec
Fort de Lucey
Fort de Point-Saint-Vincent
Fort de Frouard
Fort de Manonviller (2 off)
Fort de Pagny-la-Blanche-Côte

The *tourelles de Mougin* mounted in independent *abris* were located in the regions of:
Paris (5 off)
Maubeuge (2 off)
Lille
Lyon
Besançon
Epinal
Nice (2 off)
Fort de Barbonnet
Fort de Manonviller (2 off)
Fort de Giromagny (2 off)

Bibliography and References

A great many books and articles have been written over the years about the Battle of Verdun, mainly written in French or German. There have been even less written about the fortifications themselves and then generally concentrating on the forts and likewise hardly any have been written in English.

Therefore I have listed French, German and English

Archive Material:

Bayerisches Hauptstaatsarchiv - Abt. IV Kriegsarchiv:
Denkschriften Generalstab 179 -
Großer Generalstab. IV Abteilung Denkschriften Toul:
Beilage IIIl zur Denkschriften Toul – Fortifikationszeichnungen Fort Villey le Sec
Beilage III5 zur Denkschriften Toul – Fortifikationszeichnungen Fort de Lucey
Denkschriften Generalstab 181-
Großer Generalstab. IV Abteilung Denkschriften Verdun:
Beilage 4g zur Denkschriften Verdun – Fortifikationszeichnungen Blatt 7 (Fort de Vaux und de Douaumont; Batterie de Damloup)
Beilage 4l zur Denkschriften Verdun – Fortifikationszeichnungen Blatt 11 (Skizzen der Werke von Verdun)
Beilage 4n zur Denkschriften Verdun – Einzelzeichnungen Blatt 5
Beilage 4o zur Denkschriften Verdun – Panzertypen Blatt 1 und 2
Denkschriften Generalstab 224 -
Großer Generalstab. 4 Abteilung
Die belgischen und holländischen Befestigungen und die Grundsätze ihrer Verteidigung' – 1908

Bibliotheque Municipale de Verdun
File MS812 (Collection of Orders, Reports, Plans, Maps, Photographs et al relating to the forts of Verdun)
File MS819 (Collection of Orders, Reports, Plans, Maps, Photographs et al relating to the forts of Verdun)

Imperial War Museum, London - The Photograph Archive
Photographs

Mémorial de Verdun - Service de Documentation
Trench Maps of the Verdun battlefield from the 1916 period.

Official Publications:

Archives du service des cuirassements (1877-1927). Inventaire semi-analytique. Département de l'armée de Terre, sous-série 2V (2V 290 à 361) by Nicole Salat and Martin Barros, published by SHD/Département de l'armée de Terre, 2005.

Der Weltkrieg, Die Militarischen Operationen Zu Lande Bund 10 Die Operationen des Jahres 1916 Bis zum Wechfel in der Obersten Heeresceitung, edited by Generalmajor außer Dienst Hans von Häften, published by E.S. Mittler und Sohns, 1936. - German Text

Die Bayern im Großen Kriege 1914-1918. Anonymous published by Bayerischen Kriegsarchiv, 1923. - German Text

Die Schlacht in Lothringen und in den Vogesen 1914 Zweiter Band Die Feuertaufe der Bayerischen Armee. by Karl Deuringer (Bayerischen Kriegsarchiv), published by Verlagt bei Max Schmidt, 1929 - German Text

Erinnerungsblatter Deutsche Regimenter - Bayerischen Armee Einser Bilderbuch, by Herbert Knorr, published by Verlag Bayerischen Kriegsarchivs, 1926. - German Text

Les Armée Françaises dans la Grande Guerre, Tome IV, Volume 1. by Lieutenant-Colonel d'Infanterie Breventé Appert, Capitaine d'Infanterie Breventé Besse, Capitaine d'Infanterie Laxague and Capitaine d'Infanterie Maubert, published by Imprimèrie Nationale, 1926 – French Text

Les Armée Françaises dans la Grande Guerre, Tome IV, Volume 2. by Lieutenant-Colonel d'Infanterie Breventé Acacie, Commandant d'Infanterie Altairac, Chef d'Escadron de Cavalière Breventé Gallini, Commandant d'Infanterie Breventé Denolle, Capitaine d'Infanterie Laxague and Capitaine d'Artillerie Breventé Courbis, published by Imprimèrie Nationale, 1933 – French Text

Les Armée Françaises dans la Grande Guerre, Tome IV, Volume 3. by Lieutenant-Colonel d'Infanterie Breventé Acacie, Commandant d'Infanterie Altairac and Chef d'Escadron de Cavalière Breventé Gallini, published by Imprimèrie Nationale, 1935 – French Text.

Les Armée Françaises dans la Grande Guerre, Tome X Volume 1 by Lieutenant-Colonel d'Infanterie Breventé Pompé, Chef de Bataillon d'Infanterie Breventé Porsh, Chef de Bataillon à T.T. d'Infanterie Fargé, Capitaine d'Infanterie du Paty de Clam, Capitaine d'Infanterie Huillard, Capitaine d'Infanterie de la Charie, Chef d'Escadron de Cavalière Fauche, Chef d'Escadron d'Artillerie Pingeon, Lieutenant-Colonel du Génie Pacton and Capitaine du Génie Kont, published by Imprimèrie Nationale, 1923 – French Text

Les Armée Françaises dans la Grande Guerre, Tome X Volume 2 by Lieutenant-Colonel d'Infanterie Breventé Pompé, Chef de Bataillon d'Infanterie Breventé Porsh, Chef de Bataillon à T.T. d'Infanterie Fargé, Capitaine d'Infanterie du Paty de Clam, Capitaine d'Infanterie Huillard,

Capitaine d'Infanterie de la Charie, Chef d'Escadron de Cavalière Fauche, Chef d'Escadron d'Artillerie Pingeon, Lieutenant-Colonel du Génie Pacton and Capitaine du Génie Kont, published by Imprimèrie Nationale, 1924 – French Text

Schlachten des Weltkrieges Bund 1 Douaumont, by Werner Beumelburg, published by Gerhard Stalling 1928. - German Text

Schlachten des Weltkrieges Bund 6 Nancy bis zum Camp des Romains 1914, by Werner Beumelburg, published by Gerhard Stalling 1926. - German Text

Schlachten des Weltkrieges Bund 13 Die Tragudie von Verdun 1916 Tiel 1, by Werner Beumelburg, published by Gerhard Stalling 1926 (Tiel 1 covers the fighting on the Right Bank). - German Text

Schlachten des Weltkrieges Bund 14 Die Tragudie von Verdun 1916 Tiel 2, by Werner Beumelburg, published by Gerhard Stalling 1928 (Tiel 2 covers the fighting for the *fort de Vaux*). - German Text

Schlachten des Weltkrieges Bund 15 Die Tragudie von Verdun 1916 Tiel 3 und 4, by Werner Beumelburg, published by Gerhard Stalling 1929 (Tiel 3 covers the fighting on the Left Bank with reference to the artillery fire from the fortifications on the Left Bank, Teil 4 covers the fighting centred on the *ouvrage de Thiaumont*). - German Text

A French-English Military Technical Dictionary, by Cornelius De Witt Wilcox, published by USA War Office – Government Printing Office, 1917.

General Books:

De L'Oppidum a L'Enfouissement - L'Art de la Fortification a Verdun et sur les marches de l'Est., edited by Guy Pedroncini, published by C.N.S.V. - Memorial de Verdun, 1996 (ISBN 2 901186 10 08) – French Text

German Strategy and the Path to Verdun, by Robert T. Foley, published by Cambridge University Press, 2005 (ISBN 0 521 84193 3)

La barrière de fer: l'architecture des forts du général Séré de Rivières, 1872-1914 by Philippe Truttmann, published by Éditions Gérard Klopp, 2000 (ISBN 2 911992 37 7) – French Text.

La Bataille des Forts (Metz et Verdun dc 1865 à 1918), by Alain Hohnadel and Philippe Bestetti, published by Editions Heimdal, 1995 (ISBN 2 84048 087 5) – French Text

La Lorraine fortifiée, by Stéphane Gaber, published by Editions Serpenoise, 1994 (ISBN 2 87692 256 8) – French Text.

Le Système Séré de Rivières, by Guy Le Hallé, published by Ysec Editions, 2001 (ISBN 2 84673 008 3) – French Text.

La Voie de 60 sur less Fronts Français de la Guerre de 14-18, by Christian Cénac, published by Autoédition, 1991 (ISBN 2 9505403 0 9) – French Text.

The Ideology of the Offensive, by Jack Snyder, published by Cornell University Press, 1984 (ISBN 0 8014 1657 4)

The March to the Marne: The French Army, 1971-1914, by Douglas Porch, published by Cambridge University Press, 1981 (ISBN: 0 521 23883 8) reprinted 2003 (ISBN 0 521 54592 7)

The Price of Glory, Alistair Horne, published by Macmillan and Co. Ltd., 1962 last reprinted in paperback by Penguin Books Ltd 1993 (ISBN: 9780140170412)

Verdun – Argonne (1914-1918), anonymous, published by Michelin & Cie, 1928 – French Text

Verdun: Fort Douaumont, by Christina Holstein, published by Pen and Sword Books, 2002 (ISBN: 0850528992)

Verdun, Les forts de la Victoire, by Guy Le Hallé published by Citedis Editions, 1998 (ISBN 2 911920 10 4) – French Text

Articles:

"Fortifications in 1914-18.", by Major G.I. Thomas, D.S.O., M.C., p.s.c., R.A., published in The Royal Engineers Journal, Volume XLIV, 1930

Verdun and Metz. (Two parts), by Capt. C. La T. Turner Jones, D.S.O., M.C., R.E., published in The Royal Engineers Journal, Volume XXXIV, 1921

"Shell-Fire Versus Permanent Fortifications." – The Evidence of Verdun, 1916 by Lieutenant H.B. Harrison, R.E., published in The Royal Engineers Journal, Volume XL, 1926

"La système Péchot, 1ère partie: Coférence du Colonel Péchot du 27 avril 1903", published in Voie Etroite Part N° 75, 2/1983 – French Text.

"La système Péchot, 2ème partie", published in Voie Etroite Part N° 76, 3/1983 – French Text

"La système Péchot, 3ème partie", published in Voie Etroite Part N° 77, 4/1983 – French Text

"Locomotive Péchot-Bourdon." published in Voie Etroite Part N° 78, 5/1983 – French Text

"Numero special: Toul." published in Voie Etroite Part N° 79, 12/1983 – French Text

"Numero special: Verdun." published in Voie Etroite Part N° 85, 6/1984 – French Text

"Reseau stratégique de Belfort: Complément", published in Voie Etroite Part N° 107, 4/1988 – French Text

Internet Articles:

Les cuirassements dans la fortification terrestrial française 1871-1918, by Roland Scheller, posted 2003 – French Text
(http://www.lignemaginot.com/ligne/armes/scheller.html)

Les Fortifications Séré de Rivières et Leur Modernisation (1873 - 1914), by Alain Lecomte, posted 1988 - French Text
(http://www.clham.org/050352.html)

Les Forts Français de 1914 (Période 1874-1914) – [Part 1], by J. Harlepin, posted 1993 - French Text
(http://www.clham.org/050551.html)

Les Forts Français de 1914 (Période 1874-1914) – [Part 2], by J. Harlepin, posted 1994 - French Text
(http://www.clham.org/050561.html)

The French Séré de Rivières Fortifications, by Martin Egger, posted c1995 - German Text
(http://www.geocities.com/pentagon/1630/sdr.html)

Forum de Disscussion - Abri-Memoire 1914-1918, by Florian Garnier, posted 2005 - French Text
(http://www.abri-memoire.org/forum/read.php)

Der Festungsgürtel von Verdun, by Marcus Massing, posted 2000 - German Text
(http://www.hausarbeiten.de/faecher/hausarbeit/gew/11206.html)

The French Army, 1914, by Mark Conrad, posted 1993
(http://home.comcast.net/~markconrad/FR1914.html)

Maps:

Les Armée Françaises dans la Grande Guerre, Tome IV, Volume 1, Carte 13 (French Official History) Imprimèrie Nationale

Les Armée Françaises dans la Grande Guerre, Tome IV, Volume 1, Carte 14 (French Official History) Imprimèrie Nationale

Les Armée Françaises dans la Grande Guerre, Tome IV, Volume 1, Carte 26 (French Official History) Imprimèrie Nationale

Institut Géographique Nationales: IGN TOP25: 3112ET, Forêt de Verdun et du Mort-Homme

Institut Géographique Nationales: IGN Série Bleue: "3113E, Dugny-sur-Meuse" and "32130, Dieue-sur-Meuse"

Printed in Great Britain
by Amazon